Slow Down and Enjoy the Ride

Alistair McGuinness

Published by Discover Your Tribe, 2018.

SLOW DOWN AND ENJOY THE RIDE

First edition. July 8, 2018.

Written by Alistair McGuinness.

Into the Valley

My eyes were focused on the road, searching for potholes and scars in the bitumen. The fading light brought an ever-increasing danger. I'd just passed the stiff remains of a dead kangaroo and didn't relish the thought of colliding with a live one. I was keen to get home, but the chance to attack another downhill gradient was too good to miss, and I hadn't seen a car for hours. I clicked through the gears and raced into the valley, relishing the final minutes of my very last training session before flying into Britain next week.

It had been an arduous day, cycling alone in the countryside, churning through the hours in a last-ditch effort to get fit. In only a few days' time, I'd be tackling a 1,000-mile bike ride from Land's End to John O'Groats and my thoughts were in a spin. Had I trained hard enough? Would the hand-picked route, across the remotest parts of Britain, prove too challenging for a novice like myself? In an effort to clear my mind, I tucked my head in low and felt the cool rush of air upon my face.

Up ahead, the peppermint trees were thinning out, but within their long shadows, I sensed movement. As I studied the remnants of woodland — my senses on high alert — a stone on the road hit my wheel and interrupted my focus for a second. When I next looked up, I saw them sprinting from the trees, their high pitched screeches oscillating, their steely eyes too close, our paths set to imminently cross.

Slamming on the brakes, I fought the rear wheel as it snaked along the road. I braced my body for impact while swerving around the animals, which continued on across the road in giant strides. The nearest one to me let out a warbled cry as it scrambled up the sandy slope, flapping its flightless wings.

The bike finally came to a stop, just in time for me to turn and catch a last glimpse of the emus, bolting towards cover. Suddenly, all was silent, apart from my ragged breathing. In the last of the light, I rode quickly but carefully through the forest track, back towards the road where I'd parked my car. It was time to go home, pack my bags and prepare for the flight.

Take me Home, Country Roads

In 1996, I cycled the length of Britain with two friends, Alan and Nick. With limited planning and very little training, we set off from Land's End, determined to have an adventure. We were not disappointed. Along the way to John O'Groats, we found a secret shortcut, went in search of the remaining Beatles, endured a memorable night in a youth hostel, and met many amazing characters. We also experienced the hottest day of the year, survived two storms, and one of us fell in love.

A lot has changed since our end-to-end journey. Not least that I now live in Australia and spend more time on a stand-up paddle board than on a bicycle. My wife and I didn't move from England in search of a better life. All we wanted was a change of scenery. Fifteen years, nine jobs, two children and one dog later, we're still here.

Living in Australia has its merits, and I'm not just talking about the pristine beaches, endless skies, barbeques, and ice-cold beer. Since moving Down Under, we've had numerous family adventures, and each year I discover new reasons why so many people call it the Lucky Country. By now, I should be calling Australia my home. But like many expats, I still reminisce about the country where I grew up. Despite the fact I live close to wineries, beaches, and world class surf spots, England is often in my thoughts.

When it comes to holidays, Western Australians flock to the island of Bali, in the same way the British head to the Mediterranean. Last February, almost twenty years after our end-to-end bike ride, the only thing on my mind was a holiday to this tropical isle, along with my wife and children. We'd selected a villa, agreed on a date, and even found someone to look after the dog. We were all set.

But while searching for our flights, a phone call changed it all and our trip to Bali was put on hold. You see, Alan and Nick were planning to do the bike ride again, to celebrate its 20th anniversary. The dates were going to clash with our holiday, but how could I say no? The more that Alan spoke, the clearer it became. I had to go back and be a part of it. It wasn't just the opportunity to rekindle lost friendships, or visit my old haunts, my roots, and my home. It was the chance to once again experience a 1,000-mile adventure over thirteen long, full days. There would be places to explore, people to meet, and stories to gather.

'Cycle tracks are everywhere,' Alan promised. 'We'll go right through the heart of rural Britain with hardly a main-road in sight.'

This time, there would also be four more riders, some of whom I knew, others I'd never met. We'd even have a support vehicle. How could anything go wrong? Bali postponed, the children were devastated, and my wife is still waiting for her holiday.

'I really need to do this,' I told them. 'Besides,' I explained, 'maybe after this trip I won't talk about home so much. Surely, Britain isn't as great as it used to be.'

Day 1: Automation

'So, did you get the email from Nick?'

'Which one?'

'The one about bike computers.'

'Um, yes I think so. Although I didn't really read it properly. It's been so hectic. Anyway, you know me. I prefer maps to computers.'

Alan smiled knowingly at my deflection and said, 'Ali, maps are great, but not when the route requires fast decisions. Have you heard of Strava?'

I nodded and his face brightened. 'Okay, so as you know then, Strava is a mobile app that uses GPS to measure distance and elevation while you travel. It also creates a map of the route, which can be shared on social media.'

'Uh huh.' I nodded again.

'We're going to use something similar, but instead of smartphones we'll use another type of device, which attaches to the handlebars.'

I took a sip of summer ale and reached out to ruffle Gretna's shiny black coat. As I did so, she licked my hand in acknowledgment, her dark eyes lost behind a mass of frizzy curls. 'Good girl,' I murmured.

Alan continued, his voice animated. 'There are heaps of options available, but the type we all have is a Garmin. Our whole route is already uploaded. All we have to do is follow the directions on the screen all the way from Land's End to Scotland. Nick's done an amazing job choosing the route. He reckons we'll spend most of our time on cycle tracks, canal paths and country roads. Not like last time, eh?'

I laughed and my mind wandered back to our trip twenty years earlier and how naive Alan, Nick and I had been at the time. The year had been 1996 and we'd set off from the peninsula of Land's End in the southwest of England towards the remote, windswept enclave of John O'Groats on the northeastern tip of Scotland. Instead of using bike computers, we'd opted for

4

traditional methods and turned instead to an out-of-date road map that Nick had found in his garage.

Our itinerary was picked in a carefree manner with little rationale for the places we'd encounter along the way. In fact, in the time it took us to devour a twelve-inch pizza, every road for our thirteen-day ride was highlighted on the map in fluorescent green. Relevant pages were then torn from the AA booklet, stapled together, and then placed in Nick's panniers until we needed them.

I thought back to those torturous days, hurtling along the A9, listening to the thunderous roar of approaching lorries and silently praying that the truck drivers would see us through the torrential rain.

Now, twenty years later, it would be an altogether different experience. Not only would better mapping mean we'd find a safer route, our options had also significantly increased. This was due to a network of routes, established to encourage greater participation in cycling across Great Britain. It is known as the National Cycle Network (NCN) and was created by a charity called Sustrans.

The network of trails covers a staggering 14,000 miles and includes disused railway lines, canal paths, and minor roads. Some of these are ideally located for those, like us, cycling from Land's End to John O'Groats. Walkers, joggers, wheelchair users and horse riders also use the tracks and the numbers are impressive. It is estimated that five million people per year use the network and Nick had picked sections of these tracks wherever possible.

It sounded as if we'd have a seamless passage across Britain, including the chance to ride off-road from time to time. By using bike computers, we'd mitigate the risk of taking wrong turnings, losing valuable time. It was a perfect plan. Well, that was the theory and we were about to try it out for real.

'So Ali, now you see why these Garmin's are essential.'

I was keen to counter argue. 'We managed without them before.'

'That's true, but we ended up on main roads far too often.'

He was probably right. Ironically, though, at the time, it was our inexperience that had made the first trip so memorable. We had no idea about the merits of Lycra, had never considered cleated shoes, and certainly hadn't thought to book accommodation before leaving Land's End. But apart from those more precarious moments, there'd been some lighter moments, involving a night at the Edinburgh Fringe Festival and a search for the Beatles in Liverpool.

For Alan, the trip had been life changing. A brief encounter with Samantha in the Scottish town of Gretna Green has led to a long and happy marriage. Their jet black groodle, acquired many years after their wedding day, was named after the iconic location. Gretna still lay close to me as I supped my beer and chuckled softly at the memories.

Just then, Sam entered the living room, carrying a selection of wine, cheese and biscuits. She placed them strategically away from Gretna's drooling tongue. It was so good to see them both after so many years. Since meeting in Scotland, Alan and Sam have enjoyed many adventures, including several years living in Western Australia before returning to their homeland with their son and dog. I was staying overnight in their home in the market town of Ampthill, Bedfordshire, after flying into England that morning. Within twenty-four hours, we'd be attempting the bike ride once again.

I'd asked for a tour of their home and was suitably impressed (and a little envious) at the creative way they'd renovated. Each room was studiously detailed, and the final part of the jigsaw lay underground. Alan, it seemed, had a 'secret' cellar and he'd grinned mischievously in anticipation of my response. Once below ground, he asked me to ignore the peeling walls, broken shelves and cluttered floor space because one day it would be his very own microbrewery. He was able to fully visualise and articulate the transformation and spoke passionately about the layout, including the kegs, shelving, equipment and décor.

As I've described him in the past, Alan is *one of those characters that attracts more friends than he knows what to do with... the life and soul of the party*. Twenty years later, little has changed. He has aged a little, as would be expected, but his laughter lines are the deepest. His eyes are bright and it's clear he has a zest for life.

Although many years had passed since our inaugural bike ride, the escapades and excitement of the journey were still fresh in my mind. So fresh, in fact, that after consulting my travel diaries, I'd converted the scribbles into an adventure travel book, called End to End. Twenty years after the ride, our story was finally told. My plan was to promote the book while cycling once again from Land's End to John O'Groats.

It wasn't a complex strategy. Stored within the rear pannier would be a dozen books, and during the ride I planned to hand out complimentary copies whenever the opportunity arose. I'd started promoting the book a few weeks earlier, in a small town called Augusta, located on the coast of Western Australia. Since departing Australia I'd promoted the book during numerous stopovers and hoped to continue until John O'Groats. I'd even applied to the Guinness World Records in the hope of creating a record for the world's longest book tour!

I also planned to sell some books and donate the first royalty payment to the Primrose Cancer Unit at Bedford Hospital, a charity with which the other riders were actively involved. You see, their friend Chris had recently passed away after a battle with cancer, and the guys wanted to raise money for those that had cared for him.

During an interview for a local newspaper, my friend Mark, who was also participating in the ride, described Chris as an "amazing man" and "well-loved". He also explained that Chris himself had completed a huge fundraising drive for the Primrose Cancer Unit, including a 70-mile cycling challenge from London to Brighton, off-road. He'd completed the epic achievement only seven months before he died. We had no shortage of reasons to ride.

So here we were, on the brink of our adventure. For the majority of the group, the number one goal was to get from one end of Britain to the other to raise as much money as possible for the charity. I was also determined to carve out time during the trip to fully appreciate the sights and sounds of Britain. The talk right now was Brexit, economic growth and booming house prices, but what interested me the most, were the unique facets of Britain I'd missed since moving away. Village greens, thatched cottages, buildings full of history, roundabouts decorated with flowers, craft beers, and the BBC. The list was endless and I had to continually remind myself that it would be fruitless to seek out everything. But I hoped for at least a taste of the Britain I craved and that our journey wouldn't be *all* about bike riding.

But had I really travelled half a world away to rekindle a twenty-year-old adventure? That I knew would be impossible. Each trip is always unique. But surely half a dozen men, the British weather, the ever-changing landscape, and Nick's hand-picked route would deliver enough ingredients for an adventure worthy of the past.

There were other factors to throw in the mix too, including how I now spent more time on a paddle board than I did on two wheels — unlike Alan and Nick, who I learnt throughout the course of the evening, had significantly improved their riding skills. In fact, since our ride in 1996, Alan has rarely stopped cycling, and from the way he discussed a recent bout of cycling exploits, he obviously enjoyed it greatly.

With this thought in mind, I declined the offer to help finish off the bottle of wine and decided to catch up on my jet lag. As I climbed the stairs, Gretna bounded alongside, and once at the top she sprawled on the floor. Alan appeared at my bedroom door a few moments later.

'I'll wake you just after six and we'll go and meet Nick to load up the van.'

'What shall I do about a Garmin? After talking with you, I'm beginning to appreciate their importance.'

'Maybe you can pick one up in the next few days. If not, just stay close during the ride and you won't go wrong. We'll cycle at a steady pace.'

I nodded appreciatively, patted Gretna on the head, and closed the door. I then lay sprawled fully clothed on the bed. Alan didn't know the half of it. Within an instant, my head began to spin with endless thoughts. Why hadn't I taken the time to buy a bike computer? How many emails from Nick had I failed to act upon? Had I trained hard enough for this venture? Had I finally gone mad?

Twenty years is a long time between bike rides of this magnitude, and my training regime over the past few months had been casual and erratic. Apart from midweek bouts on a gym bike, it consisted of (mostly) Sunday rides along the sunny coast. Now, as I lay on the spare bed, it struck me that I was a fifty-year-old man, hoping to undertake a feat that proved hard when I was thirty.

Ten thousand miles away, my family would most likely be awake by now, getting on with the day — a day without me in it. My fogged mind tried calculating the exact time difference, but the numbers became scrambled. Through the open window, I thought I heard an owl, followed by absolute silence as I fell into deep sleep.

I woke next morning to the sound of whistling, as Alan knocked on the bedroom door and announced that tea and toast were ready. An hour later we were outside Nick's house. His garage door was open, and just like twenty years ago, it was filled with an extensive collection of bike parts. He wiped his hands on a rag, stowed a can of oil, and walked across the gravel drive to greet me. Like Alan, he hadn't changed much — the same style of glasses, his fair hair a little thinner, and still dressed in his trademark casual shorts and trainers.

'Morning, Ali. Ready for another adventure? You do know I'm not cycling the whole way, don't you?'

I'd heard this a few weeks before but secretly hoped that Nick and his dodgy knee would pull through at the eleventh hour. Now, it seemed, that wouldn't happen.

'My knee's stuffed,' he continued. 'So, I'm afraid you'll have to put up with me as project manager. The good news is though, you don't have to stuff all your clothes into panniers like you did twenty years ago'—he chuckled—'which is a good job, because I hear you have some books to sell along the way. You can keep them in Colin's van until you need them. I'm driving it all the way, so I'll also be the mobile mechanic.'

I felt a stab of remorse for Nick. Not only had he instigated the ride and planned every mile of the route, he'd also booked all the accommodation along the way. But his knee had flared up during the training sessions and no amount of anti-inflammatory painkillers would get him through the 1,000-mile trip. While mumbling something about microsurgery, he returned to the garage and wheeled out a jet-black, touring bike.

'Ali, meet your companion for the next thirteen days. And before you ramble on, don't thank me, thank Steve. And before you ask, you don't know Steve but he's my mate. And before you suggest it, he doesn't want any money for the loan of the bike, but I'm sure he'd appreciate a few beers when it's returned. I've put a rain jacket in the panniers as well. It's old and black but will keep you dry if you haven't got anything better.'

As I straddled the frame, he adjusted the height of the saddle and then instructed me to give it a spin before the other riders appeared. I did a quick tour of the street and then returned posthaste to the driveway.

'Did you notice you're riding a cyclo-cross bike?'

'Yes, I did actually.'

He looked impressed and beamed appreciatively. 'So you do read my emails then?'

'I may have missed a couple, sorry. Although, I do remember the one that said cyclo-cross bikes are perfect for roads and tracks.'

'Exactly,' he agreed. 'That's why we're using them. This journey will be nothing like the one we did all those years ago. You'll be impressed. Please tell me you opened the email that had all the information regarding the co-ordinates for your computer.'

'Well, now that you mention it...'

'Have you at least uploaded the daily routes onto your Garmin?'

'Well, not exactly.'

'Ali, you did get a Garmin, didn't you? Like I suggested?'

'Er, no... I'm sorry Nick. I thought I'd get one when I touched down in England, but somehow I've ran out of time.'

He shook his head in disbelief. 'Well, I guess there's no point worrying about that now. We should have enough between us, but I warn you, if you ever become separated from the group, you'll be in trouble.'

'Don't worry about that,' I replied eagerly. 'I can use a road map. Just like before.'

'But that's the point I'm trying to make, Ali. The route we're following can't be found on a map like that.'

'Well, I'll just make sure I don't get lost then.'

Nick rolled his eyes a little, and then smiled. 'Does this mean you're not going to stop a million times to talk to strangers then? Or disappear to take photos of tea rooms and castles?'

'I'll try to behave,' I replied with a sheepish grin, 'but I've been living in Australia a long time and can't help getting excited when I see thatched cottages and monuments.'

'If you miss them that much, why don't you move back to England?'

But before I had chance to reply, he looked over my shoulder and waved. 'Oh look, here's Mark! You better not tell him you haven't got a bike computer.'

I recognised the trademark mop of blonde hair the moment he cycled into view. He and I had worked together for many years at the Vauxhall Motors car plant in Luton, often played in the same football team, and also travelled together in Queensland, Australia, on an outback adventure. In all the years I'd known him I'd never regarded him as a cyclist, but first impressions were favourable as he effortlessly unclipped from the pedals and with assured confidence gave his bike a final inspection before stowing it in the transit van. It was then I remembered Alan telling me that Mark had been training hard in the last few months and was actually 'a bit of a natural.'

This came as no surprise but unsettled me a little. Was I to be the only one at the back? I waited for the other riders to appear, searching in earnest for someone of similar ability with whom I'd share stories while we laboured at the rear. But the next rider to cycle into the driveway stopped proficiently, unclipped easily, and stowed his bike within seconds. He was dressed in Lycra bottoms and a matching top. The colour had been washed out over multiple uses and his bike shoes were weathered with age. I was soon to learn his name was Colin and mountain biking had been his hobby for years.

The next to arrive was Mick. I'd met him previously on a few occasions, but only for short periods during my trips back home to England. One look at his purpose-built bike, sturdy leg muscles, and wraparound sunglasses told me all I needed to know about his passion and proficiency.

The final rider was JP, who I had never met before. He arrived with a bright smile, tentatively unclipped his feet from the pedals, and called Nick over to inspect the gears. A decade younger than myself, his comparative youthfulness looked to be offset by the same unfamiliarity around bikes as myself. Maybe I had found someone who would keep me company at the back from time to time.

While stowing my clothes into the back of the transit van, I placed my biking shoes alongside the other pairs, each scratched or pitted with battle scars. Mine, in comparison, looked shiny and unblemished.

From the back of Colin's van, we waved goodbye to family and friends, then set off towards Cornwall. Land's End is the most westerly point in mainland England and it is here that all end-to-end journeys begin or end. The peninsula is a spectacular location with steep cliffs rising from the deep blue of the English Channel. Those who like walking are spoiled for choice with a network of trails heading inland towards picturesque villages, or along windswept ridges that lead to hidden coves and golden beaches.

Upon our arrival at Land's End, we entered an archway into a pedestrianised area, passed alongside a tourist information booth, and followed the wide path to the sea front. Only a few shops were open. It was getting late.

With each step, the memories of twenty years earlier flooded back to me, and it was like I'd never left. Just like before, the sea shimmered with tiny white sails. To our right stood the Land's End signpost, positioned close to the cliffs.

Since the 1950s, visitors to Land's End have had their photograph taken under the famous sign. It's also a tradition for end-to-enders to have their photo taken by the signpost before departing on the long journey to John O'Groats where, by good fortune, there's another signpost.

The signpost at Land's End is privately owned and there's a small fee to stand under the pointers. Included in the cost is the opportunity to add your hometown onto an allocated marker, along with its distance in miles from Land's End. There are four locations permanently etched into the arrows: New York (3,147 miles), John O'Groats (874 miles), the Isles of Scilly (28 miles) and the Longships Lighthouse (1.5 miles).

We waited for our turn while a family of four from Barcelona stood proudly under the signpost. The photographer chatted freely and took the necessary shots with a big smile. After ushering them away, the letters that made up the word *Barcelona* were exchanged for *Ampthill* (for the majority of our group) and *Busselton* (for me) in Australia. I was 9,302 miles from home.

After the photo-shoot, Colin suggested it was time for a celebratory beer and the group followed in hot pursuit. But with no one else waiting for a photo, I couldn't resist taking the opportunity to chat with the photographer. I learned his name was Dan, and he was in his early twenties.

'So, how's business?' I asked, genuinely interested.

He cast his eyes towards the sky and said, 'Fantastic! Especially on a day like today.'

'Do you get many cyclists posing for photos?'

'Oh, yes. Mostly during spring or summer. That's expected, I suppose. We also meet a lot of walkers, about to set off for John O'Groats... and those who've finished the walk. You have to take your hat off to them. Mind you, after all that walking, most of them look pretty healthy. It's better than a gym membership, I reckon.'

I nodded in agreement. 'For sure.'

'Mind you, most of the people that want a photo by the signpost are just here on holiday. They're after a memento and our job is to make it an enjoyable experience.'

As we spoke, a group of women arrived for an impromptu photo, and within a few minutes, they were positioned alongside the signpost. They were from Glasgow, 564 miles away — a location we'd be cycling through in just over a week. I watched them form a semi-circle, heard something about a family reunion, and then they were gone.

I asked Dan if he could remember the longest distance that any visitor had requested for the sign and felt proud when he admitted that my hometown of Busselton, Western Australia, was a formidable distance away. But not the furthest.

'To tell you the truth, I've got no idea,' he said after pondering my question. 'But we did get a guy here from Chile last week, who lives further away than you do!'

It was time for me to find Colin and the others, but as I bid farewell to Dan, the sound of laughter caught my attention. Congregated around a small plaza, stood some people in running attire. I heard the gentle strum of a guitar and the call for a song as a champagne cork popped into the sky.

I approached the edge of the group and spoke with a woman in her early thirties with long blonde hair, pulled into a tight ponytail. Dark circles ringed her eyes, and as she spoke, I soon understood why. 'We've just run all the way from John O'Groats in nine days. I'm bloody knackered but feel ten feet tall!'

For a few moments, she excitedly explained how they'd worked as a relay team with one person at a time always running, except at night. A support van and accompanying rider made up the equation as they battled fatigue and blisters to run 900 miles between them. I wanted to talk for longer, to find out about the highs and lows, but she was being called upon to join in with a sing-song. As she approached her friends, another cork popped, followed by cheers and laughter.

I found my group, nestled together on a paved area outside the Land's End restaurant. They were sat around a wooden bench, and as Colin handed me a pint of beer, we chinked glasses and raised a toast to Nick for his hard work in making it all happen.

Despite the fact that thousands of end-to-end cyclists depart from Land's End every year, I couldn't see any more cyclists in the area. Apart from the runners — whose singing could be heard from afar — most other visitors looked to be day-trippers. They seemed content simply taking photos, enjoying a light refreshment or two, and walking sedately along the footpath. I wondered if any of them even knew about the end-to-end challenge.

On an adjacent seat, a discarded newspaper caught my attention. The front-page headline read, *ENGLAND SET TO SWELTER*, and a quick scan revealed that sizzling temperatures, up to 35 degrees, were forecast for Cornwall, Devon and Somerset over the next four days. This weather system coincided with the exact timeframe we'd be cycling through those very same counties.

It was apparent the heat wave had already begun, but at least today, the ride would be easy. We had just an eleven-mile jaunt to our overnight stay. Tomorrow would be the first real test. It wasn't just the mileage that needed to be considered. Total elevation was also a critical factor. The south-west of England is notoriously hilly, and steep inclines and long descents are characteristic. According to Nick's calculation, the ride on day two would be 72 miles long with a total elevation of 7,750 feet.

This figure prompted me to consider what our total elevation would be, over the entire bike ride. As we sat side by side, our backs to the sea, I asked him if he knew the answer.

'Yes, of course,' he replied. 'Didn't you open the email that showed all the data?'

I lowered my voice. 'I might have overlooked that one, sorry.'

'The approximate figure is 63,000 feet.'

I mulled the number around in my head for a moment and then asked, 'That's a big number. Are you sure?'

'Of course I'm sure. The numbers stack up when we're in the south-west and once again when we get to the Highlands. So, Ali, by the time you've reached John O'Groats you'll have cycled twice the height of Mount Everest!'

As his words sunk in, he followed up with a final comment, 'All those hours of training that you did in Australia are about to come in very handy.'

Suddenly, I felt totally unprepared and hid my feelings by excusing myself to take a photo of the lighthouse, far in the distance. Cornwall has long been considered to be Britain's most dangerous coastline, with over one hundred and fifty known shipwrecks recorded off the coast of Land's End. Despite GPS, lighthouses, foghorns, and lookouts, accidents still happen in the treacherous waters.

The sight of the lighthouse made me think carefully about the precautions I'd put in place to ensure I'd get to John O'Groats safely. I was reasonably fit, but it was equally important to have the right equipment. Would the lack of a bike computer influence the outcome of my ride? I hoped not. And what about the rain jacket Nick had been kind enough to lend me? Black was an unsafe option. I would most definitely have to buy a new one.

I returned to the table a little frazzled, just as Nick announced, 'I think it's time to go, lads. It's getting late and we're going out for dinner in Penzance this evening.'

There was no more time to fret. We were ready for the off. As we pulled our bikes into position, I saw Mick studying my handlebars. 'Where's your Garmin?' he asked.

I gave him a confident smile. 'I don't have one at the moment, but one way or another, I'll get to John O'Groats — with or without a computer.'

His eyes widened. 'You're not serious, are you?'

'I should have bought one in Australia but I never got round to it. Now, all of a sudden, it's real. I think I'm about to embark on an adventure I'm not fully prepared for.'

He eased out a wide smile. 'As long as you keep a steady pace, you'll be fine. Drink plenty of water and use electrolyte tablets. That's the key, believe me, especially on a day like today.'

Together, we walked our bikes away from the hotel and I took a final look at our surroundings. I could see Dan, far in the distance, standing alongside the iconic signpost, awaiting the next tourist. Nearby, the sound of laughter and music filled the air as we passed within earshot of the group of runners. I recognised the tune as their words rang out:

'*I would walk 500 miles and I would walk 500 more...*'

The wave of a hand caught my attention and I found myself grinning at the runner from earlier. She raised a bottle of champagne in the air and called out, 'Good luck!'

We turned inland, past the parade of shops, and made our way to the official starting location. It's a white painted line, now faded with time, stretched across the road. On our side of the line (nearest to Dan and his signpost), was a painted word that simply said, *Start*. On the other side of the line, on the other side of the road, I could just make out the letters that formed the word, *Finish*.

Twenty years had passed since I'd been in this exact spot with Alan and Nick. They were with me again right now but were in no way feeling nostalgic, dismissing my calls for a photo to recapture the historic moment. Instead, I sensed an eagerness to forget the formalities and just get moving.

Once again, I reminded myself that this wasn't meant to be a trip down memory lane. There were new dynamics now and other riders to consider. JP, who I still needed to get to know, Colin, who was already sitting on his saddle in readiness, and Mick, who stood alongside me, adjusting his bike helmet.

We completed our final preparations for the short ride towards Penzance, and I watched as the riders checked their computers. I switched on my own gadget then. It was a GoPro camera, attached to my bike helmet.

Clicking in our shoes, with no fanfare or cheers, we set off from the painted line. I eased towards the rear of the pack, unable to wipe the broad smile from my face. Our end-to-end journey had begun.

A few hours later, I was worried. JP, despite his lack of experience in long distance cycling, had evidently done more training than I had. And Mark, who I'd rarely known to ride, looked extremely assured and happy. From time to time, he rode no-handed, alongside the hedgerows, effortlessly making phone calls to his family as he trail-blazed along the country roads. It seemed I was alone in my inadequacy.

Soon after leaving Land's End, we diverted from the main road, opting for the quiet back roads, courtesy of the route Nick had uploaded. During the high-speed blitz towards Penzance, we encountered very little traffic. Short, sharp assaults were required to ascend steep sections of laneway, quickly followed by freewheeling descents down winding roads, hemmed in by hedgerows so tall it was impossible to know what lay on the other side. Small birds darted from trimmed hedges as we rode along cascading lanes, through whisper quiet hamlets, venturing into a series of undulating hills that cut through woodland.

On one occasion, I caught up with the front runner, just as a fork in the road appeared, and I heard the small beep of his bike computer as it recognised the location and instructed us to turn right. Suddenly, we were on a bridleway, free from cars, tractors, and tourists. The tempo was swift, and conversation was limited to snippets during the rare times when the road remained straight and even.

During the short journey, we made our way towards the coast and were rewarded with fleeting views of the English Channel, far beyond the trees. The road then dipped sharply, leading us to the fishing village of Mousehole. As we entered, my eyes were drawn to the two sturdy breakwaters, protruding from either side of the bay like a giant pair of arms about to embrace a loved one. A small fishing boat slowly made its way towards the gap, leaving a milky trail in its wake as it headed out to sea.

Granite cottages lined one side of a narrow road that ran parallel with the shore, each with a panoramic view of the mighty Atlantic far in the distance. The beach was dotted with a handful of holidaymakers, their bodies pale in contrast to the golden sands as they stretched out on beach towels or played in the shallows. One family prepared a kayak by the water's edge, while others watched boat owners go about their business. From the roadside, the clear waters this side of the harbour walls resembled a Mediterranean cove, dotted with family size craft, moored by ropes to the shore.

The main street was free from traffic but lively with families. Some carried buckets and spades, while others strolled sedately and enjoyed ice creams. Just beyond the breakwater, a cauldron of alleyways and backstreets enticed visitors with signs for restaurants, and on a street corner I noticed a shop owned by a local artisan selling handmade artefacts.

The Ship Inn took pride of place along the narrow beachfront roadway where double yellow lines had been painted, both sides, to ensure that cars couldn't stop. The pub windows were slightly ajar, and through the gaps I could see patrons enjoying a late afternoon drink. A placard by the door promised, *Fine Ales, Fresh Seafood and Live Music.*

This was the type of quintessential Britain I'd missed since moving from the UK. It wasn't just the beers on offer, but the ambience, the setting, and the views. On such a fine day, with hardly a breath of wind to stir the water, it was difficult to imagine that this was an unforgiving coastline. But a plaque on the pub wall caught my attention and I rode over to read the words.

Charles Greenhaugh
Landlord of this house
And crewman of the Solomon Browne
Lost with all hands, 19th December, 1981
Remembered with great affection

Winter months can be perilous, as demonstrated by the events of December 1981 when a vessel called the Union Star got into trouble in heavy seas. The Solomon Browne lifeboat battled wind gusts of up to 100 miles-per-hour as it headed from the Penlee lifeboat station near Mousehole towards the stricken ship. Alas, disaster struck with a total of sixteen people losing their life including eight volunteer life boatmen.

Later, Lt Commander Smith, the pilot of the rescue helicopter was reported as saying:

'*The greatest act of courage that I have ever seen, and am likely to see, was the penultimate courage and dedication by the Penlee (crew) when it maneuvered back alongside the casualty in over 60 feet breakers and rescued four people...They were the bravest eight men I have ever seen, who were also dedicated to upholding the highest standards of the Royal National Lifeboat Institution'.*

By the time we reached Penzance, the sun was beginning its descent, and along the waterfront, couples strolled hand in hand in search of a place to eat. Our first day's ride had not been arduous. But it had already stirred many emotions within me.

After showering, we ventured out for our first evening into Penzance, yet Mousehole was close to my thoughts. I wanted to return there, to watch the sun set behind the village, and to wander around its laneways. It was tantalisingly close, and as we ventured into a nearby pub in search of food, I'd made a decision.

'Look lads, I'm not sure if you are up for it, but I'd love to go to Mousehole for the evening. It's only a few miles away in a taxi.'

Nick was deliberating over which starter to choose from the menu, but upon my request he looked up. 'Ali, we were only there a little while ago.'

'Yes, I know that. But it was only for a very short time. I'd like to go back and experience the village at sunset. We could enjoy their locally brewed ales and sample the freshly caught seafood. I noticed there was live music later on, too.'

My proposal to the group was met by silence. One of the lads had not heard my appeal and wandered up, beer in hand and menu open.

'Well, I'm ready to order. How about you guys?'

I stood uncertain of my next move while everyone's eyes dropped to their menus. Nick had the final word.

'Ali, please don't take this personally, but we've all been to Mousehole before. I know you love that type of quaint stuff, mate, but we're ready for dinner and a few beers right now. Let it go. Come back again some other time. This is a long distance bike ride, not a holiday.'

Red-faced and reluctant, I grabbed a menu and fought the urge to disagree. I hardly knew some of the riders and didn't want to cause a scene on the first evening, but Mousehole was so close. I could almost smell the sea air and see the tide retreating through the gap in the harbour walls. By sunset we could be relaxing on the window seats at The Ship Inn, toasting our first day in the saddle. Travellers from across the world would share special moments about their day, while in the corner a friendly local might be willing to share a Cornish secret for the price of an ale.

Instead, we were in a non-descript pub — pleasant enough, admittedly — but in the middle of Penzance city-centre. Yes, the staff were friendly, the décor clean, and the beers were palatable, but I didn't want to be in a pub with fruit machines and tinny, piped music. I wanted an historic pub, overlooking the sea. I yearned for folk tunes, a fiddler, fishermen tales and a live band, each one heralding the summer. After the group had ordered, I made my way to the bar, still oblivious to what was on the menu.

'Do you have any seafood specials?' I asked the barmaid.

She nodded gently and shared a wry smile. It seemed my suggestion to go elsewhere hadn't gone completely unnoticed, and her green eyes were wide in acknowledgement.

She pointed to the specials board and said, 'I totally agree with you. The Ship Inn is lovely at this time of year. If it makes you feel any better we do have bass, caught fresh today by fishermen from Mousehole.'

'That will be perfect,' I said and returned to the table where JP handed me a pint of ale. I raised my glass. 'Those of you who know me will understand I'm disappointed about not returning to Mousehole. But I'm sure there will be many more evenings when we'll get the chance to experience places like it. For those who don't know me, you'll soon discover I'm a little bit prone to nostalgia. I've been living in Australia for thirteen years now, but on days like this I could move back to England in an instant!'

The speech was met with nods of agreement, and during dinner, the route for day two was discussed. Nick explained that it was imperative to stick together, drink plenty of fluids, and to set off early to take advantage of the morning breeze.

Throughout the meal, I constantly mulled over what Nick had said earlier about us being on a bike ride, not a holiday. Surely we could combine the two? I knew that anything different would challenge me. To travel so far and be unable to deviate from the plan would be immensely difficult for me. To do so would take time and lots of energy — neither of which I had.

But my allegiance had to be with the group. Not my selfish diversions. I just hoped my natural curiosity and need to *experience* (rather than just *see*) would benefit, and not hinder, our ride.

With these thoughts tucked neatly away, after dinner, I joined the group as we circumnavigated the town on foot. It was a Saturday evening and the warm breeze had enticed the locals to come out in force, many of whom had far more hair than myself, Alan, and Nick. Resident DJs ranted loudly, their music pulsating across the cobbled streets. We gave these bars a miss, in search of a place where we could exchange a conversation without yelling.

Eventually, we found a pub with a solo singer, but after Alan had placed an order for a round of beers, she announced to the small crowd it was her final song of the evening. I thought of the musician in Mousehole who by now would have finished their final set. Although, maybe there'd been an encore,

Outside, the fishing boats would be illuminated under the waxing moon and couples would be gazing over the water, in search of a shooting star.

We finished our drinks and spilled outside, greeted by a humid breeze. It was time to head home, but as the group studied road signs and weighed up various options, it was clear that no-one knew the way. Luckily, we had some common sense, and within a few minutes — without the need to study a computer — we discarded the cobbled lane and chose the quiet street that led back to our beds.

Day 2: Roll Along Summer

'We reward those who draw maps, not those who follow them.'
Seth Godin

Far out to our right, high above the glistening waters of the English Channel, the sun was a welcome sight. But with every passing hour and each new hill that we encountered, its strength increased and it quickly turned from friend to foe.

There were short interludes of relief, when we rode under canopies of mature trees, but at most other times, the trees that lined the roads and cycle paths were young, and their immature branches gave little respite from the overhead glare. Even the hedgerows that skirted the roads, neatly trimmed and taller than a grown man, were of little help when the sun was at its zenith.

When required, we stopped at various village shops to stock up on water and snacks, using each opportunity to talk about the landscape through which we passed. But with over 70 miles to travel, and an estimated elevation of 8,000 feet to climb, there was little time to rest in one place.

The aim for today was the same as every day — to reach our destination in time for a welcome shower, a hot meal, and a few refreshments before last orders at the local pub. In theory, it was simple.

The sun had continued its journey and was now up to our left, casting our stick-like shadows across the country road as we pedalled past a majestic oak tree. I searched for the slightest movement within its weeping branches, but the leaves were still. Then, the tree was gone, replaced by a hedgerow of hawthorn.

As we rode alongside it, an unexpected gap in the foliage gave us a rare glimpse of what lay beyond. The land resembled a sea of honey, each stalk of corn upright, waiting for a welcome breeze. Apart from the hum of rubber on tarmac, nothing else stirred. It seemed even the insects had ceased their buzzing and the sky held no sign of birdlife.

Each rider, lost in their own thoughts, continued to focus on the task ahead. Positioned in the middle of the pack, I watched the rear wheel of the bike in front and followed closely in its slipstream. The aim had been to cycle at pace through the final 10 miles in an effort to get to our destination before sunset, but I was struggling. The day's journey was already a hazy memory, with too many inclines, declines, sharp bends, and bike tracks to recall. Plus there was my growing list of ailments.

It had started after breakfast with stomach cramp, and by midday, my left kneecap was clicking loudly. At first, I was curious rather than worried, but soon, every other click resulted in a jolt of pain shooting up my thigh muscle to join the discomfort in my stomach. As the sun began to drop and the last of my water was drained, a dull ache began forming in the base of my skull.

It wasn't only my knee that was making unusual sounds. Since lunch, the rear sprocket of my bike had been complaining and the gnashing grew even louder when I tackled a steep hill. I'd long ceased asking how much further it was to go. Like a young child in the back seat of a car, I was in danger of sounding like a scratched record, so I'd fallen silent. Besides, each revolution of the pedals was a laboured task and I needed all my concentration.

A soft but jubilant cheer from the front rider prompted me to lift my head. Far in the distance, I noticed a road sign, shaped like a giant lollipop, positioned on the verge. As we cycled closer, my eyes zeroed in on the strategic marker, hunting for words that would declare we'd made it to our destination. I pulled off my sunglasses, wiped sweat from my eyes, and squinted at the letters. Sunlight glinted off the round plaque, forcing us to ride closer to read the words etched into the metal plate. If they dared read, *Say No to Fracking,* or, *Keep Britain Beautiful,* instead of, *Welcome to Callington,* my world was in danger of collapsing. As the sun dropped behind the hills, it seemed my life depended on the signpost.

Far ahead, Mark raised his arm into the air and I knew at once we'd made it. I looked to my right at the cyclist alongside me. It was Mick. His usual grin was replaced by a weary nod as he said, 'I think we've earned a beer, Ali.'

As he cycled on past, I pulled my water bottle from its holder in the hope of extracting a trickle to ease my parched lips. 'How long did it take?' I called out, my voice a croak.

He checked his bike computer and called back. 'Too long. Nine and a half hours.'

'Total elevation?'

'7,800 feet. There are plenty of hills tomorrow too.'

He was cycling alongside a war memorial; its granite features dark against the cobalt sky. We were now in the heart of the small town of Callington, passing shops displaying their wares. The town was winding down for the evening, and the butchers, florists, and hardware merchants had already closed. As we were close to finishing, I reached into my front panniers and pulled out the GoPro camera. It was time to capture this moment for posterity.

I switched on the video, and up ahead noticed the first rider dismounting outside a terraced house. While JP stopped to talk to an elderly lady, I pointed the lens towards my face. 'We've just finished day two and have been cycling for nine and a half hours in temperatures up to 32 degrees. Our total elevation since leaving the town of ...'

In an instant my mind went blank. Where *had* I woken up so many hours earlier? Where *had* I enjoyed a cooked breakfast before preparing for the ride?

While the video recorded, my mind scrambled to find the answer. Just then, Nick appeared from a nearby doorway. He had his hands on his hips and smiled widely at the sight before him. The memories came flooding back. I'd woken in Penzance.

*

That morning, I'd been roused by the persistent squawk of gulls outside my bedroom window and had drawn back the heavy curtains to investigate. Directly ahead was Penzance train station and beyond the russet walls of the elongated building, the dark waters of the English Channel stretched towards a pale blue sky. A gull appeared, gliding silently alongside the rooftops on an early thermal, and my eyes were drawn to my left. Just offshore, I could make out the rocky outcrop of Saint Michael's Mount, its craggy features in stark contrast to the lapping of soft waves against its edges.

I heard movement and turned to face JP on the far side of the room. He'd just woken and was already up and about, preparing for the day ahead. He grabbed his empty water bottles and urged me to do the same as he bounded downstairs for breakfast.

The owner of the accommodation was dressed in casual shorts and a T-shirt and greeted us with a cheery smile at the foot of the stairs.

'Morning lads, you can sit wherever you like — just be careful of the bikes. Tea or coffee?'

After ordering our drinks, we stepped into the breakfast room. It was bright and airy with a bay window offering plenty of natural light. Three cyclo-cross bikes had been precariously placed against the walls and tables. With no outside garage, last night the owner had kindly offered the use of his dining room as an overnight parking lot.

All the other riders were in the room, mostly wearing Lycra for the day ahead. Nick, however, was not dressed for the road and was buttering a piece of toast. I sat alongside him.

'Morning, Nick. Aren't you cycling today?'

'Not until this afternoon. I want to get you guys on the road as fast as possible. It's going to be a real hot one. Plus, my knee's aching from yesterday. I'll drive to tonight's accommodation and then I might cycle back to meet you for the last few hours.'

'What route are we taking today?'

He smiled. 'Ali, if you owned a bike computer and had read all my emails you'd know this already.'

I stared into my tea while, to my relief, he carried on. 'Tonight, we're staying in a Georgian town house. The owners are artisans. It'll be right up your street.'

I nodded in appreciation and poured more tea. 'But I warn you now,' he continued, 'not all the accommodation on our trip will be so grand.'

Before I had a chance to ask him what he meant, he launched into a brief but informative run-down on what lay ahead for the day. Our destination was the country town of Callington, located in the east of Cornwall between two expanses of open moorland known as Bodmin and Dartmoor. I learned that after a short stint on a dual carriageway, we'd mostly be using cycle paths and country roads, and we would even take a ride on a river ferry.

By the time that breakfast had finished, I'd learnt that there were literally thousands of possible routes. Apart from the roads ending at Land's End and John O'Groats, every other road, canal path and bike track in Britain — and everything in between — were available for us to use. Even a mathematician would be tested, calculating the numerous ways that you could cycle from one end of Britain to the other.

This is one of the many appeals of LEJOG. It's possible to take a unique, purpose-built route to suit your personality, fitness, timetable, or budget. You can even complete the challenge from north to south instead. This route is known as JOGLE.

After saying our goodbyes to the landlord, we stepped outside to be greeted by the warmest morning of summer so far. The sun was already high, and the road alongside the bed and breakfast was busy with passing traffic. Some cars were driven by lone drivers, their expressions blank as they commuted to work. Others were laden with people and luggage, and more than once, I noticed beach balls stuffed in rear windows. These families were embarking on their summer holidays and would soon be relaxing on one of the many beaches that help make Cornwall such a desirable location.

I had no idea when I'd next enjoy the feeling of warm sand between my toes. For now, they were snuggly fitted inside my new cycling shoes. The hard, plastic soles were not designed for walking far, and as we crossed the road towards the van, the gentle taps from each rider resonated across the bitumen.

While we prepared for departure, I noticed Nick was often called upon to assist with minor maintenance issues. A squirt of oil for JP. The loan of an Allen key for Colin and Mick. While brakes and chains were adjusted, I made an impulsive decision and cycled into town in a last-minute attempt to locate a shop that sold bike computers. Most shopkeepers were still at home. In frustration, I undertook a swift tour of the one-way system, again found no open bike shops, and returned to the car park just in time.

Nick spotted me and called us together to make his feelings known with an abrupt but riveting speech.

'This has been a poor attempt at an early start for our first full day on the road. It's going to be the hottest day of the year today, its already gone nine, and you haven't even started cycling yet.'

He then tapped my arm and said, 'Stick to the group, Ali. You haven't got a bike computer and they can't hang around if you fall behind. If you do get lost, head for the River Fal and take the King Harry Ferry. I'll be driving that way too.'

I put my thumbs up, unsure if I was already in his bad books, but the conversation was soon forgotten as Mark took the initiative and headed towards Callington.

Within minutes, we were cycling behind him along a coastal footpath. Terraced houses, dating back to Victorian times, stood alongside the road. Some gardens displayed wooden signs, informing holidaymakers about whether they had vacancies or not. Despite the sunshine, there were still quite a few to choose from. To our right, the English Channel touched the horizon, a glint of sunshine giving away the position of a faraway ship.

Despite our late departure, the mood was relaxed and the pace steady, allowing me to ride alongside Alan. He was knowledgeable about the area, reminding me that his wife, Sam, had once lived in Mousehole.

'Have you thought of a nickname for the bike Steve's lent you? Will it be called the Donegal Flyer, like the one you used twenty years ago?'

I laughed at the thought. 'No, the Donegal Flyer has retired from active service but is actually still alive and well, residing in my brother's shed. I think I'll call this bike the Bedfordshire Clanger, because the owner lives in Bedfordshire and I'm sure over the next two weeks it will make a few clanging noises.'

Alan nodded. 'You do know what a Bedfordshire Clanger is, don't you, Ali?'

'Yes of course,' I grinned. 'It's a traditional farm-labourer's meal, almost like a sausage roll. Except one half is sweet and the other is savoury.'

He grinned back. 'Looks like you haven't forgotten everything about Ye Olde England since you've been away then. Great name, Ali.'

Then he pointed to a small island, just offshore. 'Do you know what that's called?'

'I certainly do, Alan, but it's the first time I've ever been this close.'

'It's pretty cool, isn't it?'

As we approached Saint Michael's Mount, Alan chatted on about how enjoyable the day's ride would be. But I found my attention waning, drawn instead towards the craggy outcrop. I could just make out the sharp features of the medieval castle on the top. It was tantalisingly close. The sea had retracted but could still be seen, glistening at the edges of the sandbar.

The ebb and flow of the tide are one of the natural traits that help make Saint Michael's Mount such a magical location. It can only be reached on foot when the tide is out, and those that stroll across the cobbled causeway must return to the mainland before the sea creeps back or opt to pay for a crossing on one of the motorboats that service the island.

Over the centuries, the causeway has been used by thousands of people and most have walked across in peace. But in 1473, during the War of the Roses, rampaging soldiers tore across the cobblestones at low tide, intent on storming the castle. Now, the very place where these men, women and children had converged over the centuries was within my reach for the very first time.

There's a junction on the cycle path, which leads directly to the causeway. I discovered this a few moments later, but by then, Alan and the others had pulled ahead and were about to cycle round a bend in the track. I'd been so transfixed with the island that my pace had unknowingly slackened, but JP was still within earshot.

'Aren't we stopping for a group photo?' I called.

He twisted his head around and shouted something, but I couldn't hear the words. He then turned back towards the path and continued pedalling.

To my right, the cobbled causeway leading to the ancient monument looked inviting. For many years, I'd heard about Saint Michael's Mount and was intrigued that such a small outcrop could have such a dramatic history.

The island was once in the possession of monks, and during the 12th century, they constructed a church and priory. These buildings still exist, although it's the 14th century castle that now dominates the landscape. Its strategic location is an ideal fortress, and over the centuries it has been part of many conflicts, including the time when its cannons fired upon a Napoleonic ship, forcing it onto the nearby beach where it was subsequently captured.

I was now within reach of this unique location, but the riders had vanished. What was I to do? Just as I was about to change gear in an attempt to catch them up, I instinctively braked and completed a sharp U-turn instead. I couldn't just ride past, not without a gaze. It wasn't in me.

Returning to the intersection, I turned left along the footpath and free-wheeled down to the sandy beach. A small wooden boat lay on its side, not far from the edge of the footpath, giving clues to the extent of high tide.

An elderly man sat alone, perched comfortably on a wooden bench near the end of the footpath. At his feet lay a wooden cane, and by his side was a tea flask. He watched as I dismounted at speed, searched for my camera, and took a photo.

I stared longingly at the causeway. The sand to my right looked soft, stretching out towards the water. The left side of the causeway was protected by rocks, each coated in moss and glistening in the early morning sunshine. The sea ebbed sedately at the back and sides of the outcrop, held back by the force of the moon, still visible in the sky.

It was possible to reach the monument within a few minutes if I raced across. But with cycling shoes, the likelihood of falling flat on my back was high. Barefoot was an option, but it would take too much time to get my shoes on and off. Also, I didn't have a lock for my bike.

The only person within view was the elderly man and he was beginning to nod off as the morning sun caressed his rugged face. If I ran along the causeway, just quickly, at what point would I stop? At the place where the outcrop loomed from the sand? What would I see from such a vantage point? Would a hooded monk appear from the seaward gardens, greet me warmly and invite me to the island for a tour of the monastery?

I snapped back to reality and turned the bike around to face away from the island. The old man was suddenly awake, staring at me through glassy eyes.

'Are you in a hurry? It's not far, you know. I'll look after your bike if you want to take a walk to the island.'

I angled my face towards him, still straddling my bike. 'I'd love to, thank you, but I'm a bit pushed for time.'

'But it's only half past nine and the tide will be in later.'

I wanted to explain about the end-to-end bike ride and the fact that we were already an hour late and that my friends probably had no clue I was currently talking to a stranger. But the very idea of sharing this knowledge and risking a long-winded explanation was now verging on the ridiculous. I'd made my decision.

'I think I'll come back another day with my family. Do you think it will still be here in three years' time?'

He opened his mouth to reply, but without waiting for an answer, I bid him farewell and returned to the bike path, my eyes now focused on the route ahead.

For over ten minutes, my legs spun frantically on the pedals as I took the slight curves at speed in order catch the pack. Far in the distance, I noticed their row of heads just above a stone wall as they continued their steady, but determined, pace. By the time I caught up with JP, stabbing pains in my stomach reminded me that the deviation had come at a price.

He looked over at me. 'Where did you go?'

'To get a selfie with Saint Michael's Mount,' I replied between short breaths.

'Diversions will cost you, mate.'

I joined the back of the pack and mulled his words over. I knew he was right. But something was niggling me and it wasn't just the sharp pains in my stomach. Yes, the distraction had made me sweat and given me an early stomach ache. But that would soon pass, I was sure. What was really disconcerting was that the other riders were oblivious to the fact I'd doubled back.

We'd turned inland, obscuring all views of the sea. According to Nick, our next sighting of open water would be the North Sea in twelve days' time. Just ahead, a fork in the road appeared, and I heard the faint sound of a computer beep as the lead biker took the left-hand turn.

If I'd arrived at this location just a few minutes later, I wouldn't have known which path to take. The riders were following computer co-ordinates and I was meant to be following them closely. If I got lost or kept them waiting, I might drive a wedge between us. Or worse, I might jeopardise the ride.

This, I felt, was the message that JP was trying to tell me. Their ultimate goal was cycling, not sightseeing. A momentary peek at a place of interest would be more than enough for them, and I envied them in many ways. Why couldn't I be happy with just a fleeting glance? I'd been away for too long.

As we continued our journey inland, pace quickening, I kept reminding myself of Nick's advice. By the time the next bout of hills appeared, all thoughts of taking diversions had vanished.

I've always enjoyed navigating using ordnance survey maps, and in my 20s and 30s, I spent numerous weekends, striding across the English countryside with friends, armed with a compass. The maps opened up new worlds, and after numerous summers and a few arctic-like winters in the Highlands of Scotland, I'd become a competent trekker and navigator.

I've always wanted to know where exactly I am in the world. Maps fascinate me. However, I now needed to understand more about the bike computers so that I wasn't so reliant on others guiding me all the way to John O'Groats. There was no way a basic road map would be detailed enough to locate the bike paths and canal tracks he'd chosen. The only other option was to buy an ordnance survey map, but the logistics of purchasing one for every area of Britain that we needed, then finding the correct location and following the route — all while cycling — would be expensive, cumbersome, and just plain unrealistic. Only with a bike computer would I be in control and, more importantly, know exactly where I was.

At this moment in time, I had no idea of our exact location. I only knew it was day two, that hours earlier we'd ridden past Saint Michael's Mount and turned inland, and that we'd blitzed through a landscape so divine that at any point in time I could have parked my bike, plucked a wildflower from the verge, and wandered into a nearby meadow to gaze at the distant trail of clouds that clung to the stratosphere. The exact coordinates of the meadow, though? I had no clue. Without the others, I'd be lost in a heartbeat. So, until I got hold of a bike computer, I needed to stay close at all times.

Nick had transported us into another world, devoid of crowds, free from other cyclists, and at every bend in the road, there was something new to experience. At times, the route took a short sharp dip, allowing us to ride at speed before an abrupt turn forced a change of gear and an assault up another hill. Sometimes, we were cocooned by hedgerows so tall that it was impossible to know what lay beyond. At other times, we passed farmyards, and in those precious seconds, gained friendly nods from tractor drivers or stares from inquisitive cows, unaware of the yellow plastic markers pinned to their ears.

If it wasn't for the fact I had no clue where we were, I'd have been extremely happy. At this very moment, I wanted to move back to England from

Australia and live in every village we encountered. There was also a warm feeling of being part of a unique experience, part of something special.

I've known Alan, Mark and Nick for years, sharing adventures of some sort with them all. With Mark, this included a trip to Uluru in the outback of Australia. With Alan, I'd enjoyed a holiday in Tenerife as well as the first end-to-end trip. I'd lost touch with Nick since moving to Australia, but upon meeting him again a few days prior, we'd continued our relationship as if it had been weeks — not years — since the last encounter.

It was the other three riders I needed to spend time with. If only I could catch them up. They took every sudden turn, change of angle, and unplanned tractor encounter in their stride. Even JP, who I secretly hoped would wear out his rear brake quicker than mine, was proving to be a competent rider. In between hurtling down narrow roads and panting up the other side, I learned he was a musician. A pianist, to be exact, who assisted world-class pianists prepare for classical concerts. He'd joined the ride as a tribute to his friend, Chris, and like all of the riders, was eager to raise as much money as possible.

It was during a conversation with JP about the merits of catching a train to work — as opposed to an aircraft, on which I flew each week to work at an iron ore mining company in Western Australia— that he pointed ahead in excitement. We'd reached the River Fal.

The road narrowed and turned into a zig-zag before dropping towards the water. The river meandered gently with barely a ripple on its surface, and from our vantage point, the far side looked heavily wooded. On our side of the river, the foliage had been cut to make way for the road and a settlement of houses. I could see a large brick building, adorned with hanging baskets in full bloom. Its bedroom windows seemed to offer great views of the river, and I noticed that one section of the downstairs floor was in use as a ticket office and ice cream counter. A ferry in the distance filled in the missing piece of the jigsaw.

The King Harry Steam Company was formed on the 18th April 1888, to offer a ferry service to connect the settlements of Feock and Philleigh. In all this time, just seven boats have been used to cross back and forth at regular intervals.

Today, numerous cars were backed up, awaiting the boats arrival. JP and I joined a small group of passengers who had taken the opportunity to escape from their cars to admire the view. From the elevated position of the final bend, we could see it berthed on the far bank, its hydraulic platform lowered, allowing vehicles to disembark.

Suddenly, I heard the distant squeal of metal and the rattle of a chain. The ferry was now heading back to our side of the river, causing a ripple of excitement as the watching children were herded into nearby cars. I calculated that the ferry was capable of carrying about twenty vehicles. I counted the number of vehicles backed up on the road and figured there was about eighteen waiting to board. The last time I'd been on such a ferry crossing was on our previous LEJOG bike ride. The Cromarty Rose had been the name of that vessel, and I wondered if it was still operating in the waters surrounding the Black Isle near Inverness.

As the King Harry Ferry approached, I caught sight of a placard near the roadside and learned that the 300-metre crossing eliminates 27 miles of driving for those wishing to get to the small fishing port of Saint Mawes. In an age where carbon statistics are becoming popular, it's also worth noting that the ferry saves approximately 300,000 cars driving 5,000,000 miles per year. With a departure every 20 minutes, seven days a week, I thought it must be one of the most reliable forms of public transport in Britain.

The beep of a horn caught my attention as Nick's van appeared at the top of the hill and joined the end of the queue. The ramp was down now, held by two beams that jutted out to resemble a child's transformer model. As the waiting cars started their engines, I pushed off from the wall, freewheeled down the centre of the road, took the sharp turn onto the slipway, and rode up the steel ramp.

Within minutes, we were all aboard and the ferry repeated its journey, across one of Cornwall's deepest rivers. We were about to enter the Roseland Peninsula, a compact parcel of land that boasts 26 beaches, 150 miles of designated footpaths, two castles, and a sub-tropical garden. No doubt there would also be picture-perfect villages and unspoiled areas of natural beauty, waiting to be discovered by those with the time to explore. Like many other parts of Britain, it also has numerous cycle tracks and Nick had uploaded the ones most suited to our needs onto the bike computers.

For a few precious minutes, it was a relief to be moving without sitting on a saddle. During the short crossing, holidaymakers stood by the railings, taking selfies, panoramic photos and family snaps to post on social media. The water was sea green, with no other craft to be seen apart from a wooden dinghy moored to a timber jetty.

On such a humid day, while on a river shrouded by trees and with the sun blazing down from a deep blue sky, the scene was almost Amazonian. I looked upstream and then downstream, searching for other boats or signs of civilisation, but the water meandered in a lazy curve, giving no clue as to what lay beyond. I now understood why the Independent Newspaper had once voted the river crossing as one of the top ten in the world. It was beautiful. But all too soon, a car engine kicked into life, followed by another, and the ramp was lowered onto the opposite bank.

There was just a single road to follow, and the vehicles — including Nick's van — were soon swallowed up by the trees. We rode off the ramp, subconsciously selecting a low gear, and followed in their wake. I was thankful for the wide canopy that sheltered us from the sun as I settled into the back of the pack.

After a brief water stop in a village pub called the Roseland Inn, we were soon on our way again. Without warning, the road narrowed further and dipped sharply, while hedgerows grew taller and we were sucked into a spiral. It was as if we were on an Olympic luge with high banks forcing us down. Unwittingly, I was at the front of the pack, and for a fleeting moment, thought I could lead them down into the valley. But as the hedgerows turned into a hazy blur, each rider tore past me, their backs hunched and faces thrust low in an attempt to find more speed.

I focused on the road ahead, my eyes locked onto the bitumen. My mouth was wide — part fear, part exhilaration — as the Bedfordshire Clanger was unleashed. I leaned into a bend, then another, and after traversing another, slammed on the brakes, my heart lurching at the sight before me.

Alan and Mark had been the first two riders to overtake me and had silently entered into a duel. They too had been enjoying the freedom of the open road. But this wasn't an Olympic slalom competition. It was a public road. It wasn't a one-way system either. And that is why the owner of the red

Hyundai was driving towards them up the hill, no doubt also enjoying the setting.

By sheer good fortune, they'd merged on a rare stretch of straight road, and by the time I arrived, the near-miss was over. The road wasn't wide enough for a car and a bike to pass with ease, and they were forced to test their reflexes. I later learned the guys had braked, skidded, and aimed their bikes towards the gap between the car and the hedge. The skids marks on the road told me the story clearly.

After a flurry of apologies, we set off once again and soon were travelling on a busier road through a small town. Country pubs displayed large banners from windows, depicting upcoming beer festivals, and the signage promised real ales and fine food. Wooden tables adorned many of the front patios, and these were now filled with clientele tucking into Sunday specials and ploughman's lunches. Most of the adult patrons wore T-shirts and shorts, sporting their sunburned flesh with pride.

In the neighbouring village, the houses were joined together in single terraces, barely distinguishable from each other except for the differing numbers on each door. With no front gardens, many householders displayed spring flowers from their sills in window boxes. Some boxes had recently been watered and their flowers greeted the sunshine in a blaze of colour. Others had been neglected, the flowers now wilted and lifeless.

While travelling through the villages that followed, I sought quirky traits that would help me recall something about them. Maybe it was a house with a crooked chimney, a gothic figurine over a garage, or the row of whitewashed cottages that displayed the century in which they were constructed. But our pace was quick and the subtle oddities came and went as quickly as the dips and inclines. Eventually, the peculiarities blurred into one. My enthusiasm faded and was replaced by thoughts of chilled water, a shower, and a bed.

All journeys eventually run their course and the sight of the *Welcome to Callington* sign signalled the completion of ours that day. Within minutes, we found Nick, waiting outside our accommodation. The pale blue building sat close to the road, and he stood outside, resting his hands on hips, smiling at the scene before him. Most riders were silent as we dismounted and made our way towards him. I caught sight of JP, standing on the pavement in deep discussion with an elderly lady.

She was dressed in a bright yellow cardigan and held a handbag across her arm. I watched as she rummaged in her bag and handed something over before walking away. JP pushed his bike towards us, his face flushed with exertion and delight.

'Her name is Mulweena. She wanted to know why we were all riding together. When I explained, she donated a pound towards the charity.'

It was a simple gesture from a stranger, but the sight of a coin in JP's hand earned a series of grins from every rider. It may only have been a small amount, but the contribution had been priceless, especially to JP. With the thought of many more coins to earn along the way, we followed Nick's directions to the rear of the property and met with Peter, the co-owner. He had a neatly trimmed beard, which was lightly flecked with grey. He was above average height and stood straight, as if on parade. His enunciated voice implied a paid education and it carried well against the clatter of our bikes and low murmurings.

'Glad to have you all here safe and sound,' he said briskly. 'Nick's been informing me about the trip so far. You can stow your bikes inside, but go easy. One of the rooms is being converted into another art studio at the moment, so there isn't much space.'

While entering the house, Nick whispered in my ear, 'Ali, you'll love this place. It was once voted in the top ten for Cornish guest houses by the Guardian newspaper. Don't get used to it though. The one tomorrow evening is far more basic.'

After storing the bikes, Peter explained that the accommodation was primarily used as a residence for artists. Despite his enthusiasm for the topic of art, the group fell quiet, each one eager to shower and rest. He led us through a country-style kitchen and introduced us to his wife, Tessa, a pretty woman with a caring smile. After wiping her hands on a towel and exchanging handshakes with us all, Peter explained.

'Don't be fooled, lads,' he said. 'Although Tessa is an excellent cook, her domain is not the kitchen. She's the talented artist amongst us. And I'm the head chef, aren't I, Tessa?'

She grinned, nodded in agreement, and then undertook another role as tour leader as we ventured further into the house. In the hallway, she explained about the art school, then gave us the rundown of how best to appreciate their home during our brief stay.

At the foot of the stairs she turned to face us. 'It's a shame you're not eating here tonight. He really is a wonderful chef. Nick's already explained you enjoy going out to the local pubs in each new location.' She began climbing the stairs. 'I'm sure you're all ready for a shower. I'll show you to the rooms.'

As we followed, I reached out and touched the low wooden beams, my eyes drawn towards the paintings, sketches and drawings on the walls.

While we prepared for our night, Peter phoned around to ensure that we could find a suitable location to eat. He soon discovered that the pubs in the village had stopped serving, although one local publican offered us the chance to bring takeaway fish and chips into the bar so we could enjoy a beer. After a cast of votes, including one rider complaining of gluten intolerance, we asked if Peter could cast his net wider. After a series of phone calls, his voice boomed from the lounge.

'OK, lads, I've found a chef that's willing to hang around. Hurry up and I'll give you a lift.'

In an orderly manner, we made our way downstairs, and he ushered us into his people carrier. We sat in the rear seats, chatting about the day's journey, but as he drove out of the village, I cast my eyes outside. The sky was no longer a piercing blue. The light was softer but still capable of casting long shadows across the winding road. After a few moments, I turned my head to find Alan studying the book that lay open on my lap.

'What are you reading, Ali? Is that a road map of Devon?'

It was actually a gift, given to me by my wife at Christmas to use as a journal, but the leather-bound pages were still blank. My plan had been to write in it each evening, but so far I hadn't found the time or energy to capture any thoughts on paper. Even as Peter drove through the winding roads, the act of writing seemed far too difficult. I held open the cover, revealing the blank pages.

'It's my travel journal, but I haven't yet written a word.'

Alan nudged Colin and said, 'I can help you there, Ali. Just start with a few facts. Let me think. What about my record for the fastest downhill time? That's right, isn't it, Colin?'

Colin disagreed, and a lively debate ensued as the group discussed their various speeds. The banter was still flowing as Peter pulled into a car park.

'Here you go, lads. The chef is staying on especially for you, so be quick with your order. I'll be back at ten.'

An hour later, I'd stolen away from the group and found a comfy armchair nestled in the corner of the lounge. The food had been cooked to perfection and the chef had deserved our tips. JP was standing by the bar, chatting to a stranger about his day, while the others congregated by the window seats. Mick strolled over and placed a beer by my side, taking a peep at the still blank pages in my journal. I caught his stare.

'Thanks for the drink. So I'm hoping to capture a few pieces of information about the journey so far. Have you got anything that can help me?'

He smiled. 'Are you going to write a book about this ride as well?'

At this stage, the idea seemed ridiculous. For a start, I was unsure if anything of note had actually happened. Secondly, I was struggling to write a few lines in the journal, let alone consider the act of writing thousands of words.

'Maybe,' was all I could manage.

'Well, if it helps, my memory of today is that it was hot, hilly and humid. The barman reckons it'll be a scorcher tomorrow too. By the way, you did well today.'

I mulled over his comments as he returned to the others. Sipping the local ale and flicking off my shoes, I grabbed some soft cushions from a vacant chair and snuggled up. All I could recollect from today were hedgerows, inclines, sweat, and the never-ending need for water. I managed to write a few paragraphs, but the scribbles were barely legible and made me wonder how professional explorers documented their feats of accomplishment when they were half way up a mountain or sailing a boat on rough seas.

Centuries ago, the likes of Scott of the Antarctic and Dr. Livingstone kept comprehensive diaries that, to this day, paint a picture of their hardships and fortitude to overcome immense obstacles. Today, around the world, sailors push their bodies to the limit and still find the time and energy to create uplifting videos, photos or podcasts that are seamlessly uploaded onto so-cial media for their followers to enjoy.

Feeling somewhat dejected at my lack of creativity, enthusiasm and drive, I snapped the book shut then wandered towards the bar. Alan was about to order.

'You look a bit tired there, Ali. You know, sometimes you just have to let things go. I'm sure you'll remember enough to make up a good story.'

As he handed me a beer, I feigned shock. 'I don't make up stories, you know that.'

He laughed. 'Well, you do bend the truth a little. In fact, I seem to re-member that in the end-to-end book you said that I—'

We were interrupted by Nick who called out, 'Drink up, lads. Peter's just arrived. He says if we're quick, we can make last orders at his local pub. They have a pool table, so we can get a quick game in before bed.'

I finished my beer, chatting casually with Alan, all thoughts of my journal forgotten.

Day 3: Castle on the Hill

'There are no big problems, there are just a lot of little problems.'
Henry Ford

At breakfast we were spoilt with a choice of freshly cooked selections. None of us chose the herbal drinks but tea and coffee were in high demand. Peter served us with a smile and asked about our day ahead, while Tessa busied herself in the kitchen.

I wondered how we differed from their usual clientele. Here we all were, mostly dressed in Lycra, one studying a bike computer screen, two more discussing the technicalities of various bike parts, one vigorously applying sun screen to his face, and the remainder intent on eating as quickly as possible, in the politest manner conceivable.

The previous evening, we'd made a pact to set off early, but life in Callington moved at a slower pace than anticipated. By the time we finally pushed back our chairs, I could feel the tension simmering, each of us aware that the sun was strengthening fast.

As we made our way towards the bikes, there was another hurdle to face. Peter and Tessa were proud of their art studio, you see, and steered us all towards a display by local artisans. With much enthusiasm, Tessa began a spiel about the paintings.

Nick stood close to me. His voice was quiet. 'I know you like this type of thing, but we really need to get moving. *Please* don't ask any questions.'

Keeping my mouth firmly closed, I eased to the back of the group, while Nick coughed politely and insisted that we make a move. The group edged silently backwards, simultaneously donning our helmets, and soon we were out the door. No offence was taken, it seemed, as very soon, Peter and Tessa joined Nick at the door, waving us off like old friends.

Callington has at least two claims to fame. The first is that it is said to have once been the ancient site of Celliwig where King Arthur once held court. The high street gave no clues to any such past, its cream-coloured shop fronts advertising a vast selection of goods and services, ranging from curries to flooring to real estate. The second claim to fame is a very real one; the town is mentioned in the Domesday Book, an ancient manuscript that describes life in England in 1066. The book explains how the local manor once had enough land for thirty ploughs to work.

There were no horses or cultivators in the nearby fields on the morning of our departure — just a dented tractor, its young driver taking an early morning drive towards the village. After an easy climb, the land levelled out. Callington is elevated 528 feet above sea level. Not an excessive height, but the surrounding landscape boasted a multitude of ridges and valleys. Shortly after passing the tractor, we took a fork in the road, along a narrow lane, which edged close to an exposed headland called Kit Hill.

The land to our right tumbled away in a series of rolling hills, cascading into a hazy green. All conversations ceased when the front rider noticed a sharp incline, selected the appropriate gear, and changed riding position before hurtling downhill. We followed suit, passing a road sign that warned of 15-degree angles, and within seconds, the surrounding trees and hedges were blurring past.

After navigating a tight bend, I managed to lift my eyes briefly from the road to witness the riders streaming around another curve further ahead. During the downhill race, sunlight danced at the edge of my vision and wind streamed against my grinning face.

The downhill slalom ended in the hamlet of Luckett, and although we passed the first set of buildings in a heartbeat, the road soon levelled out and swept gracefully around a bend before taking us across a tributary of the River Tamar. To our right, the brook flowed towards distant fields. Those living in the terraced cottages to our left were lucky enough to appreciate the picture postcard view from their small front gardens. Ivy crept along one garden wall and up the side of a cottage, towards its slated roof.

What goes down must go up, and after passing the cottages, we clicked through the gears in preparation for the upcoming hill. Forming a single line, we passed a red telephone box in use by an old man wearing a flat cap. He watched us through the window as we laboured towards the top of the hill. As the foliage gradually dwindled, we reached for water and sucked greedily on warm air.

A sign informed us we were approaching the River Tamar. This river is the natural border between Cornwall and Devon, and we were about to cross a bridge that was built in 1437 by French Benedictine monks. It is constructed from local stone, with two semi-circular outer arches and a main arch, 15 feet high. Despite its age, it looked in perfect condition, offering far-reaching views of the wide river flowing through a wooded valley.

I stopped halfway across the bridge, waiting for the others to ride ahead, and searched for other man-made constructions. But apart from a farm building in the distance, there was nothing else. Suddenly alone with my thoughts, I wondered how much the landscape had changed since the English Civil War in 1644, when 10,000 men crossed the bridge towards Cornwall, led by the Earl of Essex. It felt comforting to know that — in contrast to those turbulent times — the bridge was now in use for much more pleasant pursuits, this time by six men on bikes whose only challenge was to reach Taunton in time to enjoy a beer at sunset.

At the far end of the bridge, a small signpost welcomed us to Devon. We were now in the village of Horsebridge, home to a building with an intriguing history. Constructed in 1480 and initially used as a nunnery, it later became a public house called The Packhorse Inn. The name remained in place until the day King Charles II stepped inside its doors. He must have been impressed, as he left his seal of approval on the steps 'for services rendered.' In memory of the visit, and from that day on, the building changed its name to The Royal Inn.

The front doors to the pub were firmly closed when we cycled past. On the flagstones outside, wooden benches sat idle, awaiting the first lunchtime patrons. For us, such pleasures would have to wait, as Dartmoor was now in our sights. This vast area of moorland is protected by its status as a National Park, and although it's home to over thirty thousand people, much of the land is deemed wild. Alas, we were only going to skirt its western and northern fringes and would miss out on the imposing sight of Princeton Jail, specifically designed and constructed to house thousands of prisoners during the Napoleonic War.

We followed tracks through woodland and found ourselves on a narrow road that dipped and angled, and suddenly we were hurtling down a steep slope towards a site known as Lydford Gorge. A signpost flashed by, directing traffic towards a lookout point for the 100-foot waterfall. We flew past to gain momentum for the incline ahead. Very soon, we were in the lowest gear possible, silently puffing our way to the top of another hill, towards the medieval village of Lydford.

It was here we encountered a castle. It was perched on top of a perfectly rounded grassy mound, adjacent to a village pub. As we approached, I expected us to ride past.

In terms of castles that I've seen, this one was small. It was about the size of a large country home with two storeys yet no roof. From the roadside, the ancient walls looked to be in excellent condition. The monument was not as iconic as Saint Michael's Mount, and by the look of the empty car park, it was evidently not a must-see tourist destination. But it was still a castle, and for some unknown reason, the front rider stopped by the roadside. Was this a landmark they were interested in exploring? I doubted my reasoning but asked out loud, 'Why have we stopped?'

One of the lads shouted back. 'Nick's been on the phone. He's driving out to meet us with more water.'

While the other riders sheltered under the canopy of a tree, I walked over the road to investigate a placard, fixed near the foot of the hill. The monument was constructed in 1195 and given the name of Lydford Castle. Its main function was to act as a medieval prison and courthouse. According to the information, it was now a free attraction, and as Nick was yet to appear, I ran up the grassy bank to explore.

Inside, there was little evidence that the building had ever been a place to house convicts. It was surprisingly cool, and the only inhabitants I could see were pigeons, roosting in the crumbling ramparts. Their soft cooing sounds felt comforting, and as I gazed out of one of the open sides of the building at the group of cyclists below, I felt my heart rate steadily fall. Somewhere in the distance, I heard the chink of a glass and the sound of laughter, then the distinctive purr of a rotor blade. It was a gentle sound, not like the whine or screech of a motor. Quite simply, it was two wheels and a sharpened blade, trimming an English country garden.

In 1510, an imprisoned MP by the name of Richard Strode described the castle as 'one of the most annoious, contagious and detestable places wythen this realme.' Now, it felt like a place of calm, not a location that had once been used as a tortuous dungeon during the English Civil War.

I dashed down the grassy bank towards the road, just as the transit van appeared. Mark had noticed my brief excursion, and as I unclipped my empty water bottles, he smiled. 'I take it there's not many castles in Australia then.'

I laughed, grabbed the large container of water from Nick, and replied, 'Not that I know of.'

I wasn't chuckling a few minutes later. When we left the village, I took the lead, certain there was one way to go. However, a shout from behind informed me that the group was about to take an unseen (by me) turning. I attempted a hasty U-turn, but my front wheel caught in a pot hole. With no momentum, I fell sideways, and despite the frantic footwork, my shoe refused to unhook from its cleats. I slammed onto the road, suppressing the urge to yell. Feeling foolish, more than injured, I scrambled to my feet. Nick had witnessed the fall, and he shouted from the van window, 'I'll adjust your cleats this evening. They're too tight for you.'

Once more, we were on the road with the forever glaring sun in the sky. Although the main road that skirts the western fringe of the national park is busy, we were able to ride in solitude by taking an inland track called The Granite Way. Offering solace and uninterrupted views, the riders seemed to appreciate the track, heads turning to take in the granite uplands, which were dominated by rocky outcrops known as tors.

Scattered across the moorland were patches of heather, the mauve a perfect accompaniment to the rich, earthy colours of the grassland. John Keats, a revered Englishman who dedicated his life to poetry up until his death in 1820, once wrote a poem that helps capture the sentiment of Dartmoor. It is called, *Where be ye going, ye Devon maid?* The third verse reads as follows:

'I love your hills, and I love your dales,
And I love your flocks a-bleating;
But O, on the heather to lie together,
With both our hearts a-beating!'

It's not only poets inspired by Dartmoor. Sir Arthur Conan Doyle used the setting to reincarnate his fictional character, Sherlock Holmes, by pitting him against a cursed country squire and a hellish hound. It is said that the inspiration for the squire came from a man named Richard Cabell, who resided in Dartmoor and bought misery to everyone he met. There were no blood-curdling cries from wild dogs to distract us, though — just the occasional bleat from lost sheep, wandering by the side of the road.

The heat, the changes of pace, and the constant twists and turns soon began to affect my ability to keep up. During the interludes without inclines, I tried to rehydrate, but before I could recover, there always seemed to be another slope to contend with. I was gradually losing touch with the entourage, but at important junctions, at least one rider stayed behind to assist. They continually called out words of encouragement and instructed me to tuck in behind them to cut down on wind drag. Sometimes when I looked up, I noticed that the rider assisting me had moved position, replaced by another. They took turns to keep me moving. Whether or not they discussed this tactic, I never found out. But time and time again, like guardian angels, they kept me moving steadily.

Villages came and went. Some had pubs and community halls, while others had shops that were also Post Offices. We encountered several remote hamlets with nothing more than a strip of houses hugging the side of the narrow road. Blink and you missed them. Did they all have names, I wondered? Maybe they were marked on an Ordnance Survey map or could be found on Google Maps. I would probably never know. During our ride, they were simply a series of homesteads that we silently rode through.

By now we'd formed two groups. The lead pack consisted of Alan, Colin and Mick, who'd edged away during a series of short, sharp hills and never looked back. They were experienced riders, and these inclines created the opportunity to push themselves into duels for the fastest times. Despite my best efforts, I was unable to keep up. Mark and JP stayed close to me and ensured our pace was steady. The miles tumbled past with pleasing consistency until the moment my derailleur snapped.

We were playing a game to take our mind off the heat, guessing popular songs from their first line. We were on a straight, level road, travelling at a fair speed, when Mark called out, 'What song starts with, *"I never thought it would happen with me and the girl from Clapham."'*

Just as JP called out Squeeze, my rear wheel locked. It caused an involuntary skid as the snapped component ripped the chain from the sprocket. The bike lurched awkwardly, pitching me towards a grassy embankment. I skidded into the foliage and came to rest on a bed of nettles. Mark and JP rode on, oblivious to my plight. I lay still for a few moments, my heart racing. Both my feet were still locked into the pedals, but there was no pain apart from a tingling in my arms. Then I heard voices.

'Ali, are you OK?'

I stared up from the verge, and their reddened faces appeared, blocking the bright sun. 'I'm just taking a quick break...if that's OK with you.'

They offered to stay, and to this day I applaud their intentions. But they'd already sacrificed an early shower by keeping me company up until that point. I insisted they carry on and they reluctantly agreed. First, though, they helped me up, dusted me down, and studied the broken component. My only option was to call Nick to see if he could assist. He answered on the first ring and, without hesitation, turned around for me. Mark and JP checked I had water, a snack, and enough charge on my mobile phone to keep in contact with Nick and — after several handshakes — set off together. I was alone again.

I found the remains of a fallen tree, close to the verge, and sat on the log to wait. I tried recalling the day so far, but the beating sun sapped my concentration. Cars drove past, but none slowed. The only other movement was a fallow deer in the field behind me, its speckled coat rendering it near invisible. I watched as it paused from grazing to study its surroundings. Eventually, I closed my eyes and lay back against the fence. When I opened them next, the deer had vanished and the sun was lower.

Nick arrived with a beep of the horn and informed me he had nearly made it to Taunton when he received the call. If he was annoyed, he hid his feelings well. With a knowing nod, he investigated the broken part and declared with an air of technical authority, 'Ali, your bike is stuffed! The derailleur must have been damaged when you fell off by the castle.'

As I took on this information, it suddenly dawned on me that without my bike in working order, I could no longer cycle. If Nick couldn't work his magic, my end-to-end road trip would be missing day three. Could I walk the bike to Taunton, I pondered? In theory, yes, but it was still 30 miles away and the very thought was quite ridiculous. Luckily, Nick had the answer. He pulled his own bike from the van, adjusted it to suit my smaller frame, and then tore out two pages from his road map.

'There you go. Paper maps at last. Now you'll be happy.' I studied the network of roads. 'Don't bother looking for the bike paths that the lads are on. Besides, they'll be nearly there by now. Your best bet is to ride directly to Taunton on the main roads.'

And with that, he let me cycle off. A mile later, he drove alongside and wound down the side window. 'Looking good, Ali!' he shouted. 'Don't fall off or get lost. I'll see you in a few hours.'

I didn't crash or lose my way but did get an understanding of how much safer the back roads would have been. While cars and trucks thundered past, I tucked my head in low, vowing to keep focused. I housed the map within a laminated pocket in my handlebar pannier, and I studied it intently while crisscrossing the countryside towards Taunton.

By the time I arrived, the others were already showered and about to go in search of a meal. The owner of the bed and breakfast appeared from a back room and shuffled towards me with a key. He was tall, slightly hunched, and had thinning grey hair. His clothes were as faded as the furniture in the dining room, but his voice had a vibrant tone, which reminded me of a school teacher.

'You're in Room Five,' he said. 'There's a pot of tea in the dining room which I made earlier, and breakfast is at seven thirty prompt.'

With that, he turned around, opened a nearby door marked, *Private,* and closed it softly behind him. From the dining room, I heard Alan call out. 'If you hurry, we'll wait while you get changed.'

But I'd had enough of rushing. I was also sure they'd had their fill of waiting. So with a brave smile, I waved them away.

Reaching for the bannister, I pulled myself up the creaky stairs and went in search of a shower. Afterwards, I lay on the single bed and stared at the yellowing ceiling. The pace during these first few days unnerved me. Surely it hadn't been this way twenty years ago?

Maybe it had.

I'd been thirty-one years old back then, riding to change my life. Now, I was cycling again. But for what reason? Was it really the challenge of a bike ride? Or was it really the thought of missing out? Just like two decades earlier, I felt completely under prepared. It seemed to me that the others had trained extremely hard and were primed for each day's ride. Even JP, with his limited time on a bike, never wavered from the daily demands. He was younger than me, so that did help, but I couldn't suppress the first seeds of doubt, creeping into my thoughts. This time, had I taken on too much?

I could see JPs freshly rinsed clothes laying across the radiator. His Lycra would be dry by sunrise, but if I didn't act fast, mine would still be coated in sweat. I packed my soiled clothes into two plastic bags and walked downstairs in search of the owner, hoping he could help me out with laundry and a Wi-Fi connection.

I found the door marked *Private*, knocked softly, and waited. After a few minutes, I tried again. This time my knock was firmer, and the door opened in an instant. For some reason, I was staring at the floor when the door opened, giving me a good view of his chequered slippers. Behind him, I could just make out the glare from a widescreen TV and heard the faint whirr of a portable fan.

His first words were not what I expected.

'You only have to knock once, you know.'

I smiled weakly, my arms full with my sweat-encrusted underwear.

'I'm sorry to bother you,' I said in my humblest voice, 'but I'm part of the group cycling to John O'Groats and wondered if you run a laundry service.'

His blue eyes bored into mine, and for a fleeting second, I thought he was going to shout. 'I'm happy to pay,' I added. 'It's just that I'm a bit worn out after our ride from Callington, and in the morning, we need to be—'

He turned his head, as if to check on something behind him. I was guessing his wife had heard my plea and had given him the thumbs up.

Believing that deep down he was a man of compassion, I feigned a crooked neck, arching my back to emphasis the pain, and let out a long low sigh. Surely he would waver now. As he faced me once again, his eyes impossible to read, he let out his surly response.

'Yes, my wife does do laundry. But not after eight o'clock.'

'What time is it now?' I asked innocently.

'Just after eight,' he replied without hesitation.

I stared up at him, hoping that my sun-baked face and creased features would tug at his heartstrings. But he didn't even take the time to reconvene with his wife. Instead, he stood his ground.

'Is there anything else?'

'Do you have Wi-Fi?'

'What's that?'

'An internet connection...'

'What do you need a thing like that for?'

'It doesn't matter. If you can't help with in-house washing, can you please direct me to the nearest launderette?'

'Yes, it's in the Polish quarter.'

'Is that an area of Taunton?'

'Well, not officially, but that's what me and the wife call it.'

'Can you direct me, please?'

'You'll find it easy enough. It's near the takeaway shops.'

As I walked away dumbfounded, I heard him shout, 'Do you want fried eggs for breakfast?'

I stopped abruptly and turned to face him. 'Perhaps I could let you know in the morning?'

'But we need to know now, so my wife can prepare.'

Was he serious? I stepped closer and dropped the bags onto the floor before replying. 'Since this morning, I've ridden 90 miles in record-breaking temperatures, fallen off twice, snapped my rear derailleur, and missed out on dinner with my mates. My underwear and Lycra are in danger of becoming a health hazard and I'm being sent on a wild goose chase to find a public laundry in the Polish quarter of downtown Taunton. So, whether I have boiled, fried or scrambled eggs in the morning is the very last thing on my mind.'

Actually, that is what I *should* have said. My mother, however, taught me to be polite to strangers.

'Two fried eggs, sunny side up sounds great,' I said. 'Free range will be even better.'

Sandwiched between a bookmaker and a Chinese takeaway, I discovered the public laundry. A sign on the window informed me it shut promptly at eight o' clock and didn't open until nine the next morning. By that time tomorrow, I would have devoured my eggs and be hurtling on a bike towards Gloucester.

While contemplating my next move, my mobile phone rang. It was Mark. My friends were in a high street pub, had already eaten their fill, and were enjoying a cheeky sundowner. I could hear their jovial banter in the background and one of them called out for me to get a move on. I thanked Mark, made a note of the pub name, and promised to be there within the hour. Hanging up the phone, I noticed my reflection in the window.

I was dressed in baggy shorts and a T-shirt and was still holding two plastic bags of clothes. I promised myself right then, I would have a good shave in the morning and then realised, for some odd reason, I hadn't urinated since lunchtime. Also, the only food that I'd consumed since breakfast consisted of a Cornish pasty (purchased in Devon) and a coffee. My wife had given me a list of superfoods to consume while we circumnavigated the UK. Green smoothies were top of that list but I'd yet to find one. The urge to eat consumed all thoughts. I chose the nearest café, picked an outside seat and asked for salad to be served with my pasta.

The spaghetti bolognaise was perfect, the spinach leaves crisp, and the ice-cold water slid down with ease. The family-run café also had Wi-Fi, and as the waiter took away my plate and placed a beer in front of me, the Face Time connection clicked into life. My wife appeared with our two boys by her side. I raised my beer in mock salute and Fran called out, 'Look at you, living it up and enjoying the weather. I hope you've been eating all the right things.'

I held up a sprig of spinach and heard her familiar chuckle.

'Now before we hear about your fun day on the road,' she continued, 'the washing machine has a slight problem...'

Day 4: Mirror in the Bathroom

'Computers are useless. They only give you answers.'
Pablo Picasso

Despite living in a region described by Lonely Planet as an ecological hotspot, there are times when I feel frustrated at the lack of cycle paths in South West Australia. The surrounding countryside is filled with wineries, forests, caves and rivers, along with small and vibrant communities, clinging to existence along the wild and isolated coastline. However, despite an abundance of natural attractions they are not connected together, except by road. Bike trails do exist. There is one long distance route, known as the Munda Biddi, but many are contained to pockets of segregated woodland.

There are numerous walking tracks throughout the state, including one of the world's longest walking trails called the Bibbulmun Track. It stretches for 1,000 km (621 miles) from the outskirts of Perth on the west coast to the historic town of Albany in the south. It's a stunning yet challenging walk through a terrain of forests, bushland, granite outcrops, valleys and cliff tops. It's important to note, however, that the track is linear and has little interaction with other public routes (apart from roads).

In contrast, Britain has an abundance of tracks, including Roman roads, converted train lines, cycle paths, footpaths, and bridleways. I like to think they resemble a spider's web, reaching far and wide into each nook and cranny. While living in the UK, I rarely gave them a second thought. They were just part and parcel of the landscape. But my extended absence had instilled a new appreciation of these trails, which were now becoming the blueprint for our daily rides.

Taunton is linked to Bridgwater by road and canal, and it was the latter that we chose on the morning of day four. While planning the route, Nick had consulted the National Cycle Network and discovered that a towpath would take us part of the way. Once again, we'd woken to clear skies, and with each new day, we improved the process of getting from our beds to our bikes in the shortest time possible.

Taunton is split into two by the River Tone, and it is this body of water that feeds the canal that then carves through the countryside in a lazy arc towards Bridgwater, fourteen miles away. For logical reasons, this stretch of calm water is known as the Bridgwater and Taunton Canal. Unlike the majority of waterways throughout the UK, constructed to aid the Industrial Revolution, this particular canal is a singular stretch of water. The initial plan was to link the canal with the River Parrett, which flows through the counties of Dorset and Somerset. And although this was successfully completed, the grander plan to link the waterway to the Bristol and English Channels was a doomed financial affair. The isolated waterway now resembles some of the Australian footpaths, which I mentioned earlier, with no connection to any other canals.

However, just like the Bibbulmun Track, this did not distract from its beauty. On the morning that we rode in single file along the towpath, the still waters acted as a near perfect mirror, the reflection of the moored boats creating a kaleidoscope of colour. Occasionally we overtook dog walkers, and we met cyclists coming the other way. The trickiest manoeuvre was riding under the road bridges. It meant riding close to the water, and entering a short tunnel while simultaneously ducking your head. With my feet clipped into the cleats, I must admit to a feeling of trepidation when entering the first few tunnels. If a water rat ran out from the shadows, I seriously doubted I'd be able to unclip my feet before I plunged into the deep.

Luckily, there were no water rats to be found, just a family of swans, paddling alongside the far bank as we rode towards Maunsel Lock. The towpath was positioned between several detached houses and the waterway. Some home owners preferred privacy and shielded their property from those travelling on the public right-of-way with trees, hedges or picket fences. Others had decided that such a view should be appreciated, allowing their lawns to sweep down to the path without interruption.

Some houses on the other side of the canal looked even grander. With no towpath to allow public access, they were able to let their gardens run towards the riverbank. Weeping willows were a common site, positioned so close to the canal that the tips of their low hanging branches brushed against the water. Many gardens had gazebos, decorated with garden furniture. People sitting or lounging outside were able to appreciate the peace and tranquility of life on the canal. I waved to a few residents as they pottered about in their gardens and, shortly after, noticed that the number of boats on the water was increasing.

We were fast approaching Maunsel Lock, where a backlog of moored boats waited patiently for the chance to navigate in turn through the bottleneck into the next section. Each boat was unique in its own way. Some were painted brightly in blues, reds and yellows. I spotted one, moored along the bank, its faded paint now peeling. In a side window, a sign read, *For Sale*. Some houseboat owners grew wildflowers in terracotta pots that lined the sterns, while one owner had strewn red, white and blue bunting across the length of their boat.

The distraction of the canals helped take my mind off the heat, which had been building all morning, and I found myself wondering how this part of Somerset was so flat. I'd always thought it to be a hilly county — not as severe as Cornwall and Devon, but with enough steepness and frequency to warrant a certain degree of fitness to traverse by bike.

I heard the sound of panting over my shoulder and, as I was at the back of the pack, was surprised to see a rider behind me. I called out a greeting but was met by a high pitched response. She was lean and fair skinned, her eyes hidden behind wraparound sunglasses, her head protected by a black helmet. She seemed eager to overtake, but the narrow path was flanked by water to our left and rutted mud to our right. Instead, she stuck close behind and uttered constant reminders we were cycling too slow.

I didn't agree with her opinion, as Colin was at the front, setting a solid pace, but with a certain edginess about her, I didn't doubt her ability. When the path momentarily widened, she rode alongside me and I thought she'd shoot ahead. Instead, she mumbled a few words before retreating to within a few inches of my rear wheel. When the next bridge appeared, Colin eased off the pace in order to circumnavigate the short tunnel to the other side. At that point, she called out, 'Too slow for me. See you later,' and veered away from the towpath up the steep track to the bridge.

In that instant, I knew her plan. She was going to ride up the embankment, directly across the bridge, and then ride down the opposite side. This would enable her to burst ahead of the front runner and speed into the distance. On impulse, I decided to follow her, grinning widely at the thought of racing down the opposite embankment, overtaking Colin, and leaving a trail of dust in my wake. At the top of the incline, as predicted, she navigated the narrow gap and rode onto the bridge. I expected her to keep going, but instead, she looked over her shoulder at me, feigned a smile, and set off at speed along the road. I searched desperately for a gap in the opposite wall, but there was none. As I stared down from the bridge, the riders rode past, eyes on the track, wheels spitting dust into the air.

The road was so narrow I had to unclip from my pedals to spin the bike around. With the smile now wiped from my face, I rushed back down the same embankment, completed a sharp U-turn by the water's edge, and raced after them through the underpass. But as I emerged from the chicane, there was no sign of them. In despair, I dropped a gear, pedalling frantically in an effort to claw back distance. When the path straightened, they were still nowhere to be seen.

A man and woman offered hope, and I slowed down to talk to them as they strolled along hand in hand.

'Excuse me, but have you seen a group of riders?' I asked.

The man pointed his walking stick in the direction they had ridden. 'Too right we've seen them. Tell them to get a bloody bell next time, and remind the one at the front that this is a public right of way not a racing track.'

A few miles further on, the riders were waiting for me. I stopped alongside and Colin spoke.

'Where did you go? You can't get lost on a single track.'

'I was led astray by the girl on a bike.'

He looked at the others, his expression as blank as theirs. 'I didn't see any girl.'

I was keen to change the subject. 'I'll explain over a beer tonight, but rest assured, I'm not taking any more diversions today.'

After leaving the canal, the road gently ebbed and dipped as we threaded our way through a mosaic of fields, each differing in colour to its neighbour. With no steep hills to worry about or a towpath to force us into single file, we were able to chat freely again. Colin informed me we were travelling through the Somerset Levels, a vast stretch of land once covered by sea. Over thousands of years, the area has been artificially drained and irrigated to allow farming to take place. With this newfound knowledge, it suddenly made sense why we were continually passing over so many man-made trenches, similar in character to canals but far narrower. They are known as rhynes, and although their primary goal is to protect the surrounding villages and farms from flooding, they also serve as essential habitat for wildlife.

Occasionally we spotted swans, normally in pairs. Dragonflies were also plentiful, buzzing past on their way to waterlogged ditches. Electricity cables ran parallel with the road, and between the tops of each pole, black sheathed wires hung in a concertina, stretching far into the distance. Crows sat side by side on the cables, watching our progress with a bird's eye view.

Our first refreshment stop of the day was in a village with the distinct name of Mark. We made our way past row upon row of cottages, then farmland, followed by houses and cottages. While riding towards the heart of the community it became clear the village was very long. A chalk board outside the Post Office tempted us with tea and sandwiches. I leaned my bike against a red post box, made a note of the collection times, and joined the others inside the white brick building. Since leaving Land's End, we'd stopped in numerous village post offices for impromptu snacks.

In a similar fashion to those in Cornwall and Devon, the post office in Mark had expanded its goods and services in an effort to survive. The interior was filled with rows of goods, including fresh fruit (from local growers), sacks of potatoes, toiletries, gloves, scarves, books, newspapers and magazines. I also spotted a bucket, sponges, batteries, lightbulbs, masking tape and dog biscuits. A glass-fronted fridge contained bacon, pork sausages, and ham off the bone, plus every possible denomination of milk. Two whole shelves were taken over by beer, wines and spirits, and crammed against the back wall, near to the post office counter, stood an ATM. I came to the conclusion that if you moved to the village of Mark, you might never have to leave again.

The front counter held the most appeal with a display of hot pies, pastries and sausage rolls, their aroma drifting across the shop front. We ate outside, seated around wooden tables that had been positioned onto a thin strip of lawn. Half way through my pie, I returned to purchase a coffee, and while waiting, stepped back into the sunlight and studied the outside window. Cards, stickers and posters were stuck to the inside glass, promoting services or products within the local community. If we had the time, there was line-dancing at the village hall tonight at seven, or a weekly slimming class run by Mary. But I didn't need a slimming class; I was already in one.

I noticed a rack of postcards. Unlike many that I'd seen in Cornwall and Devon, they were black and white sketches, depicting various locations in the vicinity. I chose one with the church, as it was the only landmark I recognised from the selection. The assistant peeped at the card before taking my money. 'That's the Church of St Mark. It's got eight bells in the tower, you know.'

I had no idea if this was a good or a bad thing but nodded accordingly as she slid the card into a paper bag and handed it back to me, along with the coffee.

'Did you know that our village is in the Guinness Book of Records?' she continued.

I sipped the coffee, keen to know more. 'What for?'

'For being the longest village in England. Don't ask me if it is anymore, but if they keep building new housing estates it might get even longer.'

'Won't that make it a town?' I asked.

Her face turned serious. 'Oh, we don't want that. We'd rather they left the village alone.' I opened the door to leave. 'Oh, don't forget to drink plenty of water. Too much coffee will dehydrate you!'

Back outside, I read the postcard and discovered that the church dated back to the 13th century. From the doorway, I could just see its granite tower, looming over the tree line, its four corners stretching towards a lonely cloud. I grabbed a pen from my panniers, scribbled a few lines to my family in Australia, and with an air of satisfaction, popped the card into the postbox. With perfect timing, the distinct peel of a church bell chimed. The riders were on the move. By the eleventh chime, they'd stood, stretched, and collected their bikes to leave.

The village of Mark might have been long, but it wasn't wide, and within a few minutes we were surrounded by farmland. Some fields had been deemed fit for livestock, while others were used for crops, like potatoes, carrots and turnips. Easy to spot from afar, were rapeseed plants. England's green and pleasant land is changing, with yellow crops becoming a common sight as farmers diversify to take advantage of the global demand for vegetable oil.

While riding alongside one such field, I got into conversation with Colin and we drifted towards the back of the pack. The road had numerous curves, twists and dips, and by the time we next looked up, the group had vanished. Colin contemplated phoning one of the riders, but decided instead to increase the pace and asked me to keep close behind as he cranked through the gears. On the level road, I was able to slipstream easily, despite the increased speed, but for all our efforts, they were nowhere to be found.

The next junction gave us a clue to our whereabouts with a sign pointing towards Cheddar Gorge. Up to that point, I had no idea we were so close. Twenty years earlier, I'd stayed in the town of Cheddar with Alan and Nick during our inaugural ride. And just like then, England's largest gorge, at 400 feet deep and nearly three miles long, was close, but not quite near enough to warrant a diversion. As we cycled past the signpost, I made a mental note to add the destination to the list for my next family holiday, along with Saint Michael's Mount and Mousehole.

Suddenly, a wide gate barred our way, forcing us to pull our bikes up vertically in order to fit through a kissing gate. A sign by the path welcomed us to a converted railway track, known as the Strawberry Line, and as we passed through, Colin checked his phone but found it had no signal.

'Ali, have you got a phone with you?' he asked.

I explained about my two phones. The smartphone had an account linked to Australia, which meant it stayed switched off unless I had Wi-Fi. The other was a pay-as-you-go phone, which I'd purchased on arrival in England. I'd only used the latter a few times to send text messages, but was yet to call anybody. I checked the screen and it also had no signal. Despite a lack of communication, there was little to worry about except the heat and humidity. The day was still young, and partial shade from a coppice of trees offered comfort. I'd long ceased trying to rub sweat from my neck. The dribbles oozing down my back were just an irritant to ignore. As for deodorant, I wondered why I'd even bothered with an all over spray after showering.

There was little point in complaining. Colin didn't seem fazed by the heat. Instead, he rode steadily and chatted easily while we travelled along a gravel track towards sparse woodland. Occasionally he spoke about his life in rural Bedfordshire and shared stories about his family, including his grandfather. They were often brief, due to sections where we were forced into single file to escape the clutches of brambles or nettles, but it felt good to hear a little about his life. Unlike myself, Colin didn't have a twenty year gap between major bike rides. This was his passion and he was a proficient rider with decades of experience.

Far in the distance, a dark shape loomed across the pathway. It was a railway tunnel, now used solely for those on foot or bike. Our path headed directly into the gloomy interior, and I slowed down in hesitation, but Colin didn't miss a beat and rode into the void without altering speed. I followed close behind, my eyes blinking as they adjusted to the sudden change in light. In an instant, we'd moved from bright sunshine to near darkness.

For a few revolutions, I pedalled blindly and fought the urge to tap my brakes, but as my eyes adapted, a row of lights appeared on the pathway, strategically located at intervals throughout the length of the tunnel. They resembled cat's eyes and must have been automatically switched on by a sensor when we entered. Without their soft orange glow to guide us, it would have been difficult to safely cycle to its end, 550 feet away. The exit was easy to spot. At first it resembled a globule of bright light, far in the distance, but with each revolution the orb expanded. Halfway through I let out a few yelps of joy and waited for the echoes to resonate off the damp walls. By the time we rode into harsh sunlight, I was eager to turn around and do it all over again.

For those that enjoy riding or walking along converted railway tracks, it is worth noting a man called Richard Beeching. During the 1960s, he became a household name throughout Britain, and during his short tenure as British Railways Chairman, produced a controversial report called *The Reshaping of British Railways*. For many years, railways had been losing revenue due to the rapid growth of motorways. In an attempt to close down unprofitable train lines, over 4,000 miles of route were stripped from the network, along with the associated stations. He was later reported as saying, 'I suppose I'll always be looked upon as the axe man, but it was surgery, not mad chopping.'

Although thousands of miles of track were ripped up and the land then sold to developers, many sections were saved as public rights-of-way and converted into bike or walking tracks. The Cheddar Valley Railway Line, where we now cycled, once carried passengers and freight between Yatton and Witham. The company existed for nearly one hundred years, but this stretch was evidently one of the locations on Beeching's long list. In memory of the summer trains, which transported freshly picked strawberries from the nearby fields of Cheddar, the route was named *The Strawberry Line.*

Our arrival at a bitumen road coincided with Colin's computer screen beeping into life. We obediently turned right and soon found ourselves outside Yatton train station. Not far from the ticket office we discovered a petite Victorian building, called *The Strawberry Line Café*, and the smell of freshly ground coffee quickly enticed us inside. There were others in the café, including a commuter, dressed in black trousers and a crisp white shirt. He was sat alongside a middle-aged couple, who were enjoying fruit smoothies and studying pamphlets on local wildlife.

The walls were adorned with framed photos of the surrounding area. Books and magazines were stacked on a shelf. While Colin rummaged in the fridge, I studied the bookshelf, discovering second-hand paperbacks and exploratory guides on the area. A quick flick through a pamphlet revealed the surrounding countryside is home to otters, grass snakes, newts and toads. The passageway we'd just ridden through was called the *Shute Shelve Tunnel* and home to a family of bats that hang from the ceiling. While skimming through the pages, Colin handed me an ice cold can of coke.

'We need to be quick, mate' he said. 'I think the others missed the tunnel and are way ahead. I'll tell them to wait.'

I held back a grimace at the thought of leaving so soon and, as he stepped outside to call them, I made my way back to the counter where a young woman with mousey hair stood patiently.

'It's a lovely little place you have here,' I said.

'Thanks. It's a community-run café. We have a few locals who visit us, as well as those passing through. Have you been cycling on the Strawberry Line?'

'Yes, it was great, but my friend and I are well behind the main group. Have you had many riders in lately?'

She pondered the question for a while, then said, 'Not that I can think of, but I have been pretty busy.'

She informed me then that the café was a not-for-profit organisation and sought to train and mentor young people with special needs. As I listened, it became clear the café served a purpose far beyond that of a daily shot of caffeine for commuters. I also learned that it acted as a hub for community events and asked if the café was quiet over winter.

'Oh, no, we're fairly busy most days. During winter, we get the log fire going and organise curry nights.'

By now, I'd drained the can of drink and was contemplating another one, but before I could order, Colin entered the café, pulled the sunglasses from his eyes and wiped away a bead of sweat. 'Ali, they're thirty minutes away.'

'Wow, really? We *are* behind.'

When he spoke next it was with disbelief. 'No, they're behind *us*! I can't understand it. Can you believe it? They know where we are now and are on the move.'

I couldn't suppress a grin. 'I suppose that means we can relax for a bit.'

'Of course,' he said with an easy smile and walked outside to make another call. I smiled widely, punched the air, let out a yelp of glee and asked the assistant for her name.

'It's Zoe.'

'Zoe, please wait here. I have a gift for you.'

In a moment of spontaneity, I dashed outside to collect one of my end-to-end books from the panniers. As I did, I noticed two people sitting on the lower steps of the footbridge. Despite the oppressive heat, they both wore Doc Martin boots and were dressed in jeans and T-shirts. The man wore a leather jacket, its edges scuffed and the sheen now tarnished with age. The girl alongside him was younger, maybe eighteen years of age. Her slender legs were wrapped around his as they lay at an angle on the concrete steps. His eyes were partially closed and he remained quiet as she called out to me. 'Hey, mate, where have you been cycling today?'

I stopped. 'We left Taunton this morning and are riding to Gloucester today. We'll keep going until we get to John O'Groats sometime next week.'

'Isn't John O'Groats in the north of Scotland? Pretty sure we learned about it in geography once.'

'Yes, it's right up the top.'

She shifted her weight and sat up. 'Why you doing it?'

'Oh, just for the adventure and to raise money for charity.'

She poked her boyfriend gently in the ribs. 'You listening? Why don't we ever do things like that?'

He grunted, and from behind his back produced a can of lager, which he swilled around before taking a swig. He then mumbled something into her ear that made her stifle a giggle. I moved away.

'Good luck!' she called out again. 'By the way, tell your mate he looks hot in shorts!'

I returned to the café, handed the book to Zoe, and explained about the Guinness World Record attempt. I then picked the seat with the comfiest cushions to drink hot coffee and tear off large chunks of my warm muffin. The interior was pleasantly cool. Now that I'd stopped moving, I was able to appreciate the background music and I recognised the singer at once. I closed my eyes as Michael Bublé filled the air.

'Dragonfly out in the sun, you know what I mean...'

The words got me thinking about a horse called Dragonfly from a TV show called Fawlty Towers. In one particular episode, the eccentric owner, Basil Fawlty, finally managed to outwit his dominant wife. After being given a tip for an upcoming horse race by a guest, he secretly places a bet on Dragonfly to win. During a series of blunders, but followed by a stroke of luck, he suddenly finds himself holding the winnings, plus ten additional pounds. Evidently unused to such good fortune, he turns to Polly, the long suffering housemaid, holds the wads of notes aloft, and says, "For the first time in my life, I'm ahead. I'm winning!"

I felt exactly the same and couldn't shake the grin from my face. For once, I wasn't at the back at of the pack, struggling to keep pace. Instead, I was able to relax in a quaint Victorian café, out of the relentless sun. If the lads had been 30 minutes in front, instead of behind, Colin and I would be back on the road by now, churning through the miles. But they weren't ahead. *We* were.

I happily slid my shoes off in an effort to enjoy every second, then leaned back and closed my eyes. I imagined how, in winter, the flames from the fireside would warm customers as they waited patiently for their food and mulled wine.

When Zoe returned for the empty mug, I asked if she was willing to help with my Guinness World Record attempt by having her photo taken by the café sign.

'I'll tell you what,' she said, 'I'll go and get Caz, the manager.'

Caz greeted me warmly and briefly studied the front cover of the book. 'Will you please sign our visitor's book Alistair? We don't get many travel writers at the café.'

A few moments later, we were outside the café, standing side by side, with Zoe taking photos. After signing the book and handing over a complimentary copy they wished me farewell and promised to shelve it at the café.

While walking away, a flurry of activity drew my attention. The white shirted commuter had left the café and was making his way to the edge of the platform. At the same time, the trundle of a train, its brakes squeaking in protest, ground to a noisy stop. The commuter got on and soon after, I spotted someone waving to me from a train window. It was the girl from the steps. Her face was partially hidden by a smudge in the glass but I could still see a grin on her face. Her boyfriend was seated beside her with his face turned away. The doors closed and the train rolled out of the station.

Familiar voices, followed by the clatter of hard plastic on concrete, sounded out from the edge of the platform. The flushed faces of our riders were coated in dust, and after removing their helmets and sunglasses, they sought much needed shade. Initially, I thought they were going to enjoy the amenities at the café, but they made a group decision to order takeaways instead. I prepared my bike for a swift departure and heard the beep of my phone from the front pannier.

The message was from Roger, a man I'd first met eighteen months earlier. It read:

Hi Alistair. Hope your day is going well. Where's the best place to meet today? Cheers, Roger.

My first encounter with Roger was on my local beach in Western Australia. He'd been sunbathing along with his wife Jean and I'd been walking my flat-coated retriever, called Peppi. As Roger and Jean were the only people lying on the white sand, Peppi ran over to investigate. The weather was certainly warm enough to warrant a T-shirt and shorts, but I've found since moving to Australia that unless it's over 25 degrees, the locals rarely strip to their bathers. And this is how I correctly guessed the two figures, sunning themselves, were on holiday from cooler climes. After Peppi introduced himself, I discovered they were retirees on a camper-van trip. Later that day, we met for a beer, and I soon learned that Roger enjoys reading travel books.

We've stayed in touch ever since, and when Roger heard I was going to complete the end-to-end bike ride for a second time, we agreed to meet during the journey. Just before I left Australia, we made a tentative plan to meet near Gloucester and then again in the evening for a meal. In truth, I was rather touched by this gesture. I hardly knew him, apart from the day we'd met at the beach, and a few emails. He was driving many hours from his home to meet me and was also keen to meet Alan and Nick, after reading about them in the end-to-end book.

So much had happened since we'd made the plan to meet and it had somehow slipped my mind. When the lads returned from the café, I relayed his message. They made a quick calculation and estimated where we'd be in a few hours to see if this fitted in with Roger's whereabouts. I messaged him back and pushed the subject to the back of my mind, to concentrate on the task ahead.

British roads are notoriously busy, especially the multi-lane motorways. Surprisingly, we were able to ride close to the M5 on numerous occasions, by taking winding back roads that continually ducked underneath or across it. Within a few minutes of crossing one of the bridges, we'd be riding solo, along narrow country lanes that offered wide-open views to undisturbed countryside.

In the village of Clapton-in-Gordano, I stopped to adjust my bike helmet strap. It should have only taken a few seconds, but a loose clip meant several minutes. By the time I looked up, the others had vanished. I set off at speed and came to a fork in the road, convinced they'd be within sight. But they weren't. I searched for a blue sign depicting a bike path but couldn't see one. They surely had to be close.

I dropped through the gears and raced up the next hill, trying to ignore the nagging feeling I was lost again. As I neared the summit, I heard the familiar din of motorway traffic and was soon back above the M5 motorway. For a few seconds, I stared at the highway, watching cars and trucks emerge from the heat haze.

Over the sound of heavy traffic, I heard the unfamiliar shrill of my brand new mobile phone. Mark had requested the number during our drive down south to commence the ride. Now it was ringing for the first ever time. I pulled it from the panniers and clicked the connection.

'Hello!' I shouted.

Above the roar of passing freight, I could just make out the sound of Mark's voice. It sounded like he was calling from a faraway country, not a few roads away.

'Ali, are you OK? Where are you?'

'I'm fine. I can't seem to find you.'

'We were all together in the last village, but somehow you've disappeared again.'

'Well, my bike helmet was slipping...'

'Where exactly are you?'

'I'm on a bridge above a motorway. I think it's the M5.'

'How did you get there?'

'Well as I said, my bike helmet—'

'Did you take the left bend after the village?'

'No, I veered right and raced after you, but—'

'I know where you went wrong. Go back down the hill, take the lane to your right and ride for about a mile until you ride under the M5. You'll see us by the side of the road, but please hurry. We're all waiting.'

Twenty minutes later, we were reunited. Maybe it was the rising humidity, but the group didn't seem to have much empathy with my unintended diversion. I felt foolish and made my apologies known.

Alan grinned. 'I think it's time you used my computer. I'll give you instructions tonight on how it works. It's pretty simple. All you need to do is follow the screen and listen for the beeps.'

To make up for lost time, the front riders set a blistering pace. I tucked myself into the centre of the pack and willed myself to make no more mistakes. There was no way of avoiding all motorways, and when we crossed the River Avon, we used the designated bike lane. Wave after wave of freight vehicles thundered along the bitumen, only yards from where we cycled. There was no danger, as we were segregated from the traffic by space and a steel fence, but it was unnerving to make eye contact with truck drivers as they whizzed past.

Within a few miles, the river would come to its natural end, flushing into the wide waters of the Bristol Channel. We, on the other hand, still had 40 miles to go. As the sun moved slowly across the sky, all conversations wilted. We rode in silence, each in our own thoughts. Sweat continually dripped from the confines of my helmet. It oozed down my back and caused me to rip off my sunglasses in frustration. I rubbed my eyes, but it did little to alleviate the stinging.

By now, both my water bottles were empty and I could feel my core temperature rising. A series of undulations tested the group and unwillingly I drifted to the rear, refusing to make eye contact with anyone as I slid to the back. Strange clouds began forming in my vision, and I knew it wouldn't be long before I needed to call out for a rest. The only thing stopping me was a foolish sense of pride.

At first, I thought it was my imagination when the rider front began to slow, but soon, I wiped my eyes and saw we'd entered a village. Up ahead, Nick's van was parked outside a pub. Alan veered from the road onto the footpath, and we followed suit. As he approached the pub, he called backwards, 'Time for a well-earned drink!'

Nick greeted us in the beer garden and introduced me to Lewis, a friend of the group who had driven up from Bedfordshire to accompany him. I recognised him from a night out, many years earlier, during a previous holiday to England. Lewis is best described as well-built and tall with friendly eyes, a booming voice and a permanent smile. I was the last to dismount and was treated to a pat on the back, followed by a bear-like handshake. He then muttered something about cold beer and steered Alan towards the bar.

I was desperate to escape from the sun and followed suit, but on reaching the doorway my legs stiffened. I held onto a nearby table, my arms trembling. I managed to venture forward and instinctively found the men's toilet. As I ran the tap and splashed cold water on my face, I looked in the bathroom mirror. My mottled face resembled a pickled beetroot, and each crease of my wrinkled brow was tainted by dust and dry sweat. Dark rings around my bloodshot eyes completed the sorry picture.

I dipped my face into the water and checked the mirror for a second time (hoping for an improvement). But apart from water droplets cascading down my face, nothing had changed.

I made my way to the lounge and asked the barman for two pints of water with crushed ice. I soon felt my body temperature begin to drop and sensed a clearing in vision. The thudding in my head also began to ease and I looked around for the others. JP was standing alongside me, studying the menu.

'You don't look too good, mate. How are you feeling?'

'Pretty crap to be honest,' I replied.

'It's hot out there for all of us, but they don't like to show it. I heard Alan has already drunk eight bottles of water.'

'That's my problem,' I explained. 'I can't seem to find the time to drink enough. How do they do it?'

'You have to remember that most of them have been cycling for years. Only Mark and I are the newbies.'

'Yes, but Mark rides like a natural and you haven't missed a beat. You know, before I came on this trip, I seriously thought I was fit enough, but you guys are superhuman!'

He chuckled softly. 'I'm not superhuman, and believe me, it's a tough ride today. Just make sure you're completely rehydrated before we leave and get a good meal inside you.'

With that advice, I called the barman over and requested another pint of water. As he poured, I asked, 'In your opinion, what meal would take the shortest amount of time to prepare.'

He placed the filled glass on the bar. 'At this time of the day, probably a packet of nuts.'

I took a long sip. 'What do you mean?'

'The kitchen closed at two, I'm afraid.'

'What time is it now?' I asked.

'Ten past two.'

'But surely—'

'Nope, the chef has left for the afternoon. A few minutes earlier and I'm sure he'd have helped, but on a day like today, I'd imagine he's on his way to the nearest swimming pool.'

JP made a groaning sound and then ordered a family packet of crisps, along with a pint of coke. I followed suit and, while waiting, noticed that the pub offered complimentary Wi-Fi. I hadn't contacted home for a while and suddenly yearned to hear the sound of Fran and the boys. On impulse, I turned on my smartphone and tapped the relevant buttons. The screen flashed into life.

'Hello, I thought you'd forgotten about us,' Fran said cheerfully.

I smiled to JP and started to reply but my voice sounded husky and I needed to sit down. One of my children called out, 'Are you in a pub?'

'Have you already finished for the day?' asked Fran. 'How lovely. I bet you're loving the sunshine. It's nippy here. Who'd have thought Australia got so chilly in winter.' The words tumbled from her mouth and I couldn't do anything but listen. 'You're acting quiet,' she continued, 'and you look a bit burned. Have you drunk enough water and used sunscreen? Where are you anyway? I know you like to keep a journal.'

I leaned over and asked a group of drinkers at an adjacent table for the name of the pub.

'The Plough Inn, mate,' one of them said.

'That sounds nice,' she said. 'Where's that then? The boys are following your progress on a map and we can mark it up.'

A barman walked by, clutching some empty plates, and I felt my stomach growl.

'Excuse me, but what village are we in?' I asked.

'The nearest village is Pilning,' he replied with a brief smile.

'Are we still in Somerset?'

He stared at me, then at the phone. 'The last time I checked we were in Gloucestershire.'

As he walked away, I checked out how much beer Alan and Lewis had left to drink. All the while I was popping crisps into my mouth like a clockwork drummer. I just couldn't eat quickly enough. Fran noticed my antics. 'What do you keep looking at?'

'Nothing, I'm just eating my crisps and talking to you.'

She persisted 'No, your head keeps turning to look at something.'

'I'm just waiting for the call to leave. I want to be ready. I didn't really want to tell you, but I got lost this morning, and to be truthful, I'm not feeling very confident.'

'Don't be silly. You'll all stick together, won't you?'

I felt my voice begin to crack and tried ending the call. But the children had their own agenda.

'What flavour are the crisps, Dad?'

'Why are you eating such a big packet?'

'How fast is your bike?'

'Have you given it a nick-name yet?'

'How's your book tour going?'

Fran popped back into view. 'Let him get a word in, boys.'

As I lifted the crisp packet to my mouth to catch the final crumbs, I heard my name being called. We were on the move.

'Gotta go!' I called. 'I love you!'

Nick put his arm around my shoulder as I broke the connection and led me to a quiet corner of the garden. I was about to explain how much better I felt, after the short break, but I sensed something was wrong. He was standing uncomfortably close.

'Ali, don't take this the wrong way, but you need to up your game. Your diversion at the canal cost us time. You can't afford to do these types of things, especially without a bike computer.'

I was momentarily stunned at the outburst and stood motionless. He was right about the computer, but I needed to fight my case. I could feel my voice straining with emotion. 'I'm trying my best here. I honestly am. I haven't even stopped to take photos, apart from the train station.'

'But you keep getting left behind and we have to wait every time.'

'Yes, I did keep everyone waiting, but do you think for one minute I meant to?'

I walked away in search of my bike, but as I clipped up the helmet, he appeared again at my side.

'Ali, look, you know me. At times I can be blunt, and you can be sensitive.'

'Forget it, Nick. As you say, I don't want to keep them waiting.'

The lads were all in line, ready for the afternoon's ride. I'd only been outside a few moments and was already wiping sweat from my eyes. Maybe it wasn't perspiration, but the trace of a tear. I ensured my sunglasses were snug and joined the riders as they cycled away from the pub. One of them rode close and patted me on the shoulders.

'You're doing well. Just stick close, OK?'

I think it was Alan but I didn't look up. In the village of Olveston, hunger and thirst drove us inside the local store. We emerged minutes later into bright sunshine, laden with pastries, water and chocolate. While refilling my bottle, my mobile phone rang for the second time. It was Roger.

'Hi, Alistair, where are you now?'

'In a village called Olveston.'

'How far is that from Oldbury-on-Severn?'

'Roger, I have no idea...'

'Don't worry, we'll work it out. I'm with my friend, Ian. I think we should cross paths at the crossroads in the village, so we'll wait there. How's your day been so far?'

'Eventful.'

'That sounds exciting. Ride carefully and we'll see you soon!'

Roger's exuberance at meeting up suddenly worried me. Since leaving the pub, the banter had fizzled out and even the strongest riders in the group were beginning to feel the heat. Like them, I was keen to reach our destination as quickly as possible to escape the glaring sun.

The landscape rarely changed as we rode towards Roger and Ian. For part of the way, the roads we travelled on were only wide enough for a single car. If two cars were to meet, one of them would have to reverse to an allocated passing spot. Luckily, we didn't encounter a single vehicle and cycled two or three aside, chatting quietly about the evening ahead.

I found Roger, or should I say, he found me, just after we'd crossed another rhyne. My mind was elsewhere, and I wasn't expecting a man to step out from the shade of a tree and call my name. He was smiling broadly, no doubt pleased that his homework had paid off.

The last time we'd met had also been under blue skies. But this time it was different. Back then, I'd been holding a beer after a relaxing Sunday by the beach. This time, I felt a mess but was determined to give Roger the respect he deserved.

I dismounted and introduced him to the group. He then introduced his friend. Ian was slightly taller than Roger with wispy hair, a grey moustache and tanned face. Both men enquired about our day, but the replies from the group were lacklustre. It wasn't ignorance but fatigue, of course.

There was time for an impromptu photo shoot, and while we lined up, Roger sought out Alan, having read about his exploits in my book. During the brief discussion, Alan explained that due to a knee injury, Nick was only riding partway and was driving to meet us in Gloucester.

The mention of our destination cut short any further conversation. The riders collected their bikes and I could sense their eagerness to depart. Considering the long day we'd already spent in the saddle and the fact that three hours of riding still remained, I could understand. I felt for Roger though. I know he was a stranger to them and only a newfound friend to me, but nevertheless, he'd driven many miles for very little in return. At least he had Ian for company.

As we set off, I promised to get in contact when we'd reached Gloucester. Hunger and thirst dictated our next stop many miles later in the town of Berkeley. On our approach through the trees, I noticed the upper ramparts of a castle and hoped the route would take us alongside. Alas, we didn't take the narrow street that led to the gates of the ancient monument. Instead, we followed the computer coordinates towards the town.

The road came to a T-junction, and at the intersection, we met a lady on a touring bike. Positioned either side of her rear wheel were two oversized panniers, protected by bright orange waterproof coverings. She'd stopped to get her bearings and was chatting away with Mark by the time I pulled up alongside. Her cheeks had a healthy glow and she looked to be in her early sixties with fine lines etched around piercing eyes. Quietly and confidently, she explained to Mark she'd also cycled through parts of mainland Europe.

'How do you know where you're going?' he asked.

She looked at the gadget on his handlebars. 'Oh, I don't go in for those computer thingies. Charging batteries and fiddling with buttons would drive me crazy. I use real maps and have a great sense of direction. As you can see, I don't bother with bike helmets either. I've never worn one in my life and I'm not starting now. Besides, I don't go fast enough to fall off.'

I'd been edging nearer during the conversation. 'Do you ever get lost?' I asked.

She studied me for a second, and then in a matter-of-fact voice said. 'Well, sometimes I do, but that's part of the adventure, isn't it? I'm on my way to Scotland as we speak but in no great hurry.'

For a brief moment, I felt like asking if she minded if I joined her. We seemed to be on a similar wavelength. But instead, I wished her the best of luck and continued on.

The centre of Berkeley proved too appealing to ignore, especially the 18th century tower, which resembled the rampart of a castle. According to the sign on the front door, we'd parked our bikes against the town hall. I don't know what prompted the stop. Maybe it was something the lady had said, or because the heat had finally sapped our strength. Either way, Mark, JP, Alan and myself soon found ourselves sitting on a bench outside the town hall, enjoying ice creams.

By the time we finished, the ancient buildings had begun casting shadows onto the road. Colin and Mick didn't stop for refreshments and had continued on together, which left four of us remaining. Alan and Mark still looked strong, but like myself, JP was beginning to fade. His neck was as red as his cheeks and his trademark smile had vanished. Alan and Mark led us home, taking it in turns to take the lead. The other one went to the back, urging us onwards in single file to take advantage of the slipstream. The strategy worked well and the miles tumbled quickly past.

Thatched cottages adorned many of the roadsides, and in the village of Frampton-on-Severn, we cycled alongside England's largest village green. All 22 acres of grass had recently been mown, and in its centre, stood a cricket pitch. Further ahead we came to The Bell Inn, a three-storey pub, constructed from sandy-coloured bricks and topped by a sharp angled slate roof, complete with single chimney.

Each of the guest bedrooms looked to have perfect views of the village green, directly opposite. Two wooden benches graced the pathway to the stout but elegant door, and patrons mulled outside, enjoying the late afternoon sunshine as we cycled by. If any of us wanted to join them, no one dared say. We still had many more miles to travel, and with reluctance, we continued our journey.

One of the most fascinating things about Nick's route were the surprises. Some good, some bad. After spending most of the day riding through remote towns and villages, we finally entered Gloucester and emerged into a council housing estate. I spent my childhood growing up in similar areas and have fond memories of the multi-racial neigbourhood with its quirky characters that played a part in my upbringing. Unfortunately, this estate didn't resemble the one I'd grown up in. We passed a car with three wheels, the missing one replaced by bricks, and the next car we saw had its bonnet open. A group of boys studied the engine.

Although some front gardens attempted a semblance of order, others were devoid of fences and littered with broken appliances or discarded litter. Some had been converted into grey slab driveways with all remnants of grass eradicated.

A group of moody-looking boys stood in the street, taking turns to kick a ball to each other. As we rode past, they stopped to stare. If they looked strange to us, I guess Lycra-clad middle-aged men on touring bikes were also a novelty. Other residents watched us with a healthy interest too. Some waved, others nodded, and then they turned back to young children, playing in the street.

The edge of the town centre looked to be plagued by a series of tired streets that had all seen better days. We rode alongside several takeaways, which offered every type of spicy meal from Chinese to Vietnamese, and a corner pub offered cheap drink deals. However, the clientele standing outside, beers in hand, didn't look too pleased with their selections and met my gaze with narrow eyes. There was a grittiness I wouldn't have associated with Gloucester.

After passing the pub, we entered bedsit land. Row upon row of three-storey houses were crammed alongside each other. Cars, mini vans and trucks fought for space along the narrow streets and a shout from a young lad caught our attention. He was attempting a wheelie on a BMX.

'Watch out!' he shouted. 'There's a bloke on the floor with blood all over him.'

A small crowd by the roadside confirmed his warning and I spotted a man lying with his head on the kerb, his eyes open, while someone dabbed a cloth against a wound. A thin trail of blood trickled onto the road. A few seconds later, we stopped our bikes. After nearly 100 miles and many hours, we'd made it to our accommodation.

Our stay for the night was functional. Most clientele looked to be transient workers and some graced the stairwells as we made our way to our rooms. They looked adequate enough for a simple, overnight stay. The décor was faded, but the sheets were clean and the shower was as hot as I dared.

Later that evening, I bagged up my soiled clothes and went down to reception. For the cost of ten pounds I was given free reign of the cellar, which had been converted into a laundry. After a short time, and armed with a basket of fresh smelling clothes, I felt a resemblance of order returning and made plans to visit Roger and Ian at Gloucester Docks. As expected, the others were not so keen to meet. I was disappointed, but I understood that with just a few hours' grace before sleep time, they wanted to relax with just each other.

Like many docks throughout Britain, Gloucester's was once an industrious hub where cargo boats from across the world converged. Back then, the ship decks would have been filled with goods from across the oceans — including exotic fruits, corn and timber — and then the imports were distributed across Britain. In time, when road and air freight were introduced, the docks became quieter and eventually fell into decline.

After considerable investment and renovation, the dockside is now reborn to become the entertainment hub of Gloucester. We met in a pub called The Lord High Constable of England, and like many other venues, it sat close to the water. Not all the buildings were new. Some had managed to survive the glory days of a working dock, including the many brick built warehouses. These are now prime real estate, having been converted into luxury apartments. Others are home to museums, shopping malls, and microbreweries.

A tall wooden ship graced the water's edge, its giant mast illuminated by a spotlight. This reminder of a bygone age didn't go unnoticed, with visitors stopping to study its distinguished features.

The pub was spacious with numerous rooms to choose from, and a small but vibrant crowd helped create a welcome atmosphere. We chose the quietest corner available so we could talk, yet despite their eager questions, I found myself answering with curt replies. To a stranger walking past, we were just three men, enjoying a social drink on a Tuesday night. No one could see the pounding in my head or feel my leg muscles stiffening as I stretched them out on a stool. I could sense that Ian was keen to share tales about his own bike ride adventure from Land's End to John O'Groats many years earlier, and on another day, I would have lapped it up. But I yearned to lay my head on a pillow and was forced to bid them a fond good night.

Before I left, I made my apologies for the other riders, as I'd hoped they'd have joined us for one drink at least. Roger shrugged it off.

'They look like a nice bunch, but I'm sure they don't want to hear Ian and I ramble on about our life as retirees. You get on and get to bed, and remember to keep in touch.'

On my way home, I decided to call Mark and soon discovered they were in a nearby pub. As we sat together, I nursed a beer, suppressing the need to yawn.

'How was your catch up?' asked Nick.

'It was good. But I'm exhausted and just need my bed.'

'Look, Ali, about today at the pub...'

'Nick, you were right. You just tell it as it is. Without a computer, I'm letting you all down. Plus, I know I shouldn't have followed that girl at the canal.'

'What girl?'

'The one that led me astray. Anyway, I'm too tired to talk now and tomorrow is my birthday, so I'm off to bed.'

I stepped outside and took a final look at Gloucester docks. Lights from the apartments cascaded across the water and the sound of revellers from a nearby pub carried on the still night air. There was a vibrancy here, pulling me to stay, but a passing taxi caught my eye and before long I was tucked up in bed.

My final thought, as exhaustion took hold and I closed my eyes, was not to get lost on my birthday!

Day 5: The Wrong Direction

'Not all those that wander are lost.'
J.R.R Tolkien

The rising sun crept through a gap in the curtains, tiptoed across the room and brushed onto my face. I woke refreshed and opened my eyes. JP was in the adjacent bed but didn't stir when I quietly collected my gear, stole out of the doorway then down the stairs towards the communal kitchen. There would be no special sausages this morning, even though it was my birthday and that was what I always had. The only food available in this hostel was a basic selection of cereals and bread.

Fifty-one is a strange age. I was nearer to sixty than forty, and I wondered where the last eleven years had gone. It seemed I was always fighting time. Even now, the sound of heavy footsteps on the stairs told me I wouldn't have enough time to speak to my family in Australia. Despite being the first to rise.

But it wasn't my fellow cyclists. Instead, coming down for breakfast were workmen, all aged under forty with wide shoulders and sunburned cheeks. Each wore steel capped boots, jeans, and T-shirts, all of which had seen better days. One of them picked up the remote control, switched on the TV and searched for an update on the news channel. The others busily set about preparing breakfast and chatted amiably about the weekend ahead.

I'd already made tea and was sitting by the bay window, trying to get an internet connection. The Wi-Fi code printed on the information pack consisted of a twenty-character string of numbers, letters and symbols, designed to foil all but the determined. To make matters worse, the final two digits were smudged with ketchup. My attempt to get an early start was quickly backfiring.

One of the men heard my mutterings. 'You trying to get the Wi-Fi, mate?'

'Yes, but the code is—'

'Too long and over complicated? I know. Here, give me your phone. I've been here for months. I've got the code etched in my memory.'

He was tall with mousey hair, a freckly face, and sharp green eyes. I handed him my phone, and he easily tapped in the sequence. I noticed that he regularly looked towards the window.

'You're connected now,' the man said.

I thanked him and watched as he buttered a piece of toast and then returned his gaze to the window. I wondered what he was looking at. Maybe he was just fed up with the politics on TV. The talk was Brexit. With the vote looming, it was a hot topic.

'We don't need any more migrants taking our jobs,' shouted one of the workmen in front of the screen.

His mate chuckled. 'It's not as simple as that, Jamie. A yes vote might mean a loss of jobs. If the economy—'

'Look out. Tim is on a roll again,' boomed another voice from the back of the room, 'and it's only half past six in the morning! Someone turn the channel over before he starts quoting Maggie Thatcher.'

Images of parliament on the TV were soon replaced by a weather report. The woman standing in front of the image of Great Britain skimmed a hand across the south-west.

'I'm sure some of you will be sad to know that the record breaking heatwave is over,' she relayed. 'Most parts of the south will return to more normal temperatures for this time of year, and we might even experience a light band of showers in coastal areas this evening.'

Her hand swept upwards. 'Spare a thought for northern parts of England and much of Scotland. While the south has sweltered, they've been under a deluge of rain which looks likely to continue into the week.'

With a wry smile, I mulled over her words, knowing that my new-found tan was soon to be washed out. I opened the birthday card that Fran and the children had stowed in my luggage and read the handwritten messages inside.

'Alright, lads, the van's here. Let's go,' the man by the window called out.

The workmen were on their feet and out the door in an instant, returning the kitchen to silence. I suddenly felt very lucky. At least I didn't have to go to work today. And it was my birthday.

Although my family wasn't nearby, I was sure they'd be happy I was on an adventure with friends! Last night, lying in bed, I'd made a pact with myself that today, on my birthday, I would do my utmost to stay with the group. According to Nick, this was one of the easiest stretches to ride, and armed with this knowledge, I decided not to take up Alan's offer of using his Garmin. All I had to do was stay close.

My only niggle during the first mile was the morning rush hour traffic. Cars continually raced, only to be caught up at the next set of traffic lights. Despite the noise, I settled at the back of the pack, whistling softly, taking in the surroundings and thinking ahead to a celebratory meal. With luck, we'd stop for lunch at a quaint riverside café or an historic inn serving ploughman's lunches. I was smiling at this thought when we approached another T-junction. Mark veered left onto a dual carriageway and we followed closely.

After a few yards, however, he stopped by the side of the road, looking at his Garmin.

'Sorry lads, it's the opposite way!'

Then three things happened all at once.

Firstly, the traffic stopped. The lights behind us had turned red, which meant there was time to race across the road and complete a U turn.

Secondly, I took a drink of water. With my head tipped back to guzzle, I watched helplessly from the corner of my eyes as the others raced across the road.

Thirdly, in my haste to join them, I dropped the water bottle onto the road.

I should have left it by the kerb and followed the riders, but instead, I made a costly decision and dismounted to retrieve it. As I did so, the traffic lights changed from red to green, and like a Formula-One start line, the sound of squealing tyres pierced the air.

For a split second I contemplated sprinting directly in front of the cars in an attempt to get to the other side of the carriageway. But such a move would have been risky. Instead, I pulled my bike towards the kerb, just as a boy racer in a Nissan Skyline whizzed past, followed by motorbikes, cars, and the rumble of heavy goods vehicles. By the time a gap appeared in the traffic, valuable minutes had passed.

I hurried across both carriageways, following their scent like a dog. Within minutes, I came to a roundabout at which I was hoping they'd be waiting.

But then it dawned on me they probably had no idea I was missing. I spotted a dog walker, emerging from nearby woodland, and stopped.

'Morning! I don't suppose you've seen any bike riders come this way?'

'No, mate, sorry. I've been in the woods. Where you heading to?'

'Shrewsbury.'

He stroked his chin and said, 'That's a long way by bike. I hope you've got a map. The roads around here are notorious for getting lost. There seem to be roadworks or new roundabouts every other week.'

'If you can just steer me in the general direction of Shrewsbury, I'd be very grateful.'

While his Yorkshire terrier strained at the lead to urinate on a wilted patch of weeds, he studied the nearby roundabout. 'Well, it's not quite as easy as that. It's a long way away and I haven't been there in years. If I were you, I'd take the left turn here to avoid the heavy traffic. That's probably what your mates would have done. Keep going for about a mile towards the next round-about. I'm pretty sure you can veer north from there.'

Turning left at the roundabout didn't seem logical to me. I probably could have studied the sun to find my bearings, but it was already high in the sky and I was beginning to doubt my ability to navigate. Also, the frustration of losing my friends so early in the day was affecting my better judgment. I briefly contemplated making a call to Mark but was determined to track them down before they noticed. Would they have turned left? They had to be close. But which way should I go?

I thanked the man, patted his dog, and decided to circumnavigate the large roundabout first of all, as the elevated position offered great views of the surrounding landscape. But alas, they were nowhere to be seen. The signs for Ledbury, Cheltenham and Cirencester meant nothing to me. It was a game of chance, and after a full revolution I decided to follow the advice of the dog walker and take the A40. With the wind at my back, I rode like a man possessed, my eyes peeled for the entourage.

The next roundabout bought me back to my senses. The whirlwind search had been utterly pointless. Panting hard, I studied the options before me. I could either head south towards Somerset, continue onwards towards Wales, or complete a U-turn and return the way I'd come. I punched the handlebars in dismay and let out a rant of obscenities.

Just as I reached for my phone, it started ringing.

'Hello,' I answered sheepishly.

'Ali, where are you?'

'Hi, Mark, I was just—'

'No, seriously, where are you? We've only just left the hostel and you've already disappeared.'

'Do you remember the dual carriageway we stopped on?'

'Yes, but where are you now?'

I gripped the phone, fighting to control a wave of anger. Not towards Mark, but myself. One thing I didn't want to do today was irritate the group — not after yesterday's mishaps. I quickly weighed up the options.

'Mark, just go ahead without me. I've taken the wrong turning and don't want to hold you up.'

His voice was softer as he replied, 'We don't mind waiting. It's your birthday and you can't ride alone. Just hurry up and find us though, because we've no idea where you are.'

Neither do I, I thought. The situation was ludicrous for such an early hour. I was in turmoil. Yes, they'd wait, but I was ridiculously off track and had no idea how long it would take to catch up. My self-esteem was slipping fast, but I was determined to make light of the situation.

'Mark, I appreciate what you're saying, but please go ahead. I seem to be on my way to Wales, but don't worry, I'll be fine. I'll grab a map and will see you later. It might make a good story over a beer tonight. Hey, don't forget to wear your Hawaiian shirt!'

I broke the connection and punched the handlebars again. A feeling of despair washed over me. Nothing was going as I'd hoped, and I was sure the others were having reservations about including me in their trip. I'd been friends with Alan, Mark and Nick for decades but felt I was in danger of damaging our relationship.

As for the others? Well, we still knew very little of each other. I'd enjoyed chatting with Colin while on the Strawberry Line, and JP — with his permanent grin — was proving to be an amicable chap. Mick was harder to read. At times, it was as though he was riding with something important on his mind. Maybe my inclusion had unsettled the group dynamics? It would certainly be fair to note I'd acted so far with a high degree of unpredictability, resulting in lost time and frustration for the group. But I had no idea if my antics were minor irritations or an absolute calamity. With these thoughts spinning round my head, I went in search of a map.

I found one in a petrol station, but it covered the whole of Great Britain and stood as tall as my knee. I only needed a few of the pages and couldn't face paying the hefty fee. In a moment of daring, I ducked below the aisle and used my smartphone to take photos of the relevant maps. At the counter I purchased a Mars Bar to alleviate any guilt.

Nick had previously informed me that the day's ride would be the easiest so far, with only 89 miles to cover and a total elevation of 5,800 feet. But his calculations were based on using bike tracks, none of which were displayed on the maps I'd photographed. If I did encounter any of the National Cycle Network along the way, it would be pure luck.

And so it was, that on my fifty-first birthday, I rode to Shrewsbury with just the clouds for company. Like me, they moved steadily across the countryside, and together we made it to the city of Worcester. I wanted to steer clear of the main roads, and travelled mostly through villages and towns. As long as I was heading towards Shrewsbury, I was happy.

In the small town of Tewkesbury, I discovered an historic pub called Ye Olde Black Bear, which claimed to be the oldest in Gloucester. It was located on a street corner, adjacent to the River Avon, and as I parked my bike outside, the main door opened and out stepped an elderly man.

He eyed the bike. 'That's a good way to avoid drinking and driving,' he said.

'Oh, I'm not after a beer. I'm just taking a photo of my bike against the pub.'

'Whatever for?' he asked.

'Because its old and I like the look of the wooden shutters and hanging baskets.'

'Are you an American?'

'No.' I chuckled. 'I'm English. But I live in Australia now.'

'Good for you. So why are you in Tewkesbury?'

'I'm on my way to John O'Groats.'

'Good grief! Whatever for?'

He was easily surprised, it seemed.

'Well, initially it was a challenge for charity. But as each day goes by, I'm finding it a great way to rediscover parts of Britain that I took for granted when I lived here. And to enjoy new locations, like this one.'

'Are you riding solo?'

'It wasn't the plan, but it seems that way today.'

'Well, if you're going to discover the inside of The Bear, you'd better be quick. There's talk in the town it'll soon be closed.'

'Oh no. How come? It looks like a pub with a lot of history.'

'It does! It even has the original ceiling beams. Why don't you take a look inside? There's not many in there at the moment. If you ask me, drinking is too expensive these days. The other day I read that twenty-seven pubs close down every week across the UK.' His voice then lowered a fraction. 'It'll be a shame if it shuts. It's a friendly pub and they say it's haunted too.'

'Haunted?'

'Yes, by a little old lady dressed in black. I think she was once a landlady. Mind you, I've been drinking here for years and haven't seen a thing.'

While he spoke, a passing vehicle caught my attention and my eyes grew wide in disbelief. 'Are you OK?' he said, stepping closer. 'You look like you've just seen a ghost yourself.'

I smiled. 'No, not a ghost. My friend just drove past in a van. I gotta go!'

The man raised his eyebrows, wished me luck and said farewell. After he'd walked away, I looked up the road for Nick's van but he was nowhere to be seen. Perhaps he hadn't seen me.

I decided to follow the old man's advice and take a look inside the pub. He was right. There were few patrons, but the low beams, soft light and musky aroma held an appeal. I contemplated walking up to the bar and requesting a local ale but fought the urge. There were still many more miles to cover and I was in need of sustenance not alcohol.

I stepped back into the sunshine and found Nick and Lewis standing by my bike. Lewis was holding a booklet, which he handed over with a smile. 'Here you go, Ali. Happy birthday!'

It wasn't wrapped, which meant I could see it was a comprehensive road map of Britain, similar to the one I'd seen at the garage. I was speechless.

'I hear you've broken a new record today and managed to get lost within the first hour.' Nick laughed.

I managed to break into a smile. 'Believe me, Nick, this is one day I didn't want to be on my own. So, are the others nearby?'

'About eight miles away, but they're on a remote bike track. Your best bet is to travel direct. Use this map and head towards a town called Bewdley. They'll pass through it later on. If you don't take too many photos on the way, you might actually meet them again before nightfall.'

I took hold of the map, thanked Lewis and explained that although the gesture was appreciated, it was too big to cram into my panniers.

'I'll just tear out the pages you need for today,' he said. 'It's only an old map from work and I'm actually due a replacement.'

He handed me the ripped out pages. 'So are you planning on going walk-about tomorrow as well?'

'Of course not,' I replied with truthfulness.

'Well, just in case,' he replied, 'here are the next few days' worth too, all the way to Scotland. Oh, by the way, I've booked us into an Italian restaurant for your birthday meal. Just make sure you're there to enjoy it.'

'I'll do my best.'

Nick started to give the bike a quick check over and then offered to top up my water bottles from a stash in the van.

'So how's your morning been, Nick?' I enquired as he worked.

'We've had a relaxing time, but you seem to be struggling. Why didn't you take up the offer of using a Garmin?'

'Believe me, I regret the decision,' I replied. 'The route sounded so easy, but as I've found out, in one moment, the situation can change dramatically.'

He handed over a packet of muesli bars and said, 'I hope you're learning, mate. Technology has come a long way since your last ride across Britain. Tra-ditional maps aren't the best solution for this type of trip anymore. By the way, they were doing a two for one deal on these oatmeal bars, so you can have these for free.'

They departed in search of a pub lunch by a riverbank while I prepared the bike. Ironically, the front pannier had a transparent plastic slot at the top, designed specifically for a paper map. I folded the relevant page and slotted it neatly inside, ensuring that Tewkesbury was at the bottom and Gloucester at the top. My first task was to cross the River Avon, then take the back roads through the villages of Church End and Kempsey.

After leaving the pub, I turned left onto a bridge. Canal boats chugged gently on the calm water, their destination and pace of travel very different from my own. With a new-found sense of purpose, I steadily made my way north, passing through villages and towns with relative ease. The land between each settlement was made up of farmland and woods.

Occasionally I spotted grand homes, with wide, manicured lawns and long driveways, but as the town of Worcester approached, the houses and gardens shrunk in size. The plan had been to divert around the fringes of the town and then head north to Shrewsbury, but instead, I was unwittingly sucked into the town centre by a series of ring roads.

Snarled by traffic, I dismounted and found myself strolling through a pedestrianised shopping strip. Thankfully, the high temperatures were dropping, replaced instead by a pleasing warmth apparent on the faces of those resting on wooden benches. I too, felt a sense of calm. Yes, I was on my own, but by travelling solo, I didn't have to please anyone else. Coffee was on my mind, but the cafés within view were either too crowded or lacked character. Worcester is an historic city and I was determined to locate a worthy place to enjoy lunch.

While searching for a suitable spot, I thought ahead to the evening dinner for my birthday. One of my brothers, Dave, was making the effort to drive many hours from Bedfordshire to join us at dinner, and I was really looking forward to seeing him.

Right now, he would be on the road with two friends, and the three of them would also join us for tomorrows bike ride from Shrewsbury to Preston. I'd been lodging with Dave at the time of completing my very first end-to-end trip, and without him, the first ride may never have happened. It was his bike I borrowed to complete the journey, and I'd nicknamed it the Donegal Flyer, in memory of our Irish mother.

The two friends with him were Paul and another man called Dave. I've known Paul for many years and it was he who introduced me to the merits of real ale and the Lake District. Over the years, he has trekked in numerous locations, including the Himalayas, the Andes and the Alps. He'd recently taken an early retirement and kept fit by running long distances. Although now nearly sixty years of age, the fact that our friends once nicknamed him The Android left me in no doubt he'd be able to keep up with the group.

Dave, the second friend, had been retired for the longest but by all accounts was an active road cyclist. I was keen to see how he faired within the group though, as he was in his late sixties, and I hoped that a degree of leniency would be taken during our long ride to Preston.

By the time I reached the end of the mall, my options had dwindled. Instead of turning back, I opted to ride on an empty stomach. At least I had Nick's organic muesli bars in my panniers. The map from Lewis was not detailed enough to depict the numerous roads in the heart of Worcester, so I followed my instincts and ducked down a side street, hoping to thread my way towards the ring road. I was hoping to make up the eight miles that Nick had mentioned and held a glimmer of hope that I'd meet the riders sometime soon.

Just before I picked up speed, I passed a parked car, its boot wide open, revealing a colourful selection of fresh fruit and vegetables. A woman emerged from an adjacent courtyard and began to unload the vehicle. Her bronze skin spoke of a faraway culture and she wore a bright yellow T-shirt with *Belize* emblazoned across it. I jammed on the brakes and stopped alongside.

'Hi, there! Sorry to bother you, but I'm after the road towards Shrewsbury.'

She pulled a box of lettuces from the boot and balanced it on one hand while trying to close the tailgate.

'Wait a minute. I'll just drop these off at the café and will be back in a second. Or you can come with me if you like?'

The mention of a café made my stomach come to life, and I quickly got off my bike to help her with the box. With a wave of her hand, she dismissed my offer, so instead I pushed my bike behind her into a small courtyard adorned with tables and chairs. The interior walls displayed a small collection of local artwork and abstract images of tropical locations. The food on the menu was described as locally sourced with a global flavour, which suited me just fine. A friendly face greeted me at the counter, and before I could think, I'd picked the all-day Mexican breakfast, complete with free range eggs, plantain, and re-fried beans. I was also going to get my special sausages.

Eager to show my thanks at finding such a café unexpectedly, I asked the cashier, 'Is this café run by Belizeans?'

'Good guess,' she said, and then waved to the lady I'd met by the car who was now returning from the kitchen. 'If you want to know more, Amanda will tell you. She's the manager.'

'Who are you then?' I asked with a grin.

'I'm Miss Bliss, the cashier, right now. But I'm also the one that's about to cook your breakfast!'

As Miss Bliss went off to wash her hands, I introduced myself properly to Amanda and commented on the exotic décor and ambience in the café. One thing was troubling me though.

'How's trade for you?' I asked. 'You know, I've just walked past rows and rows of cafés — only a stone's throw from here —but I ignored them because they looked too crowded or bland. You guys have a funky little set up here, but not a lot of customers it seems.'

She held her hands up in defence. 'It is a little quiet at the moment and I must admit we do struggle at times convincing high street shoppers to try us out. But don't worry, it's not always this quiet. We have lots of regulars, and the positive reviews on Trip Advisor help us a lot.'

While we spoke, a young couple walked in, and after ordering, they found a spot in a nearby corner. There were others too who entered the café, but they didn't all order food. Instead, they chatted with the staff like old friends. Amanda explained that Café Bliss was more than a place for good coffee and food.

'Did you read the sign outside?' she asked suddenly.

'Yes, it says Café Bliss,' I answered with confidence.

'No, not that one. There's another one that welcomes visitors to the Worcester Arts Workshop. Our café is a part of that complex. In the other rooms, we hold theatre, arts, crafts and discussion groups. There's also live music and we have Sunday sessions with musicians from across the country. They perform outside in summer and inside in the cooler months.'

By now my lunch had arrived and I was eager to tuck in. Amanda stood to leave and said, 'I'm glad you found us, Alistair. We seem to attract a certain type of person.'

I took this as a huge compliment. I tucked into the spiced sausages, deciding there and then to give away one of my end-to-end books in return for the hospitality.

Before I left, Amanda agreed to pose for a photo with the book outside the front door. Miss Bliss offered to take the photo and I thanked her for the delicious meal. When I was ready to leave, Amanda walked me to the edge of the street, pointed towards a road junction, and gave clear instructions on how best to find Shrewsbury. I shook her hand, pointed the Bedfordshire Clanger north, and set off with a smile. With clear skies, a full stomach, and a direct road ahead of me, there was little that could go wrong. And just over an hour later, I approached the outskirts of Bewdley.

The name of the town is derived from the French phrase *Beau Lieu*, meaning beautiful place, and with every revolution of the pedals, I sensed it was going to be a gem. Mighty oak trees lined the verges, joined by evergreens and silver birches. A gradual chicane led me past a row of Victorian cottages, their slate roofs angled sharply towards small front gardens.

When the road straightened out, the River Severn came into view, splitting the town into two. A riverside walkway offered visitors the chance to enjoy the views in relative peace, with park benches positioned at regular intervals along the cobblestones. Some were in use right now, all eyes on the river as a swan glided across the water towards the far side.

Soon after, I rode across a stone bridge with three arches, beneath which the river ran free, far below. The bridge was designed by Thomas Telford and built in 1798 at a cost of £9,264. This was not the first bridge to be constructed at Bewdley though. The original construction was destroyed during the War of the Roses in 1459 and its replacement was partially damaged hundreds of years later during the Civil War.

To assist with the construction and maintenance of the bridge, a toll would have once been paid by those wishing to cross over. The Journals of the House of Commons, dated 1772 to 1774, are filled with details on such matters, and with regards to Bewdley Bridge, those travelling on wagons would have had to pay a toll of three pence. Carts were considerably cheaper, costing only a halfpenny.

Tolls are no longer charged, and I rode unimpeded to the other side to join the throngs of day-trippers mulling by the water's edge. Many were seated close to the river, enjoying drinks and food from numerous cafés spread along a pedestrianised strip of land. The town square offered a selection of shops, selling ice creams, gifts, antiques, postcards and freshly baked pies. I filled up on water and opted for a sausage roll followed by a vanilla ice-cream. Then I joined the numerous holidaymakers at the edge of the river. There was an air of tranquility as lovers walked hand in hand along the pavement and toddlers threw breadcrumbs to fat ducks.

While searching for a place to sit, I passed three women sitting next to each other on a bench. They were chatting happily as they too enjoyed ice creams. I followed their gaze and watched as a small boat steered towards one of the arches in the bridge. I was transfixed. A voice from the bench roused me from my thoughts.

'Excuse me, but did you know you've dropped your wrapper?'

I reached down, scooped it up, and while depositing it into a nearby bin, called out my apologies.

'That's OK,' she said. 'This is a lovely town and we need to look after it.'

I took the cue she was keen to chat. 'Are you a local then?'

She looked over at her friends and replied, 'Well, not exactly. We live in a town called Stourbridge, not far from here.'

'I've never been to Bewdley before and hadn't expected it to look like this.'

'Oh? What had you expected?'

'I'd just forgotten how beautiful Britain can be. I took it all for granted when I lived here.'

I explained how I'd moved to Australia with my wife Francine, in 2003.

'So where's your wife now?'

'Oh, she's still in Australia with our two children. I'm here to cycle from Land's End to John O'Groats.'

The first woman stood and held her hand out in a greeting. 'It sounds like you have a very understanding wife. It's nice to meet you by the way. I'm Margitta, and this is Christine and Norma.'

Christine also stood and asked, 'Are you a solo rider? It must get lonely sometimes.'

'Oh, no, I'm actually with a group of mates, but there was a logistical problem this morning and I've found myself on my own.'

She grinned knowingly. 'You got lost?'

'Something like that,' I said quietly.

We talked for a few minutes about the bike ride, the daily mileage, the charity quest, and being so far from home. They shared secret spots where visitors rarely ventured, and I talked about flying to work each week with hundreds of iron ore miners.

'So why are you here today?' I asked. 'Is it a special occasion?'

Margitta studied me quizzically. 'No, Alistair, it's just too good a day to be stuck at home, isn't it? And we enjoy the drive out here, don't we, girls?'

While she spoke, I remembered my brother Dave again. With any luck, I'd meet him by late afternoon before we ventured into town with the others. It was time to leave Bewdley, and after picking up my bike helmet, I bade the friendly ladies farewell.

As I walked away, it struck home how much I enjoy talking with strangers. Not strange people. That's a different thing altogether and far scarier. I mean people that we meet in everyday life but, due to social restraints or the fact that we hide behind smart phones, rarely converse with anymore. As I made my way to the bridge to take a final panoramic photo, I spotted five men walking by the river. I couldn't believe it. It was my group! JP was the first to spot me.

For a few moments, we stood by the water's edge while they described the scenic but demanding route they'd taken to get to Bewdley. I could see from the strained look on their faces they were in dire need of rehydration and a rest, and the topic soon turned to food. In contrast, I was studying the map from Lewis and felt keen to depart

One rider peeled away to search for a suitable place to eat, and one by one, they followed him to a nearby pub menu displayed on a window. I sensed a distance between us — deservedly so — and I should probably have stayed with them to reconnect. But the solo ride had been unexpectedly invigorating. I'd been thoroughly enjoying the short, unplanned stops along the way. Fully aware I was in danger of alienating myself from the group, I decided to continue alone. My decision was tinged with uncertainty though, and I hoped they wouldn't take it personally.

Located just outside of Bewdley, the Wyre Forest is one of the largest remaining ancient woodlands in Britain. It isn't a pristine forest and like many similar environments has suffered from deforestation and degradation. But within an area of 10 square miles, the forest and waterways remain relatively untouched and act as an essential habitat for wildlife. Birds, including the wood warbler and the long eared-owl, call the forest home along with many mammals. Not that fallow deer, moles and water shrew are easy to spot, but I remained optimistic while riding alongside the trees.

I cycled through villages with intriguing names such as Buttonoak and Deuxhill but didn't stop. Instead, I raided the provisions in my front pannier, gulped the last of my water and kept on cycling. Just before Bridgnorth, an unexpected junction provided a direct route to Shrewsbury. I stocked up on water, decided to take the easy option, and for the next two hours, rode on without stopping.

Finally, on the outskirts of Shrewsbury, I pulled over to the side of the road to check my mobile phone. Dave had sent a text. They'd booked into a pub called The Old Bell and a few minutes later, I was freewheeling down a busy street, searching for the building.

I found the pub quite easily and leaned my bike against the wall. I gained a stare from a passerby as I took off my Lycra top and used the thin material to wipe sweat from my face and armpits. After sliding it back on, I called Dave and as expected, he answered on the first ring with a trademark, 'Hello.'

It felt good to hear his deep voice and I found myself smiling as I said, 'I'm gasping for a beer, and I'm pretty sure it's your round.'

The four of us chose a table on the verandah along with a few locals who'd also ventured outside to enjoy a drink in the late afternoon sunshine. During our first beer, I learned that all three of them were planning to undertake a cycling and walking holiday in the Hebrides of Scotland and they saw the ride to Preston as an ideal training day.

I knew from experience that Dave had accomplished many endurance feats, including a trek with Paul to the summit of Chimborazo many years before. This particular Ecuadorian summit has the unusual accolade of being the highest mountain on Earth when the measurement is taken from the earth's core, and they have therefore stood closer to the sun than any other people I've ever met. Paul's powerful legs have also taken him to the peaks of Kilimanjaro, Mount Blanc and Everest base camp.

Yet weighing up their walking prowess against the pace of the next day's bike ride, I had a niggling doubt it would be testing for us all. My main concern was for the other Dave, the one I wasn't related to, the one in his late sixties. Not that he looked unhealthy. A head full of hair and a firm but welcoming handshake matched his wiry physique. But nevertheless his age did concern me. If it had been hard for me, how would he cope?

But instead of worrying about the future, I decided to enjoy the moment. As the sun dipped below the roofline, I slipped off my shoes, took up the offer of another pint of real ale, and recited the day's events. It had been many years since I'd chatted in such a carefree manner with my brother Dave. Emigration has its merits, but precious time with close family is often the casualty. While we took turns speaking, I knew then that the decision to ride solo from Bewdley had been the right one. I didn't hesitate when Paul ordered another round of drinks.

As we supped our final beers, older Dave began talking about his hobby. Unlike the three of us, he was actually an avid cyclist and had been for generations. In fact, it was in his blood. His family owned a bike courier company, and during busy periods he still helped out. He shared stories of the numerous long distance bike rides he'd undertaken over the years. It seemed he was a hardy veteran, and as I stood to leave, I was confident he wouldn't be the one to keep me company at the back of the pack. It would be either my brother or Paul. Both were fine with me. In fact, I was looking forward to the chats we'd have.

The sun was little more than a memory now, leaving behind a trace of pink, etched across a thin trail of clouds. During the mile long ride to the accommodation, my head swam, partly due to exhaustion and too many beers without food.

I thought about the evening meal. Mark had also packed a Hawaiian shirt and I remembered Alan talking about a set of paper garlands for me to wear. I couldn't wait.

Day 6: Under the Bridge

'No journey is too long with the right company.'
Unknown

A soft tap on the door was followed shortly by another. I was already awake, showered and changed, and I opened it to find Alan standing outside, dressed for action and armed with a fresh smile.

'Good man, Ali. Glad to see you're up and about. Did you enjoy the single room?'

'For sure. It was a welcome birthday surprise. Is anyone else awake?'

'Yeah, most of us are up and ready for action. Today's the longest leg of the journey. It's about one hundred miles to Preston, so we thought we'd better get an early start.'

I heard someone call Alan's name just then and he ventured off to investigate. Quickly, I scanned the room, thankful I'd taken the time to wash and dry all my essential garments before heading out into town last night. The only casualty was my Hawaiian shirt, laying ruffled on the floor, stained with Bolognese sauce and red wine. The evening had been a huge success with just the right amount of beers to complement the spicy pizzas, but by midnight we were tucked up in bed!

I opened the curtains to check the weather and then laid out my clothes and gadgets. Most items would be transported to Preston in the van, but there were some essential articles to carry, including rehydration tablets, both phones, a waterproof jacket, maps, sunglasses, a spare top and muesli bars.

The wall-mounted TV had been a welcome luxury, even though Brexit was once again dominating the early morning headlines. It seemed that across Britain change was in the air. Except for the constant humidity. The predicted cold front was yet to materialise, and according to the forecaster, there was little chance of rain in the north-west of England.

Our first major landmark for today's journey would be Liverpool, but unlike our first ride twenty years ago, this time we'd veer away from the city centre and cross the River Mersey by bridge rather than ferry. It meant we wouldn't get the opportunity to ride alongside the impressive Liver Building, which stands over 300 feet high on the water's edge, but at least we'd steer clear of inner city traffic.

The Silver Jubilee Bridge is a 285-foot-high and 1,580-foot-long structure, originally called the Runcorn Bridge. It got its current name in 1977 when major engineering changes coincided with the Queen's Jubilee. It is estimated that 80,000 vehicles use the bridge each day — ten times the number for which it was originally designed — but at least we'd be protected from heavy freight by a designated cycle path on the eastern side. The bridge would lead our little convoy to the outskirts of Liverpool. From there, we planned to locate a converted train line, known as the Liverpool Loop, which would thread us though the suburbs.

It was time to get going. In the hallway, familiar faces made their way quietly down the stairs. We dropped our luggage at the door, then ventured back towards the dining room. The room looked eerily dark through the glass-panelled door. This was confirmed when Alan tried the handle and found it to be locked. Rattling it once again, he asked, 'What time is it, lads?'

All eyes darted to a wall-mounted clock, pointing to a quarter past seven. Nick muttered something under his breath and wandered over to the reception area. He was hoping to find someone to help but returned a few moments later.

'That's weird. I requested a seven o'clock breakfast so we could get an early start but there's no-one about.'

For a few minutes, we contemplated leaving on an empty stomach and finding something to eat on the road. However, our three additional riders for the day — including my brother Dave — weren't staying in our accommodation, and we hadn't arranged to meet until eight. While deliberating, the front door suddenly opened and in walked a dark haired woman, dressed in Nike trainers, jeans, and a puffer jacket.

She strolled towards the dining room, side-stepping our discarded bags and simultaneously removing her jacket, before placing it onto a coat hook. We stepped back, conscious of crowding her, but as she unlocked the dining room door, she turned towards us.

'You lot are keen, aren't you? Breakfast isn't 'til eight. I only came in early to grab a cuppa before the rush.'

Nick cleared his throat. 'Well, I'm glad you did. We actually booked a seven o'clock breakfast with the girl on reception.'

Her brown eyes opened wide. 'Did you now? Well, as usual, I'm the last to know.' She switched on the lights. 'In you come then, lads. Help yourself to cereals and I'll get the kettle on. I suppose you all want eggs and bacon and the like?'

'If you don't mind,' Nick said.

'Of course not. But I'm not a miracle worker, so you'll have to give me a minute.'

Initially, the clanging from the kitchen sounded worrying. But soon a sense of calm prevailed as she appeared with the first of many rounds of toast. We showered her with compliments as she dashed professionally back and forth from the kitchen.

The two Daves and Paul arrived at eight, as per the plan, tapping on the outside window to remind us they were on time. Mark opened it wide enough so we could talk.

'Bit of a delay,' he said. 'Do you want some toast?'

While they waited patiently in the early sunshine, he passed warm toast through a gap in the net curtains.

A brief interval, a few more bangs and expletives, and our host appeared with plates, brimming with fried eggs, sausages, bacon, mushrooms and beans. We devoured everything placed before us and waved away her apologies for the wait. Under the circumstances, she'd done a fantastic job.

It was approaching nine o'clock by the time we gathered outside. Out of our three new cyclists, Dave the eldest looked the most proficient. Dressed in a matching Lycra top and shorts — and with the correct type of cleated shoes — he fitted in perfectly with those among the group that took cycling seriously. The other two wore T-shirts, Lycra shorts, and training shoes, opting to use traditional pedals on their hired bikes.

'I thought you said you all left each morning with military precision,' my brother whispered just before departure.

'We normally do,' I replied. 'I really hope they won't try and make up for our late start by riding faster than normal or having less stops. My tip for the day is to stay close and avoid the urge to slow down for photos.'

As suspected, we didn't take an official break in the first hour, nor in the second or third. We did stop for fleeting moments, to give the new rider's time to adjust to their hired bikes and to wait when the group stretched out too far, but there were no pauses to enjoy coffee or mid-morning snacks.

I needn't have worried though. Throughout the morning, our oldest rider of the group proved to be a formidable cyclist. He settled into the front of the pack with ease, trading banter and sharing stories with those around him. As the order of riders changed and conversations took place along gently curving country roads, he earned himself a new nickname. Fast Dave.

In contrast, riding steadily and happily, but much further behind, my brother gained the name of Slow Dave. Paul already had the nickname of Android, earned over many decades of hillwalking and trekking, although he wasn't quite living up to any cyborg-like expectations.

The route was perfect for cycling with long stretches of quiet country roads, nestled within the soft nape of Shropshire. This was classic English countryside. Lush rolling hills to please the eye, fields of ripening wheat, rippling on a warm summer's breeze, and enough clouds to add character to the sky without the need to worry about rain.

At times we caught sight of swallows skimming across meadows, constantly changing direction as they hunted for food. Whenever we neared water — whether it was a flooded ditch, a village pond or a tributary — there was always the possibility of riding alongside dragonflies or watching formations of ducks flying in the bright sky overhead.

Just after the village of Welsh End, the glint of sunshine on nearby water signified the Shropshire Union Canal. It was partially hidden behind a row of mature trees and signified the border with Wales, but the road led us away as we continued our journey. If it wasn't for the many unplanned encounters with freight vehicles, delivering loads to rural communities, we would have had the road to ourselves. Even the tractors were sparse, although spirals of dust on the horizon spoke of their toil in distance fields.

Throughout the morning, I was determined to stay focused, despite the group being often stretched to breaking point. The country town of Whitchurch appeared like an oasis, offering numerous options for refreshments, but the lead riders rode past them all, seemingly determined to keep the momentum going. An hour later, at a critical junction, Mick stopped the pack to allow those at the back to catch up.

For once, it wasn't me. When Slow Dave came into view, I hung back to check he was OK.

We rode side by side and he slurped on the water stored in his camel-back. 'Wrenbury looked like a nice little town,' he said between mouthfuls. 'Did you see all the cafes?' Before I had time to reply, he added, 'Ali, don't get me wrong, but why are we in such a hurry?'

I grinned widely. 'Dave, welcome to my world. I guess they're simply fast riders and tea rooms just aren't their thing.'

Thankfully, I was wrong. Fifteen minutes later, the lead rider threw out an arm, crossing the road towards a nearby building where a chalk board caught my attention. *Coffee, tea and snacks by the canal,* it said. We were finally going to stop for food.

We were in a location called Venetian Marina, and after parking our bikes and ordering, I strolled towards the water. Further ahead, beyond a sign marked, *Private,* numerous canal boats were moored in designated bays, awaiting their owners or maintenance.

The marina was akin to a motorway service station. They even had posters offering several different types of service for those travelling on the water, including fuel, food, second-hand boats, and repairs. Most boats chugged sedately on towards the nearby lock, not needing to stop. But I watched as one stopped alongside the bank in order to fill up with fuel. After stepping onto the bank, the skipper was greeted by a cheery attendant and very soon they were exchanging pleasantries about the weather, the river traffic, and the rising price of diesel.

When our food arrived, I sat with Fast Dave, Slow Dave and The Android, and I waited for them to comment about the morning's ride. It was Fast Dave who triggered the discussion, asking between bites if the pace had been as quick all week.

'I think they're taking it easy today, because you three are new,' I said with a grin.

Fast Dave placed his fork on his plate, his face suddenly serious. 'I'll tell you what, they're a fit bunch. That last hour hurt, but I wouldn't let it show. I haven't been so glad of a cup of tea in years!'

It felt good to hear that I wasn't alone in thinking the pace had been brisk. Slow Dave was keen to talk. 'I'm loving the ride and the comradery, but we've blitzed through some lovely places. I'm jealous that you're riding all the way to John O'Groats. I'd love to do it, but if I do, it will be over three or four weeks, not thirteen days.'

Sometime later, the scenery began changing as we approached Runcorn. Farms gave way to small industrial estates before small pockets of woodland returned. Then suddenly, the fields were gone, replaced by new, purpose-built warehouses. Newly-built roundabouts appeared, their centres adorned with daisies, and on the grass verges, saplings waved in the breeze where once there might have been hardy oaks.

The hum of distant traffic turned into a constant drone as we rode deeper into the industrial estate and approached a looming dead end. Where the road finished, a narrow alleyway took us out of the industrial estate, under a motorway, and into the heart of Runcorn. We'd been thrust into urban civilisation and all that went along with it, including dual carriageways, traffic lights and pedestrians, as well as verges strewn with litter, heavy goods vehicles with impatient drivers, and roads stained thick with oil.

The cycle path was segregated from the carriageway by a wide strip of grass, and more than once I noted the familiar blue signs that informed us we were using one of the national cycle routes managed by Sustrans.

Further ahead, I glimpsed a section of the steel bridge we'd awaited since waking, and the gradient of the path increased. As we crossed the River Mersey, the incessant noise of high speed vehicles cut short any meaningful conversation and we made our way in single file along the cycle path, which was segregated from the traffic by crash proof barriers.

Entering the narrow track, I noticed a poster stuck to one of the bridge pillars. It said, *Need a lifeline? Give us a call,* and positioned underneath was a sticker displaying a free-to-call helpline number. I wondered briefly how many people had used this bridge for other purposes.

I peered down to search for vessels — and bodies! — but found none on the placid waterway. The Mersey looked dormant with barely a ripple on its wide expanse of grey water. My eyes sought the source of the river, far beyond the dark smudge of low-lying land, but instead they found newly-built islands within half a mile, strategically located at regular intervals across the water.

On each parcel of land stood industrial cranes, stretching far above the water. I watched as one swung into life; a steel column suspended in the air by unseen chains. They were building the new, six-lane toll bridge, deemed to be called the Mersey Gateway, and I wondered what fate lay ahead for the aging bridge I was now crossing.

I was soon joined at the top of the bridge by a feisty wind, which emitted a high-pitched whine as it tore across the ramparts. Before long, though, the wind dropped, as we changed angle and began the quick descent towards the northern side of the river. We gained lengthy stares from a group of children playing football on a street corner as we entered a housing estate after a series of turns. None of the houses had front gardens, and in every street, at least one home was boarded up.

Freewheeling towards the river's edge, the pathway led us underneath the same bridge we'd ridden over minutes earlier. For a few moments, we stopped our bikes and gazed at the water. There were no boats or ships to add to the scene, just muddy ripples, breaking gently onto the silted embankment. In this instance, far more appealing to me than the landscape was the train line, running directly above our heads and parallel with the Silver Jubilee Bridge. We were now standing alongside part of the brick-built viaduct that formed the northern section. There are forty-nine arches on the northern side in total, and we had just ridden through one of them.

I leaned against the weathered bricks, laid a hundred years earlier, and pointed my camera upwards in the hope of capturing the bridge at an interesting angle. But halfway through the photoshoot, my bladder began complaining. I quickly ducked towards the nearest tree. I wasn't gone for long, maybe thirty seconds or so, but when I stepped back into the sunlight, the group of riders was nowhere to be seen.

I ran into the clearing in panic, but a movement in the distance caught my eye. It was the back wheel of a bike, disappearing around the corner of an abandoned house! I gave chase, back towards the housing estate, fully expecting to see the riders up ahead. But nothing.

On one corner of a crossroads stood a small convenience store, offering consumers a choice of newspapers, bread, milk, wines and spirits. A man stood outside, clutching a can of lager, and took a long swig as I rode past, his calm eyes momentarily catching my panicked ones.

In desperation, I continued on to the next junction, past terraced houses with their front doors wide open. By the time I'd reached the end of the next street, my earlier smile had all but disappeared. I did a U turn and tried another road, but the street looked identical to the last one with row after row of brick houses. Only the front doors were different. Now closed, their various colours helped distinguish one home from another.

Two teenage boys crossed the street up ahead, both holding a large paper wrapping filled with fish and chips. As I rode closer they stopped to stare. The GoPro camera was still attached to my bike helmet and I heard one say, 'Give him a wave. Here comes the Google map man.'

I feigned laughter, waved a hand, and came to an abrupt halt outside a takeaway. A sign above the window told me I'd made it to the Golden Bridge Fish and Chips shop. While contemplating my next move, the phone in my front pannier began to ring. It was Slow Dave.

'Ali, I hope you don't mind me asking, but where exactly are you?'

I answered quietly because two cropped-haired youths, standing outside the shop, munching on chips, were watching my every move.

'That's easy,' I replied, hoping to mask my embarrassment. 'I'm outside a takeaway called Golden Bridge Fish and Chips.'

'What are you on about? You were just at the waterfront, taking a leak in the bushes. We called your name and set off along the path. I thought you were right behind us.'

'What path did you follow?' I asked.

'The one by the river. What other way is there? Where are you now?'

'I'm back in the council estate, and more than one person is looking at the GoPro attached to my helmet.'

'Well, I'm sure they just think you look a bit odd. Anyway, we're following the path by the river. We'll slow down until you catch us up.'

'No worries. I'm leaving now. Do you want any fish and chips? They smell delicious.'

The connection fell silent and my smile returned. Nodding to the chip munchers, I mumbled something about the benefits of gluten free and rode as fast as possible towards the river.

I sped through one of the viaduct archways and the pathway veered right, allowing me to see the route they'd taken along the water's edge. For a few miles, the track was heavily fenced on my right-hand side and I passed a series of industrial units. All the while, the riverbank remained close on my left. Apart from gulls, the only other sign of life was a mangy black cat, devoid of a collar and in need of a meal, its red eyes spying on me from the shade of a tree.

Thirty minutes since first contemplating a photo of the viaduct, I was finally back with the group and rewarded with a pat on the back by Mark. 'You never fail to keep us on our toes, do you?'

The path soon steered away from the riverbank, taking us deeper into an urban landscape. Yet even in this maze of concrete, the familiar blue signs were evident, ensuring we could still ride on designated paths, away from heavy traffic, whenever possible. Occasionally, though, we had to walk across dual carriageways, waiting with pedestrians for the flashing green symbols and loud beeps to signal it was safe to step out.

All signs of suburbia vanished when we rode onto the Liverpool Loop, a converted railway line, elevated above the streets and houses. It was a bitumen strip and proved to be a popular track. In a short while, we passed dog walkers, mums with pushers, joggers, and children on their bikes.

Mature trees stood alongside the track, and overhead their wide canopies blocked the sky. In some places, the trees were so plentiful, it was as though we were riding through countryside, not through one of the largest cities in Britain. Occasionally, the trees gave way to pockets of wildflowers, in turn snarled by blackberry bushes with dark fruit ready for plucking. We did notice some broken glass and litter strewn under the hedges, but these spots were few and far between. For the most part, it looked to me as though the track was well respected.

Mark spotted a signpost nailed to a tree, pointing to a café. Throughout the journey so far, food and water were precious commodities. We didn't always know where our next pit stop would be. Although our bike computers had pinpoint accuracy with regards to road turnings, they were unable to display the location of every bakery!

It had now been many hours since the marina, and after a quick show of hands, we followed the arrow. It led us to a narrow trail, angled through sparse woodland, where we freewheeled until we reached a quiet road. Once again we were in a housing estate, but this time with no markers to assist us. It was difficult to know if we should take the left or right turn.

Just then I spotted a group of men in a front garden. All but one was peering into the open bonnet of a car. The other was walking out of a front doorway carrying a tray of hot drinks. He looked up as I cycled to the edge of the driveway, his eyes quizzical.

'Are you alright there, mate? You lost or something?' he said.

I pointed to the other riders, most of whom were using the free time to glug on water. 'We're after the café. We were up on the Liverpool Loop and a sign on the track said to come this way.'

He grinned and said, 'I thought as much. They need to add another arrow at the bottom. Just go to the end of this road, then veer left, cross over the main intersection and you'll see a row of shops. Look for a café called Simply Coffee. They'll look after you!'

We soon discovered that Simply Coffee sold more than simply coffee. By the time we arrived, the lunchtime rush was all but over, and we had the small café to ourselves. We wandered in, one by one, each of us clutching empty water bottles.

There were two women at work. One stood behind the counter, washing a pile of pots and dishes, and the other was sweeping the floor. The nearest one greeted us warmly as we mulled around the counter, contemplating our choices. Putting the broom away, she washed her hands and stood ready by the counter. Alan was the first to order, but as he tried to pay, she waved his wallet away.

'Don't bother with that right now,' she said to his surprise. 'You look like a decent bunch of bike riders. I'll get your orders in first and we can sort out payment afterwards.' She raised her voice. 'If you're after a cold drink, grab them from the fridge and just let me know what you've taken when we settle the bill at the end.'

Alan held up his water bottle and was just about to ask the million-dollar question, when she jumped in. 'Leave all your empty water bottles on the counter. We'll fill them up for you in a minute.'

Thirty minutes later, we sat outside the café, legs stretched out, stomachs content and water bottles filled. Lunch had been a success, not only for the prompt service and tasty portions, but also for the prolonged amount of time we'd relaxed outside, enjoying the sun whenever it peeped out from behind the clouds.

As we chatted about the day's ride, Liverpool went about its business — normal day-to-day activities, but for me, worthy of observing. A courier with a cheeky smile, parking on a double yellow line to drop off a package and causing a backlog of traffic within seconds. A teenaged football fan, dressed in a bright red Liverpool football top with white track pants and Adidas trainers, striding purposefully along the pavement while being pulled along by a panting boxer dog. An elderly couple, arm in arm, dressed for winter, slowly crossing the street while cars revved impatiently from behind the lights.

I noticed that the café was positioned near a post office and this triggered off two thoughts. One, I hadn't sent a postcard to Australia for some time, and two, I needed to get another official stamp on my paperwork as proof for my End-to-End Certificate.

After paying my bill and collecting my water bottle, I ventured into the shop. The post office consisted of a single counter with two windows side by side. A shutter blocked one of the windows, but the other was available for service and a staff member waited patiently behind it.

I found the picture postcard display and picked a card that depicted the River Mersey, along with the famous Liver Birds. Unfortunately, as I studied the profiles of the mythical creatures, two more people entered the shop and walked directly towards the only vacant counter, beating me to the window by a single step.

They were both in their early twenties, fair haired, and armed with a wad of paperwork that they scattered across the counter. As the assistant made eye contact, they explained their needs, and I used the time to write my message. It was only after I'd finished that I realised they were still talking.

'No, we can't wait, can we, Steve? It's his first trip abroad, isn't it, Steve?'

Steve tried to get a word in edgeways. 'Well, I have been to —'

'Scotland doesn't count, Steve. Anyway'—she turned back to the counter—'we want to set up the card for our Thai currency and also get a quote for worldwide travel insurance. We're travelling for about three weeks. Should we get our post redirected, do you think? What do you think, Steve?'

'Well, I guess it—'

'I think we'll leave the redirection, thanks. We're going to Koh Phi Phi. It's where they made that film with Leonardo DiCaprio. We'll read the book while we're on the actual beach, won't we, Steve?'

'Well you might, but I'd rather—'

'Steve isn't a reader. He prefers Netflix and football. We haven't booked anything yet, mind you, but we hope to go next year...'

The girl was relentless and my thoughts turned to the riders, just outside. Had they ridden off again, oblivious to the fact I was stuck behind Steve and his autocratic girlfriend?

Before another word was muttered, I coughed politely and stepped forward. 'Sorry to barge in, but I just need to buy a postcard and a stamp and send it to Australia. I'm in a bit of a hurry, you see.'

I caught sight of Steve's face and found a welcoming smile as he stepped back to allow me into his space. His girlfriend was also gracious, as was the cashier.

As the cashier reached for the ink pad to add a post office stamp to my End-to-End form, proving I'd made it to Liverpool, Steve's girlfriend started up again.

'We should go to Australia someday, don't you think, Steve? Maybe after Thailand. What do you reckon?'

Before I heard his answer, I quickly thanked them all and rushed out of the shop. I expected to find the Bedfordshire Clanger parked alone by the lamppost, but instead I found the riders just getting into motion, pushing themselves up from chairs, stretching out their limbs, and slotting water bottles into designated holders.

Fast Dave approached me. 'I thought you said that lunchtimes were like pit stops. This has been very relaxing. Mind you, it came at the right time. I was beginning to feel the pinch back there.'

Mark was studying his bike computer and announced, 'OK, lads, only 40 miles to go until a shower and a beer.'

Armed with this welcome news, I ran back into the café.

'Are you OK, my love?' the owner asked. 'We're about to close.'

I was holding a giant size Mars Bar. 'I'm just after this, please.'

'Oh, you just take it, my love.' She laughed. 'It's on the house. At your age, if you're daft enough to wear Lycra and ride on bikes all day, you deserve a little treat from time to time.'

She reminded me of a younger version of my late mum, happy-go-lucky with a quick-to-smile nature, just a little shorter and rounder.

'Thank you,' I smiled and walked outside. The door closed behind me with the clunk of a lock and the, *Open,* sign was changed to, *Closed.* I waved goodbye, turned around and saw the row of riders waiting. The Mars Bar was devoured two hours later, the sugary treat a welcome boost. But as the sun began to drop, so too did our energy and enthusiasm. The road seemed never ending.

We found ourselves in the countryside again, but the cows, fields, farms and villages held less and less appeal as the afternoon wore on. By the time Preston neared, the group had divided into three, all riding separately from each other. I was with Colin and JP but had no idea if we were in the lead, in the middle, or at the end.

A signpost for Longton should have triggered a spark of enthusiasm, but I'd long forgotten this was the nearest village to our accommodation. It only dawned on me when Colin took a sharp left turn from the dual carriageway onto a shingle driveway and a sign by the verge said, *Willow Cottage Bed & Breakfast.*

Our first sighting of Willow Cottage came a few moments later, and immediately I wished we were staying longer. To me, the term 'cottage' conjures up images of quaint, thatched buildings with rose gardens and odd shaped rooms. Willow Cottage was, however, much larger; its grand and white-washed walls were adorned with ivy, which crept along the lengthy veranda to one of four bay windows overlooking an expansive courtyard.

It resembled a small country mansion, complete with views of lush green fields. From the driveway, I spotted a horse and free-roaming chickens in the adjacent field. Suddenly I felt as though I'd been transported to paradise, and my strength returned.

The interior didn't disappoint either. As Anne, the owner, led us to our rooms, past the inglenook fireplace and up the stairs, I found myself touching the exposed beams. We soon learned that the property is 600 years old and set on 20 acres. The horse out front was called Lollipop and the chickens would supply our eggs in the morning.

If there was a downside, it was purely a logistical one. There weren't enough single rooms to go around, which meant that some riders had to double up. Alan and I ended up together, which was something that hadn't happened since our bike ride twenty years earlier. He was happy to give me the side of the bed with the window view, and because it was a queen-sized mattress, any fears of rolling into each other in the night were quelled.

The two Daves and Paul were staying in a different guest house, close by, and plans were already in place to meet in the village for an evening meal. After showering and before sunset, I made a mug of tea and carried it outside in search of Lollipop. Despite my calls, the horse refused to come close to the picket fence. But as fireflies danced in the last of the light and rabbits ventured from their warrens, I clasped the warm mug and made a mental note to thank Nick for picking a top location. In that moment, the 99 miles that we'd cycled that day ebbed from my thoughts. Instead, I gazed at sun-kissed clouds and thought about the morrow.

I would miss Fast Dave with his southern style and quick-fire banter. And Paul (the Android) had kept up to the end without showing any signs of duress. He, like us, was looking forward to a pint of real ale in one of the village pubs, just across the field where Lollipop now grazed. I looked forward to chatting with him.

Most of all, though, I would miss Slow Dave, my big brother. It had been too many years since we'd shared a bike ride together, and after tonight, there would be no more time for catching up. When I finally reached John O'Groats, my time in the UK would be limited. Within 48 hours, I'd be back on a plane to Australia. Had I spent enough time with him during the ride? Probably not. That's the problem with life sometimes — we take things or people for granted and all of a sudden they're gone.

But the evening was still young. Maybe it was for this reason that I did my best to ignore the back pain that had crept up on me that afternoon. I popped two more pills, washing them down with cold tea, and heard familiar voices, calling my name. My friends were stood outside, dressed in shorts and T-shirts, smiles all round in readiness for hot food and fine ales. Mark led the way.

'OK, lads, first stop is the Ram's Head, followed by the Black Bear where I'm going to thrash Slow Dave at pool.'

To the sound of laughter, we made our way along the public footpath, passing a field of sheep along the way. The track was dry, but narrow, and led us directly to the outskirts of the village. In the last of the light, we ventured along the high street, passing a row of terraced houses. There was no-one else in sight — just us, telling jokes and sharing stories about our 99-mile-bike-ride from Shrewsbury.

Day 7: The Drugs Don't Work

'Do not judge my story by the chapter you walked in on.'
Unknown

The tingles were faint at first, sending tiny shockwaves across my shoulders and waking me from a deep slumber. I lay for a while, listless and fidgety until sleep claimed me once again. As night wore on, I woke often, silently cursing the increasing pain. Then, without warning, a shard of light struck the back of my eyes, followed by a sudden jolt that tore across my neck.

I cried out, unable to quell the sound of my voice as it shattered the still night air. My eyes shot open, but the darkened room offered little solace as my legs thrashed involuntarily on the bed. Instinctively, I took up the fetal position, breathed deeply, and closed my eyes once more. Only then did I remember I was hemmed into one side of a queen-size bed.

Across from no-man's land, Alan lay still, seemingly oblivious to my predicament. The pain had subsided, and for a few moments, I lay across the tangled sheets, convinced it had all been a nightmare. I turned to read the digital clock, but instantly regretted the decision. The slightest movement felt like whiplash, causing me to let out a low-pitched moan. I felt movement from across the mattress.

'Alan, are you awake?' I whispered.

His voice sounded distant. 'Go back to sleep. You'll be fine in the morning.'

The room fell silent then. Still groggy and without thinking, I rolled on the pillow, sending another jolt through my neck. This time my voice was louder. 'Alan, I really mean it. I've done something to my neck. I can't move it.'

His reply was low and gruff. 'Go back to sleep, Ali. It's just a headache.'

Within moments, he was asleep, his soft breathing a contrast to my gasps. I thought back to the last time I'd experienced such excruciating pain. It had been the morning after a white-water rafting trip on the Zambezi River with Fran. During the excursion, we'd tackled numerous rapids and had been flung from the inflatable many times. Over the years, those rapids have claimed lives and our guide explained the importance of the paddles. Maybe this is why I had gripped mine with such intensity during each plunge into the frenzied water. The following morning, my arms, legs and neck had seized up, rendering me incapacitated for the whole day.

Although yesterday's bike ride had been physically demanding, it hadn't been death-defying or frightening. If any part of my body was going to complain, I expected it to be my legs or bottom, not my neck. Was the pain linked to poor posture while riding? Something had to have triggered the attack, but I'd no idea what it was. Feeling confused, groggy, and restless, I closed my eyes, not daring to move, and I must have fallen back asleep.

When I next opened them, the bedroom was bathed in soft light, and I could hear the tone of familiar voices drifting through an open window. It sounded like the riders were up and about, chatting with each other in the courtyard. I also heard another noise. It was whistling in the bathroom, signalling Alan was preparing for the day ahead.

I lay still, unwilling to move, secretly hoping it had all been a nightmare. But as the bathroom door opened and I instinctively turned to face him, I regretted the decision instantly. A spasm ripped across my neck, rendering me wide-eyed.

Alan was dressed for the road and studied me with a wry smile. 'Morning Ali, it's a lovely day out there. I've just boiled the kettle. Do you want tea?'

I let out a sigh, my voice straining. 'I'm not sure if you've noticed but I can't move my head.'

He managed a half smile and said, 'Don't I know it. A cup of tea will sort you out.'

I cradled my neck and whispered, 'Are you joking?'

'You like it with milk and no sugar, don't you?'

'Alan, I can't move my head let alone drink tea.'

'Well, you look alright to me. It can't be that bad and you do exaggerate sometimes. Have a hot shower. You'll soon be alright.'

I felt the colour rise to my cheeks as I struggled to understand his reaction, but I heard myself saying, 'Tea would be great. I really do need some painkillers though. It feels like someone has pinned their foot to the back of my throat.'

He tossed some tablets onto the bed and placed a mug of tea by my bedside. 'Breakfast is anytime now, mate. We're due on the road within the hour. I'll see you downstairs.'

As he left the room, I called out behind him. 'Have you got a straw?'

There was no reply.

I felt very confused. Had one of my best friends just left me in agony to fend for myself? Or was I misinterpreting things? Did he still count me as a mate, I wondered? Had my antics and diversions during the trip finally tipped our companionship over the edge? Even if that was the case, I thought, did I really deserve this treatment?

It struck me I had two options. I could either stay in bed and hope the pain would pass, or I could get up. To remain in bed meant a subsequent solo ride, and once the pain had maybe eased or I'd sought medical help, the riders would be far ahead of me. The other option was to do exactly as Alan said. Drink the tea, take the tablets, and head for the shower. I knew the answer. I'd come too far to lie down.

My first goal was to consume the tablets, which I did while lying sideways on the bed. The next mission was to stand up, enjoy a sip of tea, and then take a long, hot shower. Easier said than done. Cradling my neck, I pivoted my body so that my legs dropped over the edge of the bed. The manoeuvre went well, my knees now resting on soft carpet. While contemplating my next move, the door opened and Alan walked in, clutching an empty water bottle.

He smiled brightly. 'Oh good, you're up and about.'

'Up? You call this up?'

'Oh, Ali, you are funny.'

'You think I'm making this up?'

'Well it can't be as bad as you're making it out to be.'

'I still can't move my neck.'

'Well, you've got this far, haven't you? You're halfway to the shower. By the way, breakfast is on the table and it smells delicious. Do you want me to fill up your water bottle?'

'No, don't worry, I'll manage.'

'Good man.'

And with that, he was gone again. I wondered if he'd informed the others. Or were they right now tucking into their bacon and free-range eggs, oblivious to the fact I was trying not to scream?

Eventually, I came up with a simple plan. It loosely involved grabbing my uppermost ear, pulling my head upwards, sliding my hand quickly into the gap, and supporting my face so I could stand. Actually, maybe it wasn't so simple.

Tea was not an option while my head leaned at such an angle, but at least the shooting pains had stopped. A mirror on the wall produced a comical sight and somehow I managed to produce the faintest of smiles. At least I was wearing underpants.

Stepping tentatively away from the bed, I could just see the paddock beneath the window. The horse grazed the edges of the field, searching for fresh green shoots in the trampled mud, and in the distance, I could see the terraced houses that skirted the village of Longton where we'd ventured twelve hours earlier.

The evening had been entertaining with an abundance of food, washed down with a selection of local ales from each of the pubs. As predicted, Mark had beaten Dave at a game of pool. It had all been lighthearted fun, tainted only by the thought that I wouldn't see Dave again until the day before my flight to Australia. As for Fast Dave and The Android, I had no idea when we'd next meet. That is part of the challenge of living the other side of the world, attempting to maintain friendships from thousands of miles away.

I stole a sideways look at the horse and studied the clouds. They were gathering fast and I hoped the rain would stay away for at least one more day. I figured if I could stand, I could probably walk, and that meant the prospect of a shower. It was slow progress, but before too long, I sat spread-eagled on the tiled floor, the power shower pounding my upper body and the water close to scalding. Not able to delay the inevitable any longer, I tentatively rotated my head, ignoring any pain as it hit resistance. By the time I turned off the taps, a semblance of movement had returned. I washed two painkillers down with cold tea before I left the bedroom.

I finally entered the breakfast room, but most riders had already eaten. Alan was nowhere to be seen and Colin looked up from his plate. 'You OK, mate? Alan said you were complaining about a sore head or something.'

I forced a grin while massaging my neck. 'Oh, it's nothing. Never felt better in my life. It only hurts if I turn my neck, but I'm sure that won't be a problem at all during our ride to Penrith.'

He chuckled softly and said, 'I must admit, you don't look the best. Can I pour you a cup of tea? That should help.'

Later, I found Nick. He was in the courtyard, adjusting the brakes on the Bedfordshire Clanger. He studied me from over the rim of his glasses. 'You don't look too good, but I'm sure you'll be fine after a few miles. Have you eaten?'

I nodded the best I could and he continued speaking. 'I've checked the brakes and lubricated your rear sprocket. I'm driving to Kendal soon and will park the van there before riding back towards you. With luck, I'll meet you all in the village of Beetham. You reckon you can keep out of trouble today?'

It suddenly struck me how much I'd missed Nick during the daily rides. His knee injury and supporting role in the van meant that he was restricted to only a few hours' ride each day. During these brief periods, I'd managed to steal some time with him, and although it was clear our personalities differed, the banter was mostly jovial. It was the fluffy stuff we didn't agree on. Unlike me, he didn't have a need for numerous photo-shoots, random conversations with strangers, collecting memorabilia, or undertaking time-costly excursions to seek out nearby attractions.

Nick's traits hadn't appeared to have changed since our first end-to-end bike ride, but Alan's mannerisms intrigued me. I've always known him to be a curious type, but on this trip his focus seemed primarily on travelling from A to B with as few deviations as possible. In Western Australia, we'd once gone walkabout with an Aboriginal guide, and during the three-day adventure, we'd hunted for kangaroo, learned to skin monitor lizards, and slept under the stars. It had been a magical experience, out in the bush, with no set plan, no detailed maps, and no idea where we were heading each day.

So far, on this trip, he'd showed little of that curiosity. But he wasn't alone. These riders were committed; of that there was no doubt. But in their haste, I believed they were missing something. Then again, it could be me that was missing the point. I didn't know anymore. What was clear, though, was that my natural curiosity was proving difficult to suppress, and this was being amplified by the words of wisdom from my Uncle Matt, which constantly mulled in my head.

Slow down, my boy, and enjoy the ride!

Nick handed me over the bike. 'In case you're wondering, we are concerned about the pain you're in. But as you probably know, we're not the most sympathetic bunch. Especially Alan.'

I'd been waiting for a chance to discuss my miserable night. 'Nick, I can't turn my head to the left. It's only just gone eight o'clock and I'm already halfway through the daily recommended dosage of codeine. You know, in the night, I called out to Alan and —'

'Ali, don't take this personally, but Alan is not going to give you, me, or anyone any sympathy, no matter what's happened. You've known him for a long time now. When have you ever heard him complain? In fact, let's face it, he's actually a bit of a machine. Sometimes I don't know how he manages to put away the amount of beer he does and he's always the first to enter the breakfast room.'

Nick was right. I'd known Alan for twenty-five years and not once had I heard him moan. Never a bad word about anyone; never a single gripe about being tired, worn out, injured, hard done by, or sick. We'd once worked shift work together, and even on the worst of nights, he'd smile, pour tea, and make light of the thought of spending your life working nightshifts at a car factory. When his mum had been diagnosed terminally ill, he didn't complain about the unfairness. 'Cancer is such a bastard,' was all he'd say, and the topic was rarely mentioned — until we'd set off to raise money for a cancer charity by cycling to John O'Groats.

While standing on the gravel driveway, surrounded by riders making final preparations, I realised that if it wasn't for Alan, I might still be lying in bed upstairs, feeling sorry for myself. Yes, I'd silently cursed him at the time, and I was still grieved at his lack of compassion, but this had made me more determined than ever.

As if on cue, he appeared from around the corner. He was clutching a collection of filled water bottles, and I recognised one as my own. While passing it over, he said, 'Good to see you up and about.' Then he called out to Nick, 'If it's alright by you, when we get to Penrith, I bagsy a single room tonight.'

I made a personal pact, there and then, not to mention the pain again. Instead of concentrating on the sights and sounds around me, I'd join in with the early morning banter. Rather than seek out photo opportunities, I'd concentrate on my posture and breathing. Besides, the drugs were finally kicking in. With ease, we circumnavigated Preston and continued our journey north. With each mile, the pain lessened, and after numerous experimental neck rotations, followed by more pills, the tightness improved.

By mid-morning, I was hungry, eager for coffee, and for the first time since leaving Preston, felt able to appreciate our surroundings. The land looked exposed and isolated; there were very few trees and only a handful of villages. A cool wind buffeted the coarse grass, but it was the panoramic sky that held my attention. It felt as though we were part of a landscape painting, each distant cloud a subtle stroke across a canvas.

Up ahead, located at a fork in the junction, stood a whitewashed building known as The Stork. Its prime position would have been a welcome site during the 17th century, when it had served as a coaching inn, offering travellers a place to eat, drink, and rest. Time had been kind to the establishment, and as we took the left fork, I gazed at the new signage, offering 21st century visitors the chance to enjoy Wi-Fi, coffee, real ale, and home-cooked food.

We were on the Lune Estuary pathway, lined to our right with an assortment of detached houses, each with uninterrupted views over open grassland. Just beyond the houses were tidal mud flats, home to numerous species of birdlife including cormorants, mallards, oystercatchers, and grey heron. We passed a farm shop, its slate roof coated in moss. A weather vane, crowned by the symbol of a cow, stood aloft against the blue sky, informing us that we were riding against a northerly wind.

Water was close by, confirmed by a small wooden boat, lying on its side in an adjacent meadow, and a series of narrow inlets, like the tentacles of a sea creature, which segregated the land ahead. I sucked in greedily. The smell of salt was strong in my nostrils. There was a feeling of untamed isolation to this place and I was keen to stay longer.

Thank goodness, my prayers were answered. A building, located near a bend in the road ahead, offered expansive views of the escarpment and the river far beyond. We'd stumbled across the Café Luna and everyone was hungry. After ordering hot drinks and pastries, we ventured outside to enjoy the view. Alan was seated close by. 'How's the neck?' he asked.

The pain had eased, but I felt reluctant to discuss the matter any further. Instead, I sat back, inhaled the strong coffee, and said, 'I'm feeling much better, thanks. I love the view, don't you?'

He nodded and sipped his tea. 'I knew you'd be OK.'

Surprisingly, he was keen to discuss the antics during the night, although I was now eager to change the subject. In the end, I couldn't help myself. 'Do you think I was making it all up?'

He pondered my question and raised his eyebrows. 'It did sound a bit melodramatic, and you do seem to have made a miraculous recovery.'

'But I was in agony, Alan. I'm telling you!'

He peered at me across his mug, a smug smile developing. 'Real agony? Are you sure? It's only pain, Ali. It always passes. That's what my dad taught us. You're as right as rain now.'

I didn't feel right as rain though. In fact, I felt slightly high. A lack of sleep, too much codeine, and a double shot of coffee — it was a wonder I was holding a decent conversation. I smiled, grateful for his honesty but eager to stretch my legs.

With mug in hand, I crossed the narrow road and stood alongside my bike. It was leaning against a National Cycle Route signpost, numbered 700. Just how many routes were there, I wondered? Compared to most countries, Britain is just a small island, but during this ride, it seemed immense. Apart from the number 700, the sign had three symbols, depicting the only forms of transportation allowed on the track. These were walking, horse riding, and cycling.

I considered taking a stroll towards the escarpment, but to do so meant squeezing through a gap in the hedgerow. Besides, the land beyond was pot-marked with channels, some glistening with mud. Travel, they say, will change you. If this trip was changing me, I was yet to grasp the meaning. For now, my thoughts were on Alan. Although I hadn't appreciated or understood his reaction, maybe I owed him a thanks. Instead of lying, tense, on a couch, while a chiropractor wielded my spine, I was now high on legal drugs, watching the water stirring alluringly in the distance.

The tide was on the turn, and within hours, the dynamics would change. Nothing stays the same forever. With the incoming tide, birds would take flight to locate new grounds for foraging and for shelter, and the flooded channels would creep towards the roadway. I wondered if the keel of the nearby boat would be lifted from the grass or if the sea would remain elusive. The answer to these questions would remain unanswered, like many others I'd mulled over on this trip.

The scrape of a chair behind me signalled it was time for us to move. Just like the tide, we rarely stopped for long. Yet, instead of the moon dictating our passage, we cycled according to time and distance. I caught sight of Mark, smiling in the mid-morning sun, a trace of ice-cream around his mouth.

We didn't encounter any horse riders or walkers along the next stretch of the journey. The only sign of life was the distant call of, 'Fore', as we passed the perimeter of Ashton Golf Course, hidden from view by an avenue of majestic chestnut trees. After a few miles, the riverside track turned sharp right and led us out onto a narrow, dead straight road, devoid of traffic. We set off along its centre, the recently trimmed hedgerows level with our eyes. The village of Aldcliffe appeared and disappeared within a few revolutions. There were no shops, churches, pubs, people, dogs, or even cats to be seen.

Then, abruptly, we were in the cathedral city of Lancaster, home to over 140,000 people. During the sixteenth and seventeenth centuries, it became known as the Hanging Town, due to the amount of executions that occurred in its vicinity. Two hundred were carried out at the castle between the tower and the terrace steps; this location was called the Hanging Corner. To warrant such a fate, the crimes committed included murder, forgery, burglary, and cattle stealing. Women were also given the rope if convicted of practising witchcraft. Times have obviously changed. The women we passed in Lancaster looked rather angelic, as did most citizens.

We breezed through the city, passing shoppers and a group of youngsters whose faces were glued to screens as they searched for virtual Pokémon. The embankment was home to two canal boats, but the hatches were closed, and drawn curtains barred any chance of peering inside. Only two lone fishermen lined the water's edge, their postures as stiff as the tall grey chimney protruding from an industrial backdrop.

After leaving the canal path, we made our way onto a one-way system, and through a gap in the buildings, I caught sight of a castle turret, far to my left and up high. Alas, too far and high for a visit. I returned my attention to the path ahead as we traversed a footbridge to take us across the River Lune. There were no boats to be seen on the murky water, but the sandy verge was populated by small wading birds, their beaks skimming across shallow pools in search of food.

Land adjacent to the river was in high demand, it seemed, with many houses crowding the waterfront. The older establishments boasted large front gardens, each with perfect views, while the newer houses further up-river, in sharp contrast, had been designed to ensure maximum occupancy in minimal space.

Suburbia returned for a while as we threaded our way through the northern outskirts of the city. Once again, we passed children playing, and for a few moments, we could have been in any town in Great Britain. In one street, a young man stood back to admire his newly washed Subaru. In another, an elderly lady, dressed in a sheepskin overcoat and sat on a park bench, waved back as we passed at speed. On one occasion, we were forced to stop at traffic lights to allow a group of mums and their toddlers to walk across.

I was finally learning that bike trails had the uncanny ability to transport us to other worlds within the space of a few turnings. After navigating a series of sharp inclines, the city seemingly vanished and our swift encounter with suburbia was over. We were now riding alongside the Lancaster Canal, following our familiar blue signs. For the next five miles, we rode in single file, most riders oblivious to the villages that lay tantalisingly close.

In the small town of Carnforth, we diverted from the canal to maintain a northerly trajectory. Here, we saw the return of winding roads, steep hills, and ivy-clad walls. The sky loomed behind a canopy of trees while the roadside foliage grew wild and unkempt, offering us the chance to reach out and touch the leaves. Further ahead, trees dwindled, their scrawny trunks strangled by thickets of wild raspberry bushes. Constant changes in the scenery helped take my mind off the pain, and like every rider around me, my remaining thoughts were of food.

The village of Beetham proved to have an Olde World charm, complete with stone cottages and whisper-quiet roads. We rode in single file, all eyes searching for a suitable spot to enjoy lunch. A corner pub looked inviting, but the lead rider rode straight past and turned into another lane. A row of cottages graced one side, while on the other, a stone church and tower completed the scene, surrounded by an ancient graveyard.

One of the cottages to our left displayed a rack of postcards outside, plus two small, round tables and chairs. According to the inscription above the door, the building had been constructed in 1881. A placard above the arched window read, *The Old Beetham Post Office*. Protruding from the stone building was another sign, hanging from a hook, informing us that it was now a tea room. An open doorway led us inside, to where the owner stood, stacking shelves behind the counter.

'Afternoon,' he said as we studied the food on display. 'When you know what you want, just give me a call. I'll be down the back, unpacking vegetables.'

Woven baskets brimming with fresh lettuces, tomatoes, and broccoli graced the shelves, and in a wooden casket, red-ripened apples yearned to be picked up and smelt. The owner returned on our signal to take our orders, seemingly happy with the varied selection of sandwiches we'd chosen, along with homemade apple pie. After paying, I made my way to the bathroom and discovered an alcove filled with locally made arts including paintings, prints, pickles and greeting cards.

By the time I stepped outside, Colin and Mick had moved the furniture onto the road, so we could eat in comfort and enjoy the sun. I sat alongside them, unable to make my mind up whether to face the post office or the church. As I flicked my head this way and that, I caught sight of Nick, freewheeling from the far side of the village, his face flushed from the ride from Kendal. He was just in time for lunch.

Although we were seated in the middle of a public road, there was little chance of interruption from passing traffic. I almost expected the next vehicle to be a horse and cart, and if anyone was going to appear along the laneway, it could well have been Robert Crawley, cane in hand, on his brisk morning walk from Downton Abbey. During lunch, the only other people we saw were two walkers, striding down the middle of the road, eager for a ploughman's at the nearby pub.

After lunch, Mick strolled towards the churchyard, his camera poised for action. I followed alongside, enjoying the sun while gazing at the weathered gravestones. I couldn't decipher any dates, but the many granite slabs protruding from the earth at strange angles told me all I needed to know. The grass around the graves had been recently cut, but unkempt clumps were left along the edges of the stones. I rested my arms on the stone wall and gazed up at St George's flag, fluttering high up on the turret.

The church looked to be hundreds of years old, constructed from rough limestone and designed in a classical, elongated shape with a clock tower at its western end. A large crow, as black as coal, sat aloft the highest rampart of this vantage point. He watched our every move and then let out a haunting cry. It was still watching us as we returned the furniture to its original spot and straddled our bikes in preparation to leave. I swallowed two more pills, catching sight of the bird while I drank. It took flight from the tower, its shrill cry cutting the silence as it flew towards distant woodland.

Our next destination was Kendal, located a few miles shy of the Lake District, a vast national park where England's tallest mountain and its deepest lake can be found. Scafell Pike, at 3,209 feet, is not high in comparison to Alpine standards, but there is still a feeling of remoteness to be found at the summit, especially if you avoid the summertime hoards.

Returning to the area triggered memories of our cycle ride twenty years earlier. We'd stayed in the town and enjoyed a pub-crawl before finding ourselves at a late night disco. Some of these pubs are mentioned in my end-to-end story, and as part of my book tour, I was keen to drop a few copies off along the way.

Since breakfast I'd been on an unnatural high, pedalling resolutely despite the pain and determined to be at ease with the world. I found myself searching for landmarks, but the streets looked unfamiliar. I was eager to find at least one of the pubs I remembered, but the others had far more pressing needs. All they wanted was to find the nearest food.

Nick had stowed his bike and slammed the van door resolutely. 'OK, lads, I think it's time for a late lunch before you tackle the long hill towards Shap.'

Once more, I was faced with a decision. Stay with my friends and let the past be the past. Or take a once-in-twenty-year opportunity and track down one of the pubs. I spoke next, my voice uneasy. 'I'll meet you at the far end of town. I'm keen to have a look around, to get my bearings. I've been away from Kendal for far too long.'

Mark held up his phone and made a gesture that said, 'Call me.'

I nodded and set off to find Ye Olde Fleece Inn. I knew it would still be open, because — twenty years ago — it had already been around for hundreds of years. Kendal looked to have prospered since then, with throngs of people filling the streets. Maybe it was just the blue skies enticing people outside, but either way — with this amount of people close by — I was sure to find help in locating the pub.

The first person I asked turned out to be a German tourist, and although his English was exemplary, he'd only arrived an hour earlier. Instead, I decided it was best to target someone who lived locally, and I made the assumption that most locals wouldn't be wearing walking boots, carrying overstuffed rucksacks, studying ordnance survey maps, gazing into gift shop windows, taking photos of quirky signposts, or standing outside the tourist information centre.

The next person to emerge from the throng of shoppers looked to be a likely candidate. She was a mother, pushing a child's buggy that had plastic bags of shopping hanging from both handles. I walked alongside and smiled politely.

'Excuse me, but I'm searching for Ye Olde Fleece Inn.'

She slowed to a crawl. 'Did you say you were after the fleece?' I glanced into the buggy, where a wide-eyed toddler stared back behind an ice cream.

'Yes, I went there once about twenty years ago and —'

Her eyes flickered towards a nearby building and she let out a faint smile. 'That's easy. You're standing right outside it.'

In terms of ambience and old world charm, the pub exterior lacked appeal, despite the baskets of fresh flowers that hung in a row outside the windows. It looked smaller than I remembered, with rendered walls, painted a conservative cream. Adjacent to the upper windows, a small metal sign protruded from the building, showing a sheep held by a sling, as though it was attempting a bungee jump. The enamel surface was streaked with rust but I could clearly read the words in black, painted below. *Ye Olde Fleece Inn. Established 1654.*

At street level, a temporary banner was strewn across the frontage and advertised the establishment as a wedding venue. I thought back to the time, twenty years earlier, when Alan, Nick, and I had entered the pub. We'd gotten this far from Land's End on a wing and a prayer and had no clue where our next resting place would be. Ironically, this had been the last public house that Alan had ventured into before meeting Samantha, the woman he was later to marry.

I parked the bike against the front door and noticed a poster, informing me that fresh food was available all day. The faint aroma of curry wafted in the warm breeze as I rummaged in my panniers for a copy of my end-to-end book. I found one easily but as I stood by the entrance, suddenly felt unsure of what to do.

The answer arrived unexpectedly with the appearance of a slim man in his mid-twenties who was walking from inside the illuminated pub towards the door. He was blonde, wore skinny jeans, a white T-shirt, and new Adidas training shoes, and was still in lively debate with an unseen patron. The distraction nearly caused him to collide with me, but I stepped back, just in time, feeling awkward in my Lycra and bike helmet. He stopped abruptly and studied me with a confident stare.

'Are you lost, mate?'

I smiled awkwardly. 'Not right at this moment,' I replied, 'but I've still got a long way to go.'

He laughed. 'Where are you heading?'

'Penrith today and John O'Groats, eventually.'

'Oh! You're one of them end-to-enders, are you?'

'Yes, but I'm just a beginner really.'

He took a step back, his eyes slightly glazed as he looked me up and down. 'Well, you look the part to me. Fancy a beer, do you? This place might not look the best from the outside, but it's a great pub and has been serving beer for hundreds of years.'

I held up my book. 'Oh I know all about the pub. It's a bit of a long story really, but I write travel stories and, once upon a time, I enjoyed a night here with two friends. We'd been on our way to John O'Groats, and now we're doing the trip all over again. I just wanted to drop a copy of my book into the landlord. I mention the pub in the book, you see.'

He stared at the retro-style front cover for a second, then without a word, walked back into the lounge. A few seconds later he returned with a barmaid.

'Here you go, mate. She'll look after you. Good luck with your ride.' He then stepped into the street and strode purposely away.

The girl was in her early twenties with long dark hair and wore a white shirt, black leggings, and boots. She curiously eyed me up and down while I quickly explained my story. After I'd finished, she took hold of the book and said, 'Well, that's a lovely story but I'm afraid the landlord is away. Would you like to come in for a drink or a meal anyway? If you don't mind me saying, you look a bit weary.'

The thought of sitting in the corner of the lounge with a local ale and a bowl of curry sounded appealing, but I had no lock for the bike and was also wary of losing touch with the group. I explained my situation but took up the offer to venture inside, just for a moment. As she made her way behind the bar to serve a waiting customer, I glanced around, catching sight of a few patrons tucking into lunch. The décor was simple with rendered walls that were decorated with photos of Kendal from a bygone age. I tried remembering where we'd once sat, but too many years had passed. I was snapped back to the present day by the soft voice of the barmaid.

'Alistair, I've put your book behind the bar for the landlord to read. Good luck with your ride to John O'Groats.'

A few customers looked up from their meals, studying the Lycra-clad man by the entrance. But I wasn't in the mood for any further conversation. Bidding farewell to the girl, I collected my bike and walked it through the pedestrian area in search of a quick snack before the long road to Shap. Up ahead, I noticed the figure of a cyclist, dressed in a yellow riding jersey. The bright image was set against black Perspex, depicting a mountain range, all of which were positioned above the frontage of a shop.

Just above the door, were the words: *Freewheel when you can...pedal when you must!*

The shop frontage displayed numerous and varied bike parts, including wheels, frames, and gear hubs. It was called Brucie's Bike Shop, and after stepping inside, I received a warm welcome from Bruce himself, who had his name etched onto his black T-shirt. His accomplice wore a similar top, albeit a size larger, and was known as Tony. Like myself, they both sported cropped hairstyles and were of an average height. We could have been triplets.

While Bruce gave me the rundown of what nutritional drinks, energy drinks, and snacks were available to purchase, Tony tampered with a bike. His eyes were continually drawn to a widescreen TV, strategically placed by the counter. I noticed they were watching the Tour De France, and after handing out the change from my purchases, Bruce updated me on the leaders' board as well as the latest news and predictions for the day's events.

For a while, I joined them, watching the cyclists approach the top of a mountain pass. All the cyclists' backs were hunched, legs straining, as they fought for position on the final bend. When the first rider reached the top, I joked, 'Is that live footage of riders on the road towards Shap?'

Bruce smiled. 'It's not the road to Shap, that's for sure. The only thing arduous about the journey to Shap is the distance. It's never quite steep enough to break a real sweat. There's far more challenging hills in the lakes, and we know most of them, don't we Tony?'

Tony nodded once and replied, 'Yes we know a few secret spots, that's for sure.'

Bruce studied my cycling shoes before continuing. 'Are you after some tips on the area?'

'Unfortunately not. My mates are nearby and very soon we'll be on the road towards Penrith. Our final destination is John O'Groats this time next week.'

'That's a pity as you're missing out on some stunning bike rides, not far from here. Maybe next time, eh.'

I handed Bruce a copy of my book, then explained about the Guinness World Record attempt and asked them for a photo outside their shop (as evidence). Tony flicked through the pages and noted that each chapter heading related to various song titles. 'I see you enjoy your music then Alistair.'

'Yes, all of us on the ride love our music. Mind you, I can't sing and if the truth be known I'm not really a bike rider. Not like you guys up here in the lakes and those professionals on the TV.'

By now we were standing outside, and as I stashed my snacks in the front panniers, Bruce studied my bike. 'I see you're riding a cyclo-cross. No doubt you're going off the beaten track then.'

Straddling the saddle, I briefly explained the journey to date. He tapped the handlebars. 'Alistair, you might not be an expert, but this time next week you'll have discovered parts of Great Britain that many in these isles have never heard of. There's not many that have ridden LEJOG and written about it too. And now you're tackling it a second time, going off the beaten track, using the national cycle networks? If that doesn't make you a cyclist, what will?'

I rode away from the shop with a broad grin, my panniers loaded with supplies, two books given successfully away, and photo evidence for Guinness stored on my smartphone. The brief but motivational speech from a stranger had boosted my confidence, but his inspirational words were not enough to suppress the dull ache in my neck. My stomach growled too, but I decided there was no time for hot food. Instead, I devoured one of the energy bars I'd just bought, popped two more pills, and rode through the green light at the end of town, heading north.

The exuberant use of codeine might explain why I decided to cycle directly out of town and commence a solo journey to the village of Shap. From what I remember, which isn't much, the Tour de France footage had triggered an idea. Up until now, most of my GoPro videos had been taken from my helmet while at the rear of the pack and the results were probably going to be a little less than uninspiring. What I really wanted was a long distance shot of the moment when our group tackled one of the longest hills in the country.

My plan was simple. After finding a suitable location to stow the camera (such as a fence post), I'd phone Mark before they left Kendal. Then, as they rode towards me, I'd click the record button, hurtle down to greet them, and tuck in alongside the pack. After cycling past the camera, I'd then return, switch it off, and race up the hill to catch them up. Yes, it was a lot of work for a few seconds of footage, but the painkillers were working their magic and, for now, anything seemed possible.

The road between Kendal and Shap is nine miles long, climbs 1245 feet (370 metres), and has an average gradient of three percent. The steepest section is just shy of 10 percent. These angles are tame compared to the French Alps but still arduous enough to test many riders, especially if the conditions are unfavourable. During severe winter storms, the village of Shap is prone to being cut off, as the road becomes impassable due to snow drifts. On this particular day, with warm sunshine caressing my face and cotton ball clouds rolling past, it was hard to imagine that the surrounding landscape ever resembles an arctic tundra.

With each mile, the feeling of isolation grew as I left behind houses and farmyards and followed the meandering road through open moorland. I should have stopped to call Mark, but instead I was solely focused on locating a perfect vantage point for the camera. From time to time, I looked over my shoulder, convinced I'd find them emerging from a faraway bend.

There was never going to be a perfect spot. Instead, I chose a wall alongside a farmyard, which offered the gentle curves of the land that fell away before rising sharply in the distance. There were no pinnacles or ridges nearby. This was open savannah where a cold wind would chill to the bone. The only prominent landmass was directly ahead, its rounded summit swathed in a sea of purple heather. Kendal was no longer in sight, hidden behind low-lying hills. Apart from my rapid breathing, the only other sound was the bleating of sheep, their gripes echoing across the windswept fields.

I plucked moss from the north side of the stone wall and used it to help level the camera. Once in position, I searched for my phone. It had been switched off to save the battery, and as it powered up, I gazed around. Far to my left, I could make out the tallest peaks of the Lake District. Although I was already involved in an epic journey, the thought of nearby tarns, crags, and hamlets tugged at my emotions. This was a location I'd once known well. At the age of eighteen I'd trekked across the lakes with Slow Dave and Paul. It had taken a week, and by the time it was over, I'd learned to map read and discovered the joys of trekking.

Alfred Wainwright M.B.E. was a fell walker, author, and illustrator, who fell in love with the Lake District and moved to Kendal in 1941. His books are still sought after, just as much for his sketches as the words that he scribed during his many years in the hills. The quote below describes his feelings towards the lakes:

"Surely there is no other place in this whole wonderful world quite like Lakeland. No other so exquisitely lovely, no other so charming, no other that calls so insistently across a gulf of distance. All who truly love Lakeland are exiles when away from it."

While gazing on the distant peaks that Wainwright had once enjoyed I contentedly decided to add another destination to my checklist for when I next returned to Britain. But as the phone screen came to life my smile evaporated, wiped away by the words, *No Service*.

In desperation, I clambered onto the wall and held the phone high, my eyes straining to view the screen. A single line crept up, just as the phone buzzed, indicating I had voicemail. I punched in the code and heard Mark's voice, but he couldn't compete with the wind that whipped down from the summit. I played the message again, and this time the single bar held.

'*Ali, it's Mark. Where are you? We're about to* (the next words were scrambled). *Call me soon* (more scrambled words) *so please don't talk to* (more scrambled words). *Colin* (more scrambled words) *ice cream.*'

And then? Nothing. Except the sound of sheep and the drone of an engine from a passing car. The driver waved as he went by. I climbed down from the wall and examined my options.

The pack of cyclists was either ahead or behind me. If they were in front, I would never catch them up. If they were behind, I still had a chance to get the footage. Either way, they weren't nearby. I decided to attempt a solo hill run.

A few minutes later, I was racing down the incline and then sweeping round the curve so I could cycle past the camera. The bout of exertion left me breathless, and as I double backed and collected the GoPro, I noticed the menacing clouds, creeping over distant hills.

I'd made a major mistake. The riders wouldn't still be in Kendal. Not after all this time. They were probably way ahead, having gone a different route to Penrith. I let out a curse, trying to remember how many tablets I'd taken. Too many; I knew that.

I set off quickly, dropping through the gears as the incline increased. Up ahead, two pylons straddled the road like giant robots guarding a mountain pass. I cycled between them, listening to the crackle from the overhead wires, and set my sights for Shap Fell Bothy, cycling solo once again.

A bothy is a term used to describe a building that acts as temporary shelter for those requiring an overnight stay in a remote location. There are approximately one hundred bothies in the British Isles, and most of these are in Scotland because it has large tracts of wilderness and a harsher climate than England, Ireland and Wales. With the assistance of a volunteer army, the Mountain Bothies Association work hard to fulfill their vision, which is to maintain simple shelters in remote country for the use and benefit of all who love wild and lonely places.

Using a bothy doesn't mean you are lost or desolate. Their rise in popularity stems from the fact that you get to spend the night in spectacular locations—for free! The only downfall is that you'll need your own bedding, and that you might either be alone or with a raucous group of Norwegian backpackers. We'd ridden past Shap Fell Bothy twenty years earlier but didn't stop to knock on the door. Instead, we continued past, cocooned in bright ponchos and surrounded by mist.

But now I was back and the sun was attempting to shine. Twenty years on, I was keen to meet whoever was staying overnight, and with each revolution, I searched for signs of the small white building. Just as the road levelled out, I recognised it immediately, positioned at the brow of the hill. Apart from electric pylons, fences, and the empty road it was the only other man-made object visible. My pace quickened as I rode towards the front door, hoping to find signs of life.

I parked my bike and walked to the rear, startling a bedraggled sheep taking shelter in an outhouse. On inspection, the front and rear doors were padlocked, and even the small windows were sealed shut. Bothies are meant to remain open at all times — so those in need can find shelter anytime — but this building had all the hallmarks of abandonment.

Wild daisies had taken advantage of muddy gaps in the flagstones, their abundance reflecting the sheer lack of foot traffic. The outer walls, although solid, were now tainted by a fine layer of mould, which crept upwards from the base. I felt a sense of loss, as I'd been looking forward to exploring the interior ever since the ride to John O'Groats had been discussed.

I'd previously learned that those who have stayed overnight refer to it as The Tardis, because the inside was far roomier than suggested by the outside. I'd also read about the Full Moon Club where musicians from near and far were drawn to the remote building to share a love of song and enjoy the sense of being in the wild. The gathering required no elitist membership. Just a passion for acoustics, a donation for the musicians, and the chance to hear storytellers, watch films, or simply gaze at the overhead moon.

There was no way to tell if the club existed anymore, or ever had. There were no flyers on the windows, no posters pinned to the weathered picket. Maybe it had all been just a myth. I reached out and touched the rendered walls, hoping that one day I'd return again to find an open door, a welcome fire, and the comforting sound of a travelling musician.

I cycled away, suddenly hungrier than I'd felt in days, and reached into my front pannier for one of Bruce's energy bars. A loud toot from a passing car forced my hand back onto the handlebars.

I veered left, looked to my right, and came face-to-face with a man leaning out of the rear window, taking my photograph. The car slowed and in that instant I recognised the face of my sister-in-law, Isabel, smiling from the passenger seat. The surprised look on my face told her I'd completely forgotten that she and my brother Matthew were driving to Penrith to meet me for the night.

The identity of the keen photographer was a mystery, though. As was the young woman who emerged from the rear seat beside him—once we'd all stopped safely by the verge.

Matthew was wide eyed with pleasure, gazing at the bike, my panniers, and my mud-stained Lycra with curiosity. After quick hugs all round, he introduced me to the dark-haired woman of about twenty years.

'Ali, this is your second cousin, Kate. She's on holiday from Florida.'

While shaking hands, I tried calculating where she fitted in our large family tree. My Irish grandmother had given birth to fifteen children, with many moving to America to start large families of their own. It was a credit to Matthew that he'd managed to stay in touch with many of these distant relations and taken numerous visits to America over the years. In comparison, since moving to Australia, I was struggling to find the time to Skype close friends and family, let alone reach out to long lost relatives.

The photographer was Kate's boyfriend. His name was John and he too was in his twenties with trimmed hair, a tanned face and a bright smile. After a week in Ireland, they were now enjoying a whirlwind visit to England, which included a short stay with Matthew and Isabel. All four of them were heading to Penrith for the night, followed by a hill walking weekend in the footsteps of Alfred Wainwright.

Matthew is exactly ten months my junior with similar looks and traits. When excited, we are prone to talk quickly, and as we stood by the verge, a barrage of questions rolled off his tongue, including the obvious one about me cycling alone.

Finally, Isabel interjected. 'Matthew, please let him get a word in.' She studied me carefully for a second or two before saying, 'You look a bit spaced out, Ali. Are you OK? Have you eaten much?'

Tears were close, but I forced a smile. How lovely it was that they had driven all this way to meet me. But we'd planned to catch up in Penrith, not on the edge of a windswept hill. I'd always envisaged meeting them in a quaint country pub after the day's ride, when I'd had the chance to enjoy a shower and unwind. But they'd caught me in the open, feeling vulnerable.

Their presence on Shap Hill told me that the afternoon was wearing on. I hadn't checked the time for hours and didn't want to ask. I looked towards the sky, hoping the sun would give me a clue, but it was blighted by cloud and I pushed the thought away.

Isabel broke the silence. 'Why don't we meet you a bit further on? I'm sure there's a pub in the next village where we can talk away from the wind.'

I thought that sounded like a great idea, and so while they headed towards the car, I set off for Shap with as much speed as I could muster. They passed me a few hundred yards further on, John hanging out the rear window with his camera pointing towards me, the horn tooting constantly while I pedalled on in an effort to look competent.

During the ride to Shap, I noted a dark scar on the hillside caused by decades of extraction for pink granite. The stone is used throughout Britain to help construct kerbstones and building frontages, and the quarry, like others in the vicinity, is one of the main employers in the region. From afar, the steep sides of the quarry resembled a Lakeland crag. These rugged bluffs are popular with rock climbers, and the sight of the jagged edge reminded me that tonight I was also to meet up with my best friend Steve and his brother in law, Craig.

Decades earlier, Steve and I had attempted to become competent rock climbers, spending many weekends in the Lake District and Scottish Highlands. With a wiry frame, a head for heights, and a sense of adventure, Steve was a natural and ended up gaining qualifications in outdoor pursuits. Although no longer an instructor, he was always seeking adventurous pastimes, and since moving to Australia, I'd missed his friendship.

The thought of such a gathering — out on a Friday night in the historic town of Penrith with its ancient pubs, quirky folk and real ales — should have elated me. But in truthfulness, all I craved was a hot bath, a meal, and a bed where I could lay my head.

After cycling along the main street of Shap, admiring the neatly kept houses and rows of grey stone cottages, I set about searching for my family. The village has three pubs, dispersed along the elongated township. I passed the first two, plus a newsagent, a post office, a butcher, a coffee shop, and the flattest playing field I'd seen since leaving Australia. For a community that can get completely cut off in winter during severe storms, they looked to be quite self-sufficient.

I located my family outside a large, whitewashed pub called the Crown Inn. The pub is set slightly back from the main road and located directly opposite the local school, its playground eerily quiet due to the holiday period. For some reason, we chose the outside courtyard instead of the cosy interior, and I found myself reaching for a jacket to ward off a chill as the sun continued to fall. Although their road stories sounded jovial, I felt slightly adrift from the scene. My long-lost cousin described a recent trip to London, but my head spun with fatigue and my stomach growled at being fed beer.

Just as Matthew rose from the bench to offer another round of drinks, a man walked out of the pub, chatting into a phone. If he had a signal, then so did I. But somehow, I couldn't muster the energy to call Mark, let alone explain the situation. I felt a pang of jealousy, knowing that I'd forsaken the chance to ride with them in exchange for a short visit to Ye Olde Fleece Inn. By now, they'd probably be showered and rested in Penrith, discussing plans for dinner.

With this thought in mind, I declined the offer of another drink, made plans to meet in a few hours, and set off solo once again. I was cycling far more slowly when they next passed, and this time there was no one taking photos.

Penrith is a bustling market town, located just outside the Lake District, in the Eden Valley. Like many towns in the area, tourism and agriculture are integral to the local economy and it was pleasing to see the streets filled with so many people. It might have helped that it was a Friday evening, and according to a wide banner at the entrance to the town, there was a country show on the following day.

As feared, I entered the accommodation just as they were heading to the first pub. Mark straddled an arm around my shoulders. 'We called, but you never answered. Don't you like riding with us?'

I patted him on the back and smiled weakly. 'Believe me, Mark, I'm not trying to avoid you, however it might seem.'

'That's good to hear, mate. Let's see if you can stick with us tomorrow. After you've showered, meet us in the pub and we can catch up.'

As they made their way to the street, Nick stopped alongside me. 'You've made good time for a man that refuses to consult a map, answer a phone, or use a bike computer. I've arranged to meet Steve and Craig at the Dog Beck pub. Don't be too long as they're keen to see you.'

It's a strange feeling to walk into a pub after a 90-mile bike ride and come face-to-face with someone you haven't seen in years. Especially when that person is your best friend and surrounded by a group of riders you've been cycling with for seven whole days. Throw into the mix my younger brother and his wife, my long-lost cousin and her partner, and I was positively reeling. All in all, twelve people were sitting around a large wooden table, many holding drinks as they relaxed in soft leather chairs.

Maybe it was my imagination, but in those first few seconds, as I stood by the doorway, I felt they all wanted different things from me. Steve and Craig would want to hear about the trip to date. Mark would be curious to know how I'd managed to once again spend the day cycling alone. Nick would ask me how the bike was faring, and JP would enquire about my neck.

Mick was about to order more drinks and he asked me what I wanted, while Kate approached me, eager to find out if I knew any stories about Celine (her Grandmother). Matthew was soon after a recommendation for a day's walk in the lakes for two novices from America, and Colin later asked if I needed any new batteries for the bike computer.

As for myself, all I wanted was to get through the night and start afresh on the following day. We were heading for Scotland, and with luck, I wanted to track down a woman called Daphne that we'd stayed with twenty years earlier in the spa town of Moffat. None of the other riders knew that I wanted to play detective, not even Alan or Nick. I'd inform them tomorrow when the time was right.

Halfway through my second beer, Isabel chaperoned me to a nearby booth where Matthew, Kate and John were also seated. It felt good to sit and talk, but despite all efforts, the long day was catching up with me. I felt out-of-sync, unable to converse without mixing up my words. Eventually, I gave up talking, leaned back against the soft cushion, and decided to listen to their stories. A waitress appeared with perfect timing and placed down plates of spicy chicken wings, French fries, an assortment of dips, and a bottle of water.

While Matthew spoke, I heard a familiar tune in the background. The pub was playing a David Bowie song. I plucked a few chips from the dish, smeared them in ketchup before taking a bite, and mimed the words in my head.

This is Major Tom to Ground Control
I'm stepping through the door
And I'm floating in a most peculiar way
And the stars look very different today

Day 8: Have You Seen Her?

'As long as one keeps searching, the answers will come.'
Joan Baez

The search for Daphne started a few months before I left Australia. It was triggered by an email from Nick, the contents of which included the estimated total elevation that we'd cycle over the trip. While studying the email, however, it wasn't only the figures that drew my attention. I was also fascinated by the towns, villages and cities we'd be visiting. Some — like Shrewsbury and Liverpool — were familiar, but there were others — such as Callington and Altnaharra — I'd never heard of, and I was excited to find out more about them.

One familiar location stood out amongst the list. It was the spa town of Moffat, located in the Scottish Lowlands. We'd stayed there during our inaugural ride, and that day our paths had crossed with Nick's wife and her friend Samantha, who were embarking on a week's touring holiday. Although Alan and I both knew Karen, this was the first time we'd set eyes on Samantha, who would later become Alan's wife.

Twenty years ago, the girls had booked us into a quaint, white-washed bed and breakfast called Spur Cottage, owned by a couple called Daphne and Jack. It must have been a combination of our cycling adventure, the warm summer's evening, a gathering of new friends, and the kindly welcome by Daphne and Jack, which helped create a memorable evening. Especially for Alan.

Now, twenty years on, we were returning to Moffat, and I wanted to rekindle the memories. With this thought in mind, I located a copy of my end-to-end book, found the relevant chapter and read a few words about Spur Cottage.

The house smelt of freshly cut flowers, and each room was adorned with little knick-knacks, which added a sense of character...

At the time, Daphne and Jack had been a sprightly pair, probably in their early sixties. Luckily, I'd kept the photos taken on that day, and I studied the grainy images, convinced — after all this time — they'd still be alive.

The email from Nick also explained that Karen and Samantha were planning to travel to Moffat, just like before, and that during our journey, they'd also meet us in various locations throughout Scotland, including John O'Groats. But was a reunion at Spur Cottage part of their plan? I'd never known Nick to be overly sentimental, and so I suppressed the thought. From what I knew of him, the decision to pick Moffat was purely a logistical one; it would be a perfect location to rest after the seventy-mile jaunt from Penrith.

Just north of the town of Moffat, you can turn right and head towards the historic city of Edinburgh. We'd taken this option two decades earlier, which then led us through the Highlands and along the eastern coastline. This time, however, we'd veer north-west after Moffat, towards Glasgow. From there, we'd cycle through Glencoe and Fort William before setting our sights on Loch Ness. Moffat would be a staging post — no more, no less. But I couldn't help but ponder how our visit also presented me with the perfect opportunity to locate Daphne and Jack. It sure would be a rewarding feeling to knock on their front door once again.

A noise from the hallway broke the spell as Noah, my twelve-year-old, walked into the study where I was reading. 'Dad, what are you doing?'

'I'm checking the route and have just discovered that I'm going back to a lovely little Scottish town, called Moffat.'

He gave a nonchalant shrug, picked up the photo, and studied it carefully, pointing out the younger versions of me, Alan, and Samantha. Before placing it down, he asked, 'Who are the other people?'

'The man in the middle is Nick. He was our project leader back then and is also organising the trip this time. The woman on the right is Karen, his wife.'

'What about the other two?'

'That's Jack and Daphne and they're the reason I'm excited. I can go back to their cottage and say hello again.'

He stared at me, his soft green eyes narrowing.

'But they won't remember you after twenty years, will they?'

'They might,' I teased.

'Daaad!'

'Maybe you're right, Noah. But that's not the point. When I last cycled to John O'Groats, I didn't have a mum anymore. She died when I was twenty-four. One of the reasons I did the ride back then was to raise money for a cancer charity.'

I paused. 'I also needed to get my life back on track and the ride gave me time to think. And a goal. Sometimes adults have to do this type of thing.'

Noah didn't seem to mind me talking candidly, so I continued. 'I remember, Daphne was kind and reminded me a little of my mum. That's why I wrote about her in the end-to-end book.'

He nodded politely and turned his attention to our dog, Peppi, who had made an appearance in the study. Before he became distracted by the dog, I grasped him playfully in an overdue hug. 'Soon I can ride all the way to Moffat again, say hello, and give her a signed copy of the book.'

He tried wriggling free, and I ruffled his curly hair. 'Look, I'll show you the route that Nick sent. From Land's End, we cycle towards—'

Just then, Fran appeared at the doorway. Her face was flushed and she stood in mock annoyance, hand on hips. 'Noah, did you tell dad that dinner is ready?'

Before he had chance to reply, she smiled. 'Come on now, the pair of you! Turn off that computer, or else the dog gets your dinner. Have you finished packing and printing your boarding card yet, Ali?'

Nick's email had distracted me and I grinned sheepishly. 'No, I got side-tracked. Give me a second and I'll be at the table with some exciting news. I'm going to become a detective!'

Fran left the room, mumbling something about burnt potatoes, and I opened up the browser for Qantas Airlines. In the morning, I'd be flying north to spend eight days away on an iron-ore mine site, located within a remote, semi-arid area of Australia known as the Pilbara. I'd be working twelve-hour shifts, then returning each night to a small, purpose-built cabin that Australians call a 'donga.'

Temperatures were forecast to be in the low forties, but the job had its perks. The mining camp had an air-conditioned gym, complete with static bikes, which I planned to take advantage of most evenings. It wasn't the perfect scenario for getting fit, but in such remote conditions, was my only option. While the printer spat out the boarding card, I thought about Nick's email and the chance to track down Daphne and Jack. But right now, I had other priorities. Dinner was going cold, my children were asking to play beach cricket, Peppi needed a walk, and I was yet to pack.

During the first evening at the mine site, I managed to spend thirty minutes in the gym, and while in the canteen, I obeyed the healthy eating guidelines. It was eight in the evening by the time I ventured into a small outbuilding, kitted out as an internet café. Above the doorway, an air conditioner rattled and groaned, cranked up to maximum as it struggled to cool the air. The room was occupied by numerous miners, some showered and changed after their long shift, others still wearing their yellow work shirts, faded by the sun and stained with red dust. They all sat quietly, surfing the web or connecting with friends on Facebook.

I took a seat and found myself making eye contact with the man to my right. His eyes were bright and sharp, but the sun had etched numerous tiny lines deep into his forehead and neck. His scraggy beard was also tainted with red dirt, and the luminous shirt that he wore was soiled. Alongside his computer screen stood five empty beer cans, scattered across the table. He was peeling back the tab from another and acknowledged me with a slight nod of the head.

I noticed a buxom brunette on his screen, and realised he was on the lookout for love. I followed suit. Not with the search for a young lady, but with the act of opening a beer. It tasted good, and I happily clicked onto Google and began searching for Daphne and Jack. At first, I thought it would be easy. Surely Google and Facebook knew all the answers. But after three beers and much finger tapping, I felt light headed, frustrated, and ready for bed.

The next evening, I tried a different tact by targeting Facebook groups associated with Moffat. I found a few and posted about my search for Daphne and Jack, convinced that success was just hours away. I returned the following evening to find that no-one had replied. In desperation, I contacted nearby churches and got a chirpy reply from a local vicar who promised to ask his congregation. Sunday came and went, and I never heard from him again. I then targeted local pubs and other community groups, but still there was radio silence.

On my final evening in the Pilbara, I returned to the internet café. The bearded miner had been a constant companion all week and sat alongside, just as before. Unlike myself, he'd been successful, eventually connecting with a Russian blonde who was searching for an outdoorsy man. While he tapped on the keyboard, humming quietly and sinking another six-pack, I sat nearby, trawling my way through Google's search pages.

On my return home, the search was postponed as family life took over. With four weeks to go before my departure to the UK, suddenly a message appeared via Facebook, the words, *Daphne and Jack*, halting me in my tracks. I clicked on the link and noticed my earlier appeal in the text below. The next line read, *Daphne is still at Spur cottage. Jack died a few years ago.*

In an instant, I felt a surge of elation, tinged with sadness. I stared at the message, resting my head in my hands as I contemplated its meaning. I had no idea who'd replied and so I clicked the link again, but the message vanished. Despite a frantic search, no amount of mouse clicking helped bring it back.

Eventually, Fran appeared at the doorway. 'Will you ever get off that thing? What are you up to now? You're off to England in a few weeks, and just lately, all you seem to be doing is working, riding your bike, or staring at a computer screen!'

I sat up straight. 'I'm sorry, and yes, you're right. But you won't believe it. I've finally got a reply about Daphne and Jack.'

Her eyes opened wide as I explained the chain of events. I wanted to continue the search but knew that time was running out. Fran and the boys needed my support and attention. I pushed the thought of Daphne to the back of my mind and walked out of the study.

Four weeks later, I crossed the border into Scotland. The ride from Penrith had been surprisingly easy with Steve and Craig comfortably fitting in with the dynamics of the group. Although I'd arrived in Penrith feeling physically drained, I managed to find my second wind as the night wore on. After the meal with my family, we ventured into the high street and found a quiet pub serving craft beers. Later, I caught up with the other cyclists at an Indian restaurant.

During the late-night curry, I learned from Steve and Craig that they belonged to a cycling club and were used to long distance rides. The following morning, they met us outside our accommodation, fully prepared for the day ahead. Initially, it felt strange to see my old best friend wearing Lycra. Not that he looked odd. His lean physique suited the stretchy white top and matching shorts. But up to now, we'd only ever undertaken our adventures with backpacks, walking boots, maps, and compasses.

I needed to remind myself that those days were gone. In reality, we rarely kept in touch anymore, apart from random Facebook posts. Today's ride, although only a short distance, presented a chance to rekindle our friendship.

Craig was also kitted out in Lycra, and both men sported neatly-trimmed goatee beards and lightweight racing bikes. They were using smartphones to monitor their progress and cheerfully informed me that our route would be 61 miles long, with a total elevation of only 2,750 feet. This far north, I'd expected steeper terrain but was happy for the respite. The undulating landscape was easy on the gears as we made our way across a sparsely populated landscape. Occasionally we spotted tractors. Some were parked in farmyards, one or two shared our road, and others were in use, carving up distant fields.

The historical city of Carlise soon crept up on us, the way that many big towns and cities do. Within the space of a few short miles, hedgerows disappeared and open fields were gobbled up by seventies-style housing estates. For fleeting moments, we caught sight of everyday life in this part of Cumbria. Boisterous children played football in the streets, and young mums congregated in parks, chaperoning toddlers and pushing buggies. We passed a row of shops including a post office, bookmakers, and a newsagent. The corner shop had a *Closing Down Sale* plastered across its front window. Up ahead, an overweight man walked along the pavement, the plastic bags at his side bulging with unseen items.

Very soon, we were riding single file and totally focused on getting through the network of dual carriageways, traffic lights and roundabouts. We briefly entered a noisy world of lorries, cars, motorbikes and pedestrians. Befitting such a city, the prominent landmarks were medieval churches and ornate buildings, fighting for attention alongside shopping malls and high-rise car parks.

We rarely stopped, and with Carlisle soon at our backs, conversations returned as the miles tumbled. Craig proved to be a confident rider, willing to take the lead to pull the group along. When opportunities arose, I chatted to

Steve about his life in England and we found the time to chitchat about family and friends. The discussions were lighthearted, and we reminisced about past endeavours. Steve explained his latest exploits, including a dog sledding and winter bush-craft journey into the Arctic Circle.

Would I have been part of that adventure if I'd stayed in the UK, instead of moving to Australia? Possibly not. Steve still seemed to possess a hunger for exciting challenges. Such feats sounded far less appealing to me than they had a decade earlier. Maybe it was down to the way I was feeling at that moment or because he was younger than me. He asked about the types of activities I planned for the Australian summer months. 'Paddle boarding and fishing with the family,' was the only answer I could think of between breaths.

I enjoyed our chats, side by side on the open road, but they were short-lived. The pace was fast and the front riders were constantly changing direction as we crisscrossed our way towards the border. I heard the M6 traffic before I saw it, and very soon, talk faded as we rode parallel with the motorway. All eyes were drawn left towards the wide, sedate waters of the River Esk.

There wasn't a hill or ridgeline to be seen — just a gentle river flowing through lush meadows. Eventually, the road drifted away from the motorway but remained close enough for us to spot the turnoff to Gretna Green. The gap widened further after that, and as the drone of traffic melted away, we rode two by two towards the border.

The welcome sign to Scotland looks remarkably similar to the one I'd stopped at two decades earlier. A thistle is displayed at its centre, and underneath the national symbol are the words, *Scotland Welcomes You,* written in bold font. A square patch of land, adorned with a colourful display of wildflowers, creates the perfect backdrop to the sign for obligatory photos.

The nearest building to the border, in the village of Gretna Green, is called the Old Toll Bar and describes itself as the first (and last) house in Scotland. Its walls are painted white and in stark contrast to the black outline of its front door and leadlight windows. According to a large placard screwed onto an outside wall, the building was constructed in 1830 and has witnessed over 10,000 weddings!

Gretna Green has been synonymous with weddings ever since Lord Hardwicke introduced the Marriage Act in 1754. The aim of the act was to stop English minors from marrying if their parents or guardians objected.

However, at the time of its introduction, Scottish law still allowed irregular marriages to take place. From the ages of twelve for girls and fourteen for boys, the only legal requirement for marriage in Scotland was that two adult witnesses were present.

During the 1770s, the opening of a nearby toll road presented elopers with the opportunity to reach Scotland with greater ease than ever before. Gretna Green is the first village over the border and the logical place to tie the knot. As well as the Old Toll Bar, the blacksmith's workshop also held great appeal for couples.

During the 18th and 19th centuries, a blacksmith was a highly regarded figure in the local community. Apart from making horseshoes, fixing carriages and farm equipment, he would often take on other duties including civil marriage ceremonies. Over the centuries, as the popularity of weddings in this area increased, one single blacksmith could no longer keep up with the demand. Those that assisted became known as the 'anvil priests', one of whom was a man called Richard Rennison, who married 5,147 couples at the blacksmith's.

The anvil soon became a symbol to forge two people together in matrimony, and to this day, even though Scotland has long since updated its laws, Gretna Green is one of the most popular locations in the world to get married. The days of the eloping couple may now be over, but the appeal of the blacksmith's draws thousands of people to the town each year.

Although I was aware that my friends weren't interested in visiting tourist attractions that deviated from the main route, I was hoping that hunger would entice them to make a minor diversion. However, as we rode through town, the front rider ignored the signs for the *Famous Blacksmith's* and *Gretna Green Restaurant* and took another route instead.

For half a mile we fringed the town centre, bypassing a housing estate to our left and large detached houses to our right. Some of these homes had been converted into bed and breakfast establishments or small hotels. After passing a primary school, the front rider turned left, heading directly out of town. We were leaving Gretna Green within minutes of our arrival.

Immediately, I sped forwards from the back of the pack, followed a tractor as it overtook the group, and then waved the riders down. They made their way onto the pavement with puzzled looks all round as they stopped to listen. I pointed to where we'd just come from.

'Didn't you see the signpost? We're just around the corner from the tea rooms at the blacksmith's. I don't know about you, but I'm hungry and would appreciate visiting it again.'

I was met by momentary silence, broken by one rider who announced, 'But it isn't on the route. According to the computer, we have to turn left here.'

I felt the colour rise to my cheeks but remained outwardly calm. I looked around for support, glad to see a few nods of agreement. To confirm how near we were, I asked a passerby for the quickest route. He pointed towards the town. 'It's dead easy. Follow the road and you'll be there in a few minutes. They have a wee café there, as well as a restaurant if you're really hungry.'

Very soon, the sounds of bagpipes filled the air as we cycled alongside a white-clad building and turned into the village complex. By luck, a newly-wed couple were standing arm in arm, underneath an archway. Nearby, a piper dressed in tartan belted out a Celtic wedding tune with professional ease.

An official photographer jostled for space alongside a few excited family members, and I was silently pleased to see that some of my friends had parked their bikes to take photos of the ceremony. With the photo shoot over, the newlyweds headed back inside the blacksmith's, and we made our way to the café. By the time we'd ventured outside again, the bagpipe player was busking in the plaza, standing close to a sculptured archway with two stone hands joined together.

The outside seats of the café were in high demand with many visitors crowding the space. There were no others cyclists among them, and many of the patrons looked and sounded like they'd come from foreign lands. I studied Alan as he ate, my eyes drawn to the rosy stripes across his scalp where the sun had penetrated the gaps in his bike helmet each day.

If the grey sky threatened to ruin the buoyant atmosphere, no-one seemed to notice. Most patrons looked happy enough to watch and listen to the piper. Children stood nearby, gazing up at him, while couples strolled past and placed coins into a metal bowl balanced on an anvil. As soon as the group had eaten, they stirred to life and rose from their seats. I could sense their keenness to get to Moffat, but on impulse, I decided to stay longer. I didn't expect anyone to hang back with me though. Although Gretna Green held some appeal for these well-travelled riders, it wasn't going to hold their attention for very long.

As a ten-year-old, I'd visited the blacksmith's with my dad and younger brother, Matthew. I still have the photo of us by the entrance, displayed proudly in my home, and for this reason alone, I wanted to stay a while, enjoy the sun that was threatening to shine, and explore the shops. I was yet to purchase a gift for my family, and also wanted to give away another complimentary copy of my end-to-end book as part of my quest to become a Guinness World Record holder.

My announcement didn't surprise anyone. I hoped that, by now, they understood I was on a different type of journey, feeling the need to linger whenever possible. As Craig walked past me, he spoke quietly. 'Good luck, mate. I hope you find what it is you're looking for.' Then he asked, 'Are you still using your bike computer?'

I opened my arms wide in mock surrender. 'Well, I have been, but the batteries went flat about an hour ago. Don't worry. I'll find my way.'

'I'm sure you will, but luckily it's easy from here. Just turn right when you leave the courtyard and stay on the B7076. We'll see you later for a well-earned beer!'

He joined the others and they waved goodbye as I rose from my seat and held my hand up high in acknowledgement. Rightly or wrongly I'd broken away from the group again. Steve and Craig had travelled all this way to ride with us and I'd peeled away halfway through the day. Was I being selfish? My mind wrestled with the worry that I was acting strange or downright rude. But as I finished the last of my tea, the words from my Uncle Matt slid into my thoughts once more, clear as the brightening sky.

'Slow down boy, and enjoy the ride.'

Ah, I love those words. That was the difference, you see. Although I wanted to ride alongside the others, I couldn't suppress my natural yearning to explore each place of interest that I passed. I couldn't ignore my own desires, and also the thought that this might be my last visit to Gretna Green for a very long time. Britain was my friends' home, and they could visit any of these attractions during a weekend away. For me, this was a rare opportunity.

Some visitors had arrived by coach. I could see a small group being rounded up at the café by a pot-bellied coach driver, wearing a white shirt, black blazer, and grey nylon trousers. The tourists in his group would soon be sitting in modern comfort on their way to another iconic attraction, hot showers and fine dining in their thoughts.

My shower would come, but much later, after many more hours and miles, and well after the other riders. I briefly contemplated a hasty exit, as there was still time for me to catch them up, but instead I found myself in a nearby gift shop. After a successful shopping spree, I decided to promote my Guinness World Record attempt. I left the precinct and strolled towards the archway where the wedding couple had stood earlier for photos. At the very least, I could get a quick selfie beneath the iconic sculpture and then be on my way.

Approaching the arch, I noticed a rope in front, which hung in a series of loops, close to waist height. I slipped underneath, and as I took a step towards the archway, heard a shout from the front entrance of the blacksmith's. A middle-aged lady appeared, armed with a clipboard, which she thrust into the air. She was dressed in a navy-blue suit, with a name tag pinned to a lapel, but I was too far away to read it. Instead, I focused on her face, which was showing signs of a scowl.

'Excuse me, sir. But that's private. Didn't you see the sign?'

I stepped back under the rope. 'Oh, I'm sorry. But why is it private?'

She stopped alongside and answered briskly. 'The official archway is for wedding parties only and the next ceremony is about to finish.'

I made my apologies, a little peeved, and ventured towards a nearby shop. This one offered free tastings of whisky and had a large collection of spirits for sale, along with an array of Gretna Green memorabilia. Many had been created by local artisans and included landscape paintings, digital prints, and wood carvings. On other shelves, I noticed hand-knitted scarves, ointments, creams, jams, and preserves. Depending on your budget and taste, there were also racks of cuddly toys, fridge magnets, postcards, miniature bottles of whisky, clay models of the blacksmith's building, and even a doll-size bagpipe player.

I picked up a postcard, wrote a few lines, and presented it at the counter for payment and a stamp. As the cashier took my money, she studied my clothes. 'Heading to John O'Groats, are ye? We get a lot of long distance riders in here.' I nodded and she continued. 'It sounds like a lot of hard work to me, but good on you!'

She looked around for other riders, but I was the only Lycra-clad person in view. I could read her thoughts, but before she asked, I got in first, explaining my reasoning for staying behind. I then presented her with a copy of the end-to-end book, which she reached out and accepted with a smile. After signing the inside cover, I requested a photo with her by a local landmark. She stared at me from across the rim of her glasses, her puzzled look hard to hide.

'It's to do with my quest to become a Guinness World Record holder. The photo will help prove that I've found a new reader in a faraway location.'

'Oh, aye,' she said with a hearty chuckle. 'I know just the place. Come on, follow me. But we'll have to be quick, as there's a wedding underway at the blacksmith's and they'll be out soon.'

We returned to the courtyard and strolled towards the rope. As we reached it, she said, 'We can head across to the archway for a quick photo. Off you go and I'll see you there in a second. I just need to let my manager know where I am.'

I ducked under the rope a second time and managed a few more steps before hearing a familiar voice. This time, the tone was sharper. 'Excuse me, sir. I thought I told you the arch is private. There's a wedding taking place right now and the couple will be out at any—'

Just then, the shop assistant appeared, dashing across the courtyard. 'Sorry, love. Alistair's with me. He's on a book tour and is cycling to John O'Groats.'

The woman held up a clipboard, her voice higher pitched than earlier. 'Mary, that's all well and good, but they're about to step outside at any second.'

I stood under the archway, camera in hand, my face impassive. Mary let out a nervous giggle and whispered, 'Be quick with the photo, will you, please?'

I captured the moment perfectly, ensuring the book cover was displayed according to Guinness's rules. Just as we ducked back under the rope, the rear door of the blacksmith's opened and a newly-wedded couple stepped outside, followed closely by an excited entourage. They were met by a wail of music as the Highland Piper came to life and a photographer chaperoned them into position by the archway.

At this point, I should have made haste, but with over 30 miles still to cover, it made sense to eat again before riding any further. This time I opted for the restaurant and once inside, stacked up my tray with soup, bread and salad. By luck, the crowded room offered a vacant table, ideally situated at the far end, offering prime views of the ceremonial archway.

The restaurant also had Wi-Fi, and on impulse, I sent Fran the picture with Mary by the archway. Partway through the soup, I received a reply.

How lovely. We're visiting Mickey and Rose and they saw your picture. Guess what! They were married at Gretna Green!

While wiping the bowl clean with the remaining crust, my phone buzzed, followed by a request to accept a Face Time call from Fran. I tapped the screen and she came to life, smiling from the far side of the world. In the background were our friends, Mickey and Rose, calling out a cheery greeting. Noah and Sebastian made a swift appearance too, ushered in from the garden to say hello. After a quick chat, they rushed back to their game.

Yards away from where I sat, the piper was still playing, so I decided to turn the camera towards him and live stream the ceremony across the globe. Partway through, the signal vanished. I was just about to leave the restaurant when my phone buzzed again. Within a few short steps, I would lose the Wi-Fi signal and had no idea when I'd next be in touch with home. Conscious of time, but intrigued by the message, I stopped by the exit and checked the screen.

I'd received a photo from Rose and Mickey. It was of a wedding couple, standing under an archway, alongside a bagpipe player. The words underneath read:

That's us at Gretna Green over twenty years ago.

I studied the musician displayed on my screen and compared it to the piper walking towards me. The ceremony was over, and I watched as he lay down his pipes, discarded the bearskin hat, and rummaged through his bag. Could he be the same man displayed on my camera?

As he stood, we made eye contact and I moved closer. Only now, up close and personal, could I really appreciate the attention to detail he'd taken with his traditional costume. Every nuance of dress had been meticulously addressed, down to the tartan kilt, horse hair sporran, and bright white piper stats, traditionally worn to keep dirt and debris out of soldier's boots. After exchanging pleasantries, he gulped on a water bottle, then wiped a bead of sweat from his brow.

'I guess it's warm with that on,' I gestured, pointing to the black hat laying near his feet. It was a foot long and made from fur. It certainly wasn't designed for wearing on a warm day.

'Oh, aye' he replied with a smile. 'Mind you, I'd rather the wee bit of sunshine we have now than the rain they're forecasting over the next few days.'

I looked up to the sky with expectant eyes. The sun had struggled to make an appearance most of the day, fended off by a persistent layer of grey. But the clouds were thinning, allowing the sun to shine through in short, sharp bursts. If the piper was correct, this might be the last sunshine on my face for a few days.

After taking a drink, he deduced that I was a cyclist on my way to John O'Groats. Before he asked if I was riding solo, I showed him the photo of Mickey and Rose with a piper. He held the phone, turned towards the shadows and studied the image. In a soft voice, he explained, 'Oh, aye. I know that man well. It's my elder brother, Billy.'

A moment of silence passed between us. 'He's been passed away a few years now. But we used to play here together.'

We chatted for a few minutes more, and in that time, I shared how Gretna Green was dear to me, with childhood visits and my first bike ride with Alan and Nick. I then discussed my Guinness attempt and the desire to give away a few copies of my book along the journey, while collecting photos as proof. I handed him a copy of the book, and after studying the cover, he said, 'Would you like a photo with me holding it?'

'Yes, please.'

'Of course. It's good to meet you Alistair. I'm Alan Marshall.'

His handshake was firm but polite, and he turned towards the archway, steering me towards the rope. As we approached, my eyes scanned the courtyard for the lady with the clipboard. To ease my conscience, I asked, 'I'd love to have a photo by the archway, but isn't it only for wedding parties?'

He studied me with wide eyes and smiled broadly. 'Oh, dunnee worry about that. I work here, and besides, there's no one using it at the moment, is there?'

Although the far door to the blacksmith's was closed, I wondered how long it would be until another wedding party appeared. We made our way under the rope, towards the archway, and as I prepared the smartphone for a photo, he stopped in his tracks. 'Wait here a minute, I'll go get my hat.'

He ducked under the rope, and as I watched him walk away, the front door of the blacksmith's opened and out stepped the woman with the clipboard. There was no wedding party alongside her, and it was for this reason alone that she only looked perplexed more than annoyed. I managed a weak smile as she held the rope aloft and strolled purposefully towards me.

Then came the call from afar that I'd been hoping for. 'He's with me. I just went back to get my hat.' She stopped abruptly and shook her head in disbelief. His voice carried far as he explained. 'Can you believe that his friends in Australia just sent through a picture of their wedding day, years ago? Billy was the piper at their ceremony.'

The woman smiled and shook her head. 'Nothing surprises me anymore, Alan!' She then turned her attention to me and smiled. 'Looks like you've been lucky today!'

After the selfie with Alan, he recommended that I take a tour of the blacksmith's, as part of it was set aside as a museum, with numerous exhibits. In the entrance hall, I was half expecting to see the woman again but she was nowhere to be seen. Instead, an amiable, grey-haired man took a few of my pounds and steered me towards a turnstile. After pocketing the change, I asked, 'Can I have a look at the area where the weddings take place? I'd love to see the anvil.'

He pointed to a wall clock. 'Yes, but only if you're quick. There's a ceremony starting in ten minutes so you'll need to be out of the marriage room before that. It's easy to find. Just follow your nose.'

I followed his advice, spending only a few short minutes studying the numerous displays that told the story of how Gretna Green became synonymous with marriage. Black and white photos of newlyweds, dating back over a hundred years, adorned many of the walls. Glass fronted cabinets offered illustrations of elopers arriving at the village by horse and cart. In a far corner, I found framed photos of famous visitors and letters of thanks from across the world.

A handful of visitors stood nearby, studying the various artefacts, but I didn't have the time to join them. I wanted to find the anvil. So, I followed my nose and walked into the furthest room. Aesthetically, it was perfect and still managed to capture the look and feel of a blacksmith's workshop. The brick walls were painted white with antique hand tools scattered around, including some rusted parts secured to the ceiling. The flagstone floor was devoid of furniture except the infamous black anvil, housed on a block of timber. Written on the side of the anvil in white paint were the words:

Gretna Green Old Smithy Marriage Anvil

I gave the anvil a tap with my knuckles, nodding in appreciation at its solid feel, and decided it was finally time to get back on my bike. As I did so, a woman entered the room and I recognised her at once. It was my friend with the clipboard, and with practiced ease, she connected a rope across the entrance to the room. She then ushered me away, gave a sly smile, and announced cheerily, 'Sorry, my dear, but this is out of bounds from now on. Even for you. I have a wedding party on the way. Good luck with your bike ride!'

With a loud swish, she pulled a heavy curtain across the entrance, blocking all views of the room. I then heard animated voices and the sound of laughter. The wedding party had arrived. I didn't want to eavesdrop and searched for the exit. As I did so, the curtain rippled. I watched for another movement and found myself smiling as a tiny gap appeared, and for a fleeting moment, caught sight of a young bridesmaid.

She wore a pink dress and her hair had been styled in soft ringlets. Her blue eyes followed me while I walked away, and with each step, the curtains closed, inch by inch. By the time I reached the exit, all I could see was her round face and mischievous grin. I waved and in return was greeted by a tongue poke. I opened the exit door, looked over my shoulder, and watched as she smiled and snapped the curtains shut.

While riding away on the Bedfordshire Clanger, I stole one final look around the courtyard. Alan was already in position with his bagpipes, waiting for the wedding couple to appear. Any second now, the anvil would strike and another chapter would be added to the history of Gretna Green.

Moffat couldn't come quick enough and for the next three hours I rode without stopping. The sun had once again been vanquished and the clouds that blanketed the sky resembled a pale sheen. I rarely looked up from the road, but on the occasions I did, the undulating terrain rarely changed. I passed disinterested sheep and curious cows, but neither distracted me from my mission. Villages came and went, but the names, streets, and landmarks were ignored. I had tunnel vision, with Moffat in my sights. As the miles tumbled, the thought of Daphne came to mind. But with no strategy in place to locate her, I knew the chances were slim.

Moffat has a claim to fame, namely the Star Hotel. According to the Guinness World Records, it is the narrowest hotel in the world with a width of just twenty feet. Twenty years earlier I'd enjoyed a memorable night in the lounge bar with Alan, Nick, Karen and Samantha. Now I was outside, sitting astride my bike, contemplating the best way to start the search for Daphne. But my legs felt hollow, my bones were weary, and my stomach was grumbling again. I needed to stock up on fresh fruit and muesli bars, as there was no guarantee of having time in the morning. The ride to Helensburgh tomorrow was going to be another testing one.

Unwilling to walk far, I peered up the street, hoping to see a shop, but was distracted by a man walking out of the hotel. He was dressed in newly pressed jeans and leather shoes, and he wore an open neck flannel shirt. His tousled hair had turned grey at the temples, and in his hand, he held a half finished pint of beer. He stood on the outdoor paving, lazily watching over the street while enjoying a drink. Oh, how I envied him. To me, he looked like a man who had all the time in the world with nowhere to head to in a hurry. With no shops in sight, I walked up both steps towards him.

'Have you cycled far?' he asked immediately.

I made an effort to smile. 'A fair way. We left Penrith this morning and are heading to Helensburgh tomorrow.'

His eyes darted around and then rested back on my own. 'Did you say, we?'

'Yes, I'm with a group of friends, but it's a long story.'

He shrugged. 'No matter. You know, it's a nice enough evening and you look ready for a beer.'

'A beer sounds great. But first I need to stock up on food and I'm gasping for water.'

'Well, that's easy enough. There's a shop just around the corner. If you entered the town from the Gretna road, no doubt you'll have passed it.'

I thanked the man and then realised there was a fair chance he was a local. If this was the case, he might know Daphne.

'I know it's a long shot, but I stayed in a place called Spur Cottage twenty years ago. A couple called Jack and Daphne used to run a bed and breakfast. I don't suppose you've heard of them. Jack has passed away, but I'd love to find Daphne.'

Suddenly, my voice sounded strained and I felt my head swimming. Was it emotion or fatigue? The man didn't seem to notice and stroked his fingers across a day's worth of stubble. I inched closer, hoping to see his eyes widen in recognition.

'I used to be a local taxi driver but I cannee remember a bed and breakfast called Spur Cottage. Maybe it closed a long time ago.'

He pointed to a faraway ridgeline. 'There's a retirement village on the edge of town. Maybe Daphne lives there. Sorry I couldn't be more helpful.'

I thanked him again and watched as he drained the glass and strolled back into the narrowest hotel in the world. I followed him and stood by the entrance. I couldn't remember anything from twenty years ago. No-one looked up as I ventured a few steps inside the dark interior. Why would they? Most were dressed for a Saturday evening on the town, sitting in couples or small groups. The aroma of grilled meat wafted from the kitchen, reminding me once again that I needed to end the day's ride.

I made a hasty exit, found the grocery store, and stocked up with essential items. I then found my bearings and headed to the bed and breakfast. While riding past the hotel, I saw the man again. He was holding a freshly poured pint and raised the glass high. 'Have you found Daphne yet?'

With false bravado, I replied, 'Not yet, but hopefully I'm getting nearer.'

Within minutes, I was admiring the white, freshly painted exterior of Seamore House, our accommodation for that night. The front door overlooked the pavement and this too looked to have had a recent coat of paint. My knock on the door was met with a swift response, revealing a slim, middle

aged man. He held out a hand and smiled. 'You must be Ali. I've been expecting you. I'm Allan, and my wife Heather is inside.'

He stepped outside and gestured to a side gate, which he pushed open.
As I positioned my bike alongside the others, he said, 'Your friends have all
showered but they thought you'd be later than this. I guess you didn't stay too
long in Gretna Green.'

Allan handed me a key and pointed me towards the stairs. Partway up I
heard familiar voices — and new ones too — as the men, two women, and
a teenage girl prepared for a night on the town. We'd been joined by Samantha, Karen and her daughter, Tilly. Although it had only been a week since
I'd met Samantha, it somehow felt much longer. I received a warm hug and a
'what-have-you-been-up-to-now?' type look.

Many years had passed since I'd met Karen, but I recognised her friendly
smile immediately. We too shared a hug and chatted for a few minutes about
Nick's knee, the route he'd picked, and how he was faring as project manager.
I got a high five from Tilly, who stood close by, listening to her mum. While
I chatted to the girls, the riders emerged from their rooms, freshly scrubbed
and eager to enjoy a Saturday night in Moffat. Once again, the greetings were
heartfelt and tinged with humour.

'What took you so long?'

'You were quicker than I thought.'

'Did you get married in Gretna Green?'

'How was the bike computer?'

Mark appeared, fresh faced and wide eyed, as though he'd spent the day
at a spa retreat, not cycling many hours from Penrith. I stole a look in the
corridor mirror and felt a tremor of remorse at the reflection. Dark smudges
had formed around my eyes and the skin on my face resembled the mottled
walls of the guest house.

It wasn't that the day's ride had been arduous. Far from it. In fact, it had
been the easiest so far. Maybe the culmination of numerous diversions was
finally catching up with me. Mark didn't comment on how I looked. Instead,
he smiled and said, 'Well done mate. If you hurry, we can wait, but be warned
— we're eager to get out!'

I didn't have the energy to rush and instead promised to meet them in
town soon. I appreciated the Samaritan that had carried my overnight bag

from Nick's van to the room and also valued the fact that they were willing to wait. But we only had twelve hours left in Moffat. Their time was precious and the sun was already low in the sky.

After showering, I chose the Hawaiian shirt, hoping it would somehow energise me. A short while later, at the foot of the stairs, I caught sight of Allan with his wife Heather. They were both in the kitchen and came out to check if everything was OK with the room.

'All good, thanks. I'm finally off to meet the others.'

In my hand was a copy of the end-to-end book, which I held up. 'Can I interest you in a complimentary copy of my latest travel book? It's about cycling from Land's End to John O'Groats.'

He took a look at the retro cover and nodded approvingly. 'Does this mean you've done the ride before?'

'Yes, but just the once, a long time ago. It took me twenty years to write the book.'

'Well, maybe we'll see you all in another twenty years for the third attempt,' he jested.

I laughed and mentioned the chapter about Moffat. 'I don't suppose you've heard of a lady called Daphne? She used to run a bed and breakfast with her husband Jack in a place called—'

'Spur Cottage. Of course! We know Daphne well, don't we, Heather?'

In that instant, my heart gave a soft flutter as a series of questions spilled from my mouth. 'You know her? Is she still living at Spur cottage? Is she nearby?'

Allan laughed softly and opened the front door. 'She lives just around the corner in the next street. Just the other day, I saw her at the shops and she looked just as sprightly as ever.'

I raced to my room for another book, taking the steps two at a time. When I returned downstairs, Allan was standing on the pavement, pointing to a nearby side street.

'That laneway will take you straight to her house. You'll see Spur Cottage at the end. I'm sure the sign is still above the door. Good luck, and if she is in, please tell her we said hello.'

The lane was narrow and whisper-quiet. But my mind whirred incessantly, bombarded with conflicting thoughts. How would I start the greeting without sounding like a door-to-door salesman? What if she mistook me for a Jehovah's Witness and the travel book as a bible and closed the door within seconds of opening it? There was always the possibility that she wouldn't be home, of course. What if she was at bingo or having tea with neighbours? She could have even been on holiday in Benidorm! I hoped not.

With each step, the unanswered questions continued. The street was narrow with no cars in sight, or the space to park them. The houses either side were as mixed up as my thoughts. Some were terraced, their front doors adjacent to the lane. Others were set back behind low stone walls, some single-storey, some cottage-sized, some painted in pastel blues or pink. One house was adorned with hanging baskets, each one blooming with wildflowers.

At the end of the lane, I came to a junction and stopped. Just to my left, instantly recognisable, was the corner house that Daphne called home. I crossed the road and found myself staring at an inscription above the lintel, which read *Spur Cottage*. I knocked softly and waited. I counted to ten, then tried again, this time with a firmer knock, my nerves jangling. *She wouldn't be in. She had to be out.*

The door creaked open and in the doorway stood a lady who was instantly familiar. She was smaller than I remembered, but not as elderly as I'd imagined she would be. Maybe twenty years earlier, I'd misjudged her age. There wasn't a trace of grey in her highlighted hair, which looked as though it had recently been in curlers. She wore a red jumper and tanned trousers and stood with a straight back. A small dog came into view and stopped alongside her heels as she looked up and down the street. She held the door with one hand, and rested the other by her side.

The words blurted out. 'I'm sorry to bother you, but is your name Daphne?'

Her answer was clear, but understandably guarded. 'Yes, it is. How do you know that?'

At that moment, I wanted to give her a gentle hug and plant a soft kiss on her forehead. But such an act would have warranted the door being slammed in my face. Instead, I raised the book into view and said, 'I'm a travel writer, Daphne. My name is Alistair and many years ago I stayed here with some friends during our ride to John O'Groats.'

With this information, she seemed to relax a little. 'Oh, I'm sorry, my dear, but I don't run a bed and breakfast anymore.'

I held up my hand to dismiss the idea. 'No, that's OK. I'm staying around the corner at Seamore House with Allan and Heather. They said to say hello. By the way, I've bought you a gift. It's the book about my bike ride.'

She clasped her hands to her chest and smiled. 'I dunnee understand. A book for me? Whatever for?'

I handed her the copy and explained. 'As I mentioned, I stayed here twenty years ago with friends on our way from Land's End. You and your husband Jack made us feel very welcome. I wrote about the experience in this travel book.'

The mention of Jack's name caught her by surprise. 'So you met my Jack. How lovely.'

The door opened wider and she took a good look at me. In the doorway, she studied the cover, then allowed me to locate the section on Moffat. She began to read a few words, then stopped and wiped away a tear as her name, and then Jack's, appeared on the pages.

'Oh, my goodness me. This is lovely, thank you. Now, what am I thinking? Come in, please. Don't stand out there on the street!'

I was ushered into her kitchen, and for a few minutes, explained everything I could without overwhelming her with too much detail. I asked her to sit so I could read a small passage. As I did so, she listened, but the sound of Jack's name triggered another tear and I decided to put the book down.

'I'm sorry, Daphne. I didn't mean to upset you. One minute you're pottering around in your kitchen and the next, a strange Englishman with bloodshot eyes is standing in your kitchen reciting an incident that took place twenty years ago.'

'That's fine, Alistair. I can't believe you came over to say hello. You must be so tired. Where did you cycle from today?'

'Well we left Penrith this morning and to be truthful it wasn't too bad. We're off to Helensburgh tomorrow with rain forecast for most of the day.'

'That sounds like a long way. Can I offer you a cup of tea, my dear?'

The offer was tempting but I didn't want to overstay my welcome. Instead, I asked to go into the garden where the photo of us all had been taken twenty years earlier. We were joined by the dog, and as I stroked his ears, Daphne gave me a tour.

In that instant, the memories flooded back — standing around on a warm summer's evening after the long ride from Kendal, enjoying a cold beer and listening to Jack tell a story about life in Moffat. Very soon we were back inside and Daphne picked up a framed photo from the table.

'That's my daughter with the Queen.'

Gently, she put it back. 'It's funny how life turns out, Alistair. Family is so important, you know. I do miss my Jack. Are you married?'

'Oh, yes,' I explained. 'Fran and I have two boys, Noah and Sebastian. And I can't wait to let them know the search for Daphne is finally over.'

At the front door, she looked up at me. 'Will you pop by in the morning for a cup of tea before you go?'

Although I wanted to say yes, I sensed this would be my only visit. Unable to admit it, I promised to try.

I think she knew we wouldn't meet again. It had been a bizarre but blissful encounter, twenty years after our first. I took her hand in mine, reaching forward to give her a hug. She wiped away the slightest of tears and stood by the doorway as I walked away smiling.

I knew where my friends would be. The narrowest hotel in the world has two bars and they'd chosen the public one at the rear. The clientele consisted of a healthy mix of locals and visitors, spanning many decades in age and demographics. I found them easily, spread across the corner seats, chatting, laughing, and sharing jokes. Mark was ordering drinks and handed me a pint of local ale, his smile wide. 'Glad to see you again, Ali. Get that down you.'

It had been a most unusual day, and for a few minutes, he shared their ride from Gretna, off the beaten track. His description sounded far more exciting than my frontal assault along the B7076.

We made our way towards the tables and I plonked myself down next to Samantha. She took a sip of wine and grinned mischievously. 'So, Ali, how is the bike ride going for you?'

'To be truthful, it's a lot harder than I remember it. But I guess I am older now, and the route is far tougher, even though I seem to miss out on most of the difficult bits.'

She chuckled, took another sip of wine and glanced towards Alan. He was close by, in deep discussion with Nick.

'Ali, don't take this the wrong way, but you know those two aren't in the least bit sentimental. Not like you. They rarely think about the past. To them, it's all about the now.'

I stifled a yawn and nodded in agreement. 'Believe me, Sam, I admire their focus, and know I dwell on the past too much. I'm trying hard to be in the now, but this ride keeps revealing parts of Britain I'd forgotten all about, or rekindling long lost memories.'

'Ali, you're not a spring chicken anymore. You can't do a massive bike ride and expect to see and do everything too.'

'I totally agree. Right now, I'm feeling every one of my fifty-one years.'

'Did you find Daphne?'

With a sense of pride, I sat up straight. 'Yes, I did! And to be truthful, it made my day.'

'Good on you. You don't give up, do you? How are you getting on with using Alan's bike computer? I've heard you've made a few wrong turnings!'

I took a gulp of beer and parked the glass on the overcrowded table. 'I'm learning the hard way, but I'm determined to stay with the group for the remainder of the trip.'

'Well, I'm glad,' she said.

I didn't have the heart to tell her that the batteries had recently died and I'd forgotten to purchase anymore.

'One way or another,' I continued, 'I'll be in Helensburgh tomorrow!'

And with that, I made my way over to the jukebox. Craig and Steve were about to make a selection and I slid between the two of them. Without turning his head, Steve scanned the songs on offer. 'I've found a song for you.'

He punched in the number and we watched silently as the vinyl flipped onto the turntable. The band were The Specials. An old favourite. I knew the first line and caught a glint in Steve's eyes as he raised his glass and mimed.

"You've done too much, much too young. Now you're married with a kid when you could be having fun with me!"

Day 9: The River

'There's something about childhood friends that you just can't replace.'
Lisa Whelchel

Eight weeks before the end-to-end bike ride began, I decided to beef up my training. Spin classes were going well but I needed to spend time on the road, not in a gym. A friend lent me his cyclo-cross bike, and another loaned a set of panniers, which I strapped to the rack and filled with house bricks. I then set myself a goal.

Each time I returned from the mine site, I'd commit at least one day per week to bike riding. I chose the coastal road most times and followed it for many hours, through ancient woodland and alongside fields of ripening vines. It's hard to imagine that far below my feet lay a vast network of caves, stretching towards the Southern Ocean.

Occasionally I'd divert along narrow tracks and ride alongside tracts of parched farmland, waiting for the rains. Then, I'd leave the escarpment and veer towards the ocean, the road sweeping through perfect curves, offering expansive views of the pounding surf.

I'd then turn the bike around and race against the autumn sun, my eyes peeled for kangaroos, mysteriously drawn to the roadside each sunset. I repeated the route numerous times, leaving home progressively earlier as winter approached. After clocking up 700 kilometres over numerous weekends, I unloaded the bricks and returned the bike, convinced I was now ready to tackle the long road to John O'Groats.

During the evening meal at Moffat, those training rides along the coastal road felt totally inadequate. Rain was on its way tomorrow, and the thought of waking early to ride towards Glasgow filled me with trepidation rather than intrigue. All I craved was a bed, but instead, I held up my glass for a refill and toasted Karen, Samantha and Tilly, who were to cook us a home-cooked meal in Helensburgh.

Those around me looked the picture of health, their faces flushed by the elements and glasses of wine. The conversation was relaxed, the pizzas kept coming, and someone ordered another bottle of Chianti. I sat close to Craig and Steve, listening to stories about their biking exploits in England and abroad. I asked questions, traded jokes, and joined in with the banter.

Throughout the meal my head swam, not from excessive alcohol, but a sense of overwhelming weariness. Instead of declaring an early night, I stayed put, determined to join in with the banter and unwilling to let my guard down. Afterwards we passed a pub. I should have kept on walking. Instead, I suggested one for the road and soon found myself sitting alongside Alan and Sam. It was late and most patrons had left.

Sam chose a corner table, and over a nightcap, we reminisced about our time in Moffat two decades earlier. I was keen to delve deeper, but Alan soon changed tack. 'I've heard it's going to be wet tomorrow. Just remember to stay close and we'll tackle the route together.'

He made it sound so simple, and maybe — in theory — it was. The landlord called time and we ventured outside. The town was settling down for the night, wrapped in a blanket of cloud. We walked in silence, listening to the faraway sound of late night revellers searching for a party. Outside the bed and breakfast, Sam stopped by the front door. 'Please stick with them tomorrow, Ali. There's going to be a pot of chili con carne waiting for you all at the other end. We might even have a few drinks to celebrate!'

Although the thought of a home-cooked meal sounded appealing, it was a comfortable bed that occupied my thoughts as I climbed the stairs. But although I slept soundly, my body was sheened in sweat when I awoke.

The lads were already tucking into cereals when I entered the dining room. Allan appeared from the kitchen, armed with plates of hot food. While dishing out eggs, bacon, sausages, and fried potatoes, he gave a rundown of the latest weather report. A cold front was forecast, with squally showers and a chance of flooding in regional areas. This news, although expected, caused a murmur within the group, and one or two began checking their watches.

Instead of tucking into the food, I played with the eggs, unsure why my appetite had vanished. Allan collected the half-finished plate and asked, 'Aren't you hungry this morning? By the way, did you manage to find Daphne?'

I explained what had happened and he nodded enthusiastically. 'So, are you going to see her this morning?'

'It's not likely at the moment,' I replied. 'I can't seem to get into gear.'

I glanced at the riders, who were now wiping their plates clean and draining the last of their drinks. Despite the fact that Daphne was close by, I'd been unable to move with any sense of purpose since waking. Each step, thought, and action seemed arduous. Time was running away.

I picked up a piece of toast and hurried upstairs, aware the other riders were eager to depart. While searching for my cycling shoes, I heard numerous calls from each room. I tried to remain focused but felt anything but ready. Somehow, I managed to wheel my bike outside, and to my surprise, I was out before the others.

My eyes instinctively turned to the laneway towards where Daphne lived, but raindrops sent me racing to the van to fish out the waterproof that Nick had lent me. By the time I found it, the other riders were emerging from the side garden.

Their jackets were striking in bright orange and fluorescent green. My top was as black as night, totally unsuitable for the squally clouds hurrying across the rooftop, yet well suited to the way I was feeling. Especially as I'd left it too late to say goodbye to Daphne.

Colin had been riding up and down the road, checking through the gears. 'Good to see you're ready,' he said. 'Looks like you're all set for action.'

I'd hardly murmured a word all morning and still felt listless but managed a smile.

'By the way,' he continued, 'Mark is making a phone call to home, and JP is staying behind with him. They'll catch us up soon.'

My heart leapt at this unexpected news. There was suddenly a way I could see Daphne. If Mark and JP could come and collect me when they were ready, I'd be able to ride with them instead. But they didn't know where Daphne lived.

While the group made last minute bike adjustments, I ran into the house, hoping to locate JP so I could let him know my plan. I called his name, fully expecting to see his bright face appear around a doorway. But despite a frantic search, I couldn't find him anywhere and daren't shout too loud while guests were sleeping. Finally, I came back downstairs, searched the kitchen and TV room but to no avail.

Reluctantly, I stepped outside to find the riders lined up, waiting patiently for my arrival. Within seconds, we were on our way to Helensburgh.

The town looked deserted as we made our way along the high street and turned north along a narrow road, shrouded by mist. Very soon, the houses and streets dissipated, replaced by damp fields and a scattering of lonely trees. We came to a pine forest, eerily quiet in the early hours. The seedlings had once been planted in rows, with gaps to allow maximum sunlight and growth. But as we passed alongside, I stared deep into the woods and found them to be lifeless and cold. The earth was darkened by recent rain, with droplets of water clinging to the edge of each pine needle. A bend in the road led down to a stream, and as we crossed over towards a wooded valley, the small drop in altitude freed us briefly from the mist.

After another turn, I heard the familiar drone of faraway traffic, but before we ventured nearer, the lead rider pulled over and announced we were waiting for JP and Mark. They appeared on the scene within minutes, their bright tops glowing against the murky tree line. They cycled in perfect symmetry, side-by-side, and smiled broadly as they passed by, before leading us towards a dual carriageway.

Only then, while at the back of the pack, did I truly appreciate the full merits of wearing vibrant colours on such a day. I could see each rider clearly, and as the angle of the main road increased, I clicked through the lower gears and made a pact to buy a brighter top before the day was through.

All too soon, I began falling away from the second last rider and muttered in annoyance as the gap quickly widened. The incline wasn't excessive, but I struggled to find a steady rhythm and began faltering. I reached for my water bottle and thought back to the unfinished breakfast. I had no idea if the front riders knew I was far behind and contemplated calling out. There was no need though. Alan and Mark peeled away, slowed their pace, and rode alongside me so we became three abreast.

Although we hugged the left lane, traffic was light and approaching cars could be heard from afar. They both rode without grimace, heads aloft, scanning the road ahead. I remained silent, unable to respond to their small talk. Each breath was ragged as I sucked in the cool air and tried replying, but the words that stumbled out were incoherent. I could sense their frustration, but they persevered with the casual conversation, offering to share memories of times they'd met my dad. Just why he became the topic of conversation was lost to me. I presumed it was because we were cycling towards Glasgow, close to where dad was born and raised. I sensed they were trying to take my mind off the hill, but the conversation was too one-sided.

When the front riders increased the gap further, Alan suggested we act to catch them up. In our threesome, Mark would take the lead, I'd tuck in behind, and Alan would take up the rear.

The plan failed. Within moments, Alan and Mark were two bike lengths in front of me. Dropping their speed, they attempted the strategy once more. But as before, despite all efforts and a series of grunts, the result was just the same. I hadn't expected to be sweating at such an early hour. When they dropped back a third time, it wasn't to talk about my dad.

Alan asked, 'What's up, Ali? The hill isn't that steep.'

'I've no idea. But I can't go any faster. Maybe it'll be better if you all go ahead.'

'We can slow down for a bit, until you catch your breath,' Mark suggested.

I appreciated the gesture, but knew, deep down, that today was going to be a go-slow. Each revolution of the pedals felt restrictive, as though I was cycling through treacle. It would be better to let them go. We'd only been cycling an hour and I didn't want to spend another long period on my own. It was getting to be a lonely trip at times. But I didn't want to hold them back any longer. I replied in short, sharp bursts, my eyes locked onto the road.

'Please, go ahead. Maybe I'll catch you up, once I've recovered.'

'Is your computer turned on?' Alan asked.

'Yes, it's all good.' I'd managed to find some old batteries last night.

'See you later then.'

Although the parting had been my suggestion, I still felt a stab of disappointment as they nodded in response and increased their speed. Within seconds, they were yards ahead.

I pedalled frantically, focusing on the white line that segregated the bitumen from the verge, and counted to a hundred in a last-ditch effort to make up lost ground. But when I next looked up, they'd vanished, swallowed by the mist. I wouldn't see them again for another nine hours.

I didn't feel pity or anger. For the first hour, I just felt numb. The mist was a constant companion. It sat on my shoulders most of the time, while at other times, whenever the road dipped, it hung above my head. The clouds gathered broodily at the edges of my vision, and all morning I fought a feisty headwind. Then came the drizzle, so fine at first that I hardly noticed the droplets forming on my jacket. They were followed by unexpected bursts of bright sunlight, which penetrated any gaps in the iron blanket.

For a short while, I became so preoccupied with cloud watching that the towns and villages I passed through left little impression. The bike computer beeped at strategic intersections, and I followed the prompts with ease. If I'd been handed a map and asked to mark my position, I'd have prodded a finger halfway between Moffat and Glasgow and hoped for the best.

I skipped the chance of a mid-morning coffee at a roadside eatery in the vain hope that the steady pace would reacquaint me with the pack. But with each mile, the realisation hit me that it was going to be a solitary day. Signs for Glasgow appeared from the gloom, counting down the miles to the city. The computer route had been meticulously plotted, and with each beep, I found myself crossing over or under busy roads as I weaved towards the city along the designated cycle ways.

Without warning, the deluge of rain, which I'd managed to avoid so far, arrived in force. There was little to do but cycle onwards, but with the squally rain came decreased visibility and, with that, a further reduction in speed.

According to a road marker, Glasgow was still twenty-five miles away, but the surrounding suburbs had already swallowed most of the greenery. Over the rumble of faraway thunder, I thought I heard the bike computer beeping and rather than studying the screen, I decided to take the next turning. Within seconds, I found myself on a main road filled with freight traffic.

I decided to turn around at the next roundabout, but another deluge hit me square on, obscuring all views of the computer screen. I could still hear it, though, beeping frantically, as if to tell me to turn around. But with heavy traffic thundering past, I was forced to ride onwards in search of a safe place to stop.

White arrows, painted on the road long ago to assist users with decision-making, had worn off, and all that remained were grey smudges, stained with diesel oil. To amplify the problem of not knowing which way to turn, the traffic had intensified, and unwittingly I was now riding close to the exit lane of a motorway.

I gripped the handlebars hard as the roar of approaching juggernauts grew louder. Every second I expected to hear the sound of a horn rammed in anger at the senseless rider in black. But the trucks skimmed past, forcing me sideways towards the puddles.

I ignored the computer beeps and concentrated on keeping the bike upright and moving. The constant worry that I was dressed unsafely, without lights, during an unseasonal storm at a major road intersection, didn't help. But I was determined to stay calm. The Garmin would get me out of the problem, once I could find a resting place.

Up ahead, a set of traffic lights blazed red, and I came to a stop by a faded white line. I was at a major roundabout, complete with traffic lights to manage the flow of vehicles. Set high above the lights were various road signs, depicting nearby towns and cities. I read them all, searching for Glasgow, but it was nowhere to be seen. How could a city so close, filled with millions of people, not be signposted?

A thought struck me. Maybe I had to circumnavigate the roundabout to find the sign for Glasgow. The lights turned green and I joined the race, pedalling hard to keep abreast of the vehicles either side of me. My eyes darted for a sign, but there was only a side road for local traffic. Up ahead, another light shone green and I rode quickly before it changed.

Cars beeped and I wondered if it was at the lone, dark rider, partly covered in mud. I rode on, peering through the rain and frantically searching for a sign to Glasgow as cars overtook and cut in sharply. The next set of lights were on red. I came to a stop and realised I'd gone full circle. In desperation, I wiped the computer screen and caught sight of a map of Scotland, obscured by raindrops. In a desperate attempt for freedom, I pushed numerous buttons at random, just as the traffic lights turned green. Despite the engine noise of the cars and trucks, I heard the robotic voice of the computer. *Day One: Land's End to Penzance.* Not helpful.

Ignoring the computer, I followed in the rain-splattered wake of a Heavy Goods Vehicle, veered into the left-hand lane, and rode hurriedly away from the roundabout. As quickly as it arrived, the rain eased. I found myself on a bridge, its red railings protecting me from the meandering river, far below.

I should have done a U-turn at that point and retraced my tracks but decided to find a safer route until I could purchase a fluorescent jacket. After cycling across the bridge, a *Welcome* sign up ahead grew closer. Like it or not, I was now in Motherwell.

In an attempt to catch my breath, I turned left through an area known as Strathclyde Country Park. A roadside map depicted a stretch of land, dominated by an expanse of water called Strathclyde Loch. A single road ran parallel with the lake, which was buffered by an expanse of lush grass and rows of newly planted saplings. The feeling of relief at escaping the traffic was marred because I was so far from where I needed to be. As for the bike computer, it stared back blankly and had long ceased beeping.

I had to find someone to talk to. But as I rode deeper into the park, there was no sign of anyone on foot. Cars passed by, but I couldn't find the courage to wave them down. Instead, I admired the manicured gardens and gazed at the nearby lake. While cycling, I plucked my water bottle from its holder and guzzled greedily, safe in the knowledge that my day had turned to shit.

To my right, partially shrouded by shrubs, I noticed a single-storey building with three doors set in dark bricks. In contrast to the pleasant surroundings, the public convenience was a cheap, functional construction. Sandwiched between the gents and the ladies was another room, and a placard above the door said, *Private — Keep Out*. The door was partially ajar, and through the gap, I noticed a man, lounging on a seat.

After a swift visit to the gents, I studied the surrounding area and decided that on a sunny day, the park would be ideal for the folks of Motherwell to enjoy a gentle stroll. It was bigger than I'd initially anticipated, but seemingly devoid of anywhere to purchase food. Luckily, Nick had insisted on stuffing a packet of muesli bars in my panniers a few days earlier. 'In case of emergencies,' he'd said.

I was now able to appreciate his foresight. While unwrapping the cellophane, my mind focused on the tasks ahead. The main priority was the bike computer, and after a simple diagnosis, it became clear the batteries had died.

I had no spares or a local map. A quick scout of the brooding sky told me that rain was on its way again. I needed to act decisively and there was only one man who could help me. I finished my snack, knocked on the open door and called out.

All I could hear was the animated voice of a TV presenter, describing an action-packed moment in a football match. I knocked harder, which caused the door to open further. Sat on a chair, his legs perched on top of a desk was a man of similar age to myself. Conscious of the fact that it might be a tentative moment in the game, I held my palm towards him in a nonchalant fashion. 'I'm sorry to bother you but I'm after some batteries for my bike computer.'

His eyes flicked from the screen to the doorway and back again. I made a gesture with my thumb and forefinger, rubbing them together. 'I'm willing to pay, of course.'

He still didn't move but did reply. 'Sorry, pal, but I cannee help you. There's no batteries here, I'm afraid.'

His eyes returned to the TV just as I heard the shrill of the final whistle. This seemed to please the man and he punched the air in delight. In doing so, he noticed I was still in the doorway. His tone was a little sharper the next time he spoke. 'Are you after anything else, as it's my lunch break? The toilets are open if you need them.'

I backed away, not wanting to harass him further, and felt the patter of fresh raindrops on my bike helmet. I stared at the darkening sky and knew the time for politeness was over. I needed to get into and through Glasgow as soon as possible, and every minute standing here was time wasted. I stepped back into his view and raised my voice. 'It's me again. I appreciate that it's your lunch break and it sounded like a great game, but I'm cycling to Helensburgh today and need some help.'

He sat up and eyed me thoughtfully. 'Did you say you were on a bike? Why are you going to Helensburgh?'

I smiled uneasily. 'Oh, we're cycling from Land's End to John O'Groats. Helensburgh is our stop for the night.'

He stood and turned the TV off. 'It was a friendly match and both teams played shite,' he said curtly. Then he ambled towards the doorway, peered at my parked bike and asked, 'Where are your mates? You made it sound like you're in a group.'

'Well, it's a long story, but the bottom line is I'm here and they're many miles ahead.'

He whistled softly and ran a hand through greying hair. He was short and stocky with friendlier eyes than I'd previously thought. In the awkward silence, he kept looking at the bike and then me. Something was troubling him and I couldn't think what it was. To break the silence, I began talking.

'As I was saying, I'm after batteries, but if you haven't got any, I'd really appreciate some directions to—'

'I thought the swimmers that raced in the nearby loch were half crazy, but you must be friggen mad as well.'

I grinned sheepishly, not sure if he thought I was mad for cycling to Helensburgh on such a dismal day, or for attempting to cycle to John O'Groats. The concept of cycling seemed to amuse him further as he asked, 'Where did you start from this morning?'

'Moffat.'

He nodded thoughtfully as if in agreement and then said, 'Land's End to John O'Groats on a bike. What will you people think of next? How old are you? I can see you're not a spring chicken.'

'I've just turned fifty-one.'

'Sorry, pal, but you look a wee bit older than that today. You should take up darts and drinking beer rather than cycling and eating muesli bars. It cannee be healthy — all that adventurous stuff at your age.'

Although the discussion was intriguing, I was acutely aware that once more I was getting nowhere fast. I needed information.

'I really need to get through Glasgow and make my way to Helensburgh before nightfall. Please help. I don't want to go back the way I came. I'm not in the mood to play cat and mouse with more trucks while wearing black.'

'I was wondering about your jacket. I thought cyclists wore fluorescent tops.'

'Well, I'm a bit of a beginner.'

'A beginner! It's a bit late to be a beginner when you're cycling in this weather and about to enter the Highlands. You need to get yourself a fancy wee top like the other cyclists around here.'

I smiled wearily and informed him that I planned to do exactly as he advised. But my priority was Glasgow. The rain eased and he walked outside. His shirt emblem displayed the local council logo and he also wore an unzipped windcheater, jeans, and work boots. He pointed down the road that I'd travelled on earlier. 'I'm sorry to tell you, but you've wasted your time. There's only one way from here to Glasgow and it's the way you came.'

I shook my head in disbelief. 'What about the road through the park? Doesn't it lead to somewhere useful?'

'The only useful thing about that road is the work they're doing to repair it. It's a dead end at the moment. Come back in a few months and you'll be laughing.'

He could see his jest hadn't hit home. The thought of all that wasted time, plus the fact that I had to circumnavigate the roundabout again, sent an involuntary shiver down my spine. I thanked the man and made my way to the bike. He watched as I gave a mock salute, followed by a faint smile, and then turned my bike to face the road.

While cycling away, I heard a shout from behind and saw him trotting towards me, his arms waving. Had I dropped something? I completed a U-turn and we met again, this time under the canopy of a tree. He was panting softly. 'Look, there is one way,' he said. 'But you might end up getting lost in the suburbs.'

I chuckled softly, my heart racing with anticipation as he pointed to a bitumen footpath. 'You see that laneway? Just follow it through the woods until the end. It will take you through some fields. You cannee go wrong. Go over a railway bridge into a housing estate. Take the left turning, go past the houses, and continue for as long as you can. Don't deviate down any side roads. Just go straight. If you see a children's playground, you're on the right track. Look for an alley alongside a set of garages and follow it to the end. If you get lost, tell someone you're after McDonald's. They'll know where that is.'

He took a short breath. 'It's located near a roundabout. From there you'll find the road to Glasgow. It's not pretty and there are big lorries, mind. If ya cannee find McDonalds, look for signs to Coatbridge. That'll get you close to Glasgow, for sure. There are plenty of shops along the way too. You might even find a new jacket!'

A sudden downpour dampened any further need for conversation. He hastily pulled the jacket over his head and stabbed a finger towards the path. 'Good luck! I hope you find your friends and make it to John O'Groats. Remember, look out for McDonald's!'

He ran back towards the building, hunched against the wind and rain, while I set off along the track. It was exactly like he said it would be. I emerged into the housing estate and took the first turning on my left. Most houses were cream-coloured with slated roofs, and many overlooked a wide stretch of grass. In the centre, a football pitch and two goals stood empty, waiting for the sunshine. Apart from parked cars along the roadside, the estate looked deserted. The rain intensified and the only residents I discovered were those running for cover.

The road ended at a T-junction and on instinct I turned right. With a sense of pride, I passed a sign towards Coatbridge and silently thanked the Good Samaritan. I was still mystified why Glasgow didn't own a signpost but within minutes was rewarded twofold. Out of the clouds emerged the golden arches of McDonald's, and at once the hunger pains started. Near the entrance, an arrowed sign by the road acknowledged I was finally within sight of Glasgow.

I didn't want to leave McDonald's. For one thing, it was lovely and warm inside. The bright décor, comfortable seats, simple food, hot coffee and piped music were soothing as I listened to the storm raging outside. Upon entering, I'd been oblivious to how wet I actually was. This became apparent while I stood in the queue, studying pictures of fast food on the illuminated display. A pool of water began spreading across the tiled floor towards the adjacent queue. A teenager sniggered and nudged his mate, and I smiled in the acknowledgement that I looked like an odd sort.

I was carrying my front panniers, as they contained my GoPro camera, smartphone and pay-as-you-go phone. They were also home to the muesli bars, a print out of the accommodation for that night, and the form for post office stamps to prove I was a valid end-to-ender. I reached inside to study the paperwork, as it had been some time since it was stamped. As I feared, it was sodden.

'Excuse me, sir. Why don't you move over this way and we can speed up your order.'

The young girl at my side was slim with dark hair and a beaming smile. She held a mop, which was soon in action, swishing the puddle. As I stepped back, she ceased mopping and pointed to an unmanned till. 'Jimmy, would you take this man's order on the end till, please?'

A teenage boy appeared from the kitchen, stepped behind the till, and gestured me forward. I said yes to all the supersize options, and then Jimmy instructed me to take a seat until the order was ready.

McDonald's was filled with a multitude of people, ranging from mums with toddlers to old age pensioners. One table was surrounded by a group of spotty youths, more interested in their phones than their companions. While searching for a free table, I found a cleaning trolley and ripped off a handful of paper-towel, which I placed onto my seat. Then I pulled the paperwork from the panniers and laid it on the melamine table in the vain hope it would dry.

The girl that had mopped the puddle appeared by my side and placed a tray of food onto the table. 'Here you go, sir. I'll grab your drink when it's ready.'

I hadn't expected table service and smiled as she busied herself at another table before detouring to the bistro and returning with a steaming mug of coffee. After placing the drink down, she noticed I was studying the damp form. 'Looks like you're on a treasure hunt,' she said with a shrug.

'Well, I am on the hunt, but not for treasure. These are stamps from some of the places I've been to. Now I'm searching for Glasgow, and after that I need to get to Helensburgh.'

Her head tilted slightly, as if confused. 'Glasgow's impossible to miss. You're nearly there and it's a massive city!'

Then she looked at my discarded bike helmet and asked the obvious question. 'Are you cycling all the way to Helensburgh in this weather?'

'Yes, and in four days' time I'll be in John O'Groats. That's the plan, but I've taken a bit of a detour today for various reasons. By the way, the coffee is delicious and I appreciate your help.'

She was being called to deal with a mini crisis, but before departing, she said, 'That's OK. To be truthful you looked kind of spaced out when you walked in. We thought you might have been on drugs or something. But you look normal enough now. Well, normal enough for someone that wants to cycle for hours in this rain.'

I held up my mug and bid her farewell. But she didn't wander away. Instead she said, 'You might be soaking wet today, but at least you're on an adventure. This time tomorrow you could be gazing at Ben Nevis. If you are, spare a thought for me back here while I clean the windows and watch cars go round the roundabout.'

Then she laughed and walked away. I was still pondering the drugs comment. Did I really look that crazy?

The route from McDonald's to Glasgow was direct, although the busy road did little to inspire me. I was repeatedly forced to stop at traffic lights along with throngs of motorists. Occasionally, I was rewarded with smiles from some of the passengers, but on most occasions, their faces were hidden behind steamed windows. The route took me alongside a retail centre, and it was here that I discovered a shop, which catered for outdoor enthusiasts. Finally, I was the owner of a sleek, bright orange, fully waterproof top — its price slashed by half, thanks to a mid-summer sale.

I also purchased new batteries for the bike computer and selected the route from Moffat to Helensburgh. The computer located my current position and selected a course to merge with the nearest coordinate Nick had uploaded. The screen created a maze of lines, which I could have deciphered with patience. But I decided to switch it off and take the most direct route instead. It was only when traffic hit a snail's pace, that I realised the direct route went right through the heart of Glasgow.

It was hard to imagine that this was their summer. Pedestrians scurried along damp pavements, dressed in jeans, jackets, shoes and hats. Some carried umbrellas, and in pub doorways, smokers made small talk, huddled under the eaves to escape the drizzle. I've heard that Glasgow is a vibrant location with a strong sense of culture. Famous musicians from across the world travel to the city to play to thousands of fans. It's not only music that Glaswegians enjoy. They are obsessive about football and have a strong connection to arts and history.

But I wouldn't have made a connection with any of this while cycling alongside the bargain shops, bookmakers, nail salons, and run-down pubs. Maybe it was the oppressive sky, but this section of the city looked dreary and worn out. I passed a pawnbroker, its windows adorned with a poster stating they buy and sell gold. The shop next door was boarded up, and the one after needed new window frames.

I approached an intersection, dominated by a stone column, which stretched proudly towards the granite sky. Tolbooth Steeple was constructed in 1625 and is all that remains of the original Tolbooth buildings, which were home to the council hall and city prison. At 126 feet high, the steeple once served as the location to undertake public executions. Those accused of practising witchcraft were prime candidates for the gallows, along with convicted thieves and murderers.

These days it's an historical landmark and an accurate timepiece. By the time I rode alongside it, the hands were pointing to three o'clock. Even if I were able to get through Glasgow without a glitch, it would be many more hours before I sighted Helensburgh.

I tried pushing away thoughts of the other riders, but they were constantly on my mind. No doubt they'd be moving at speed and within touching distance of our overnight accommodation. Maybe they were already there, enjoying the facilities and checking their bikes over for the big day tomorrow.

After passing through an area called Trongate and battling my way through snarled traffic, I finally caught sight of the River Clyde and stopped at the banks to admire the view. At this stage of its journey it was maturing, and within 30 nautical miles would merge into the Firth of Clyde, the largest and deepest coastal waters in the British Isles.

For now, the river was approximately 100 yards wide, moving slowly but steadily with small eddies swirling between the steel columns of the bridge. Something struck me as odd. It felt strange, standing beside Scotland's second longest river, not far from the city centre, without sighting a single craft bobbing on the water. This waterway was once the powerhouse that helped Glasgow prosper. In 1812, the world's first commercial steamship was launched on the Clyde after being constructed in the local docks. This was the beginning of an era of unprecedented growth, with Scottish shipbuilding skills in demand from customers across the world.

Nowadays, the river remains intact, but the frenzied days of mass construction are over. Shipbuilders still exist but not in the vast scale that bought prosperity and growth to the city. With each mile that I cycled, the dark, historic part of the city gave way to a sparkling, modern world. Only a red brick rotunda, now converted to an upmarket restaurant, gave any further clue as to how Glasgow once looked in this particular location. With its steep sided roof, elongated windows and rounded walls, it would have made an imposing administrative building for the construction industry. Since the demise of the industry, buildings like this have fallen into disrepair or are threatened with demolition.

Common sense prevailed on this occasion though, and the rotunda lives to fight another day. I stopped to grab a coffee and a muffin, which the rotunda now offered, and from one of the outside windows, studied the plush décor. Despite the ambience, I didn't relish the thought of sitting on luxury seats wearing damp shorts and a wet anorak. Just before setting off, I overheard two women discussing its history. One was pointing to the far side of the river.

'Yes, I tell you, there's an underground foot tunnel that goes from this rotunda to the one on the other side. They say it could open soon as a tourist attraction, but it's been sealed up for years.'

While riding away, I made a mental note to put the secret tunnel on my wish list for when I next returned to the UK. Adjacent to the rotunda, I sighted a vital clue to Glasgow's history. It was a steel structure, jutting skyward from a car park. The Finnieston Crane was once an important piece of machinery in the construction of ships. The men and shipyards are all but gone now and the crane now stands alone, towering over the riverbank, its oversized jib still capable of a decent day's work, given half the chance.

The city centre with its historic buildings, dark alleyways, snarled roads, and tired shop fronts soon receded, now replaced by a riverside setting with a sense of space. Even the clouds were peeling back their layers, allowing the sun to pierce through. The skyline altered, revealing modern buildings, constructed from steel. Each was a different size and shape to the last, with manicured lawns and new roads in between them.

One building resembled a giant armadillo, its steel ridges catching a rare glint of sunshine. I was determined to cross the Clyde and rode onto the Millennium Bridge. On the far side, a large rectangular building made from glass and steel dominated the waterfront. I'd found the headquarters of BBC Scotland. I rode across the narrow bridge, drawn to the impressive building, and found myself freewheeling around its perimeter. The sky was clearing and the sight of the Clyde lifted my spirits. I was no longer in any hurry. I cycled back to the bridge, and this time I stopped halfway to stare down at the murky waters swirling far below.

The first time I'd ever set eyes on the Clyde was as a thirteen-year-old boy. Along with my younger brother Matthew, we'd travelled to Scotland with our dad. The reason, dad said, was a longing to return to his roots and to share places of his childhood with his sons. Matthew and I were glad of the trip as it also meant we'd be spending a week at a Butlin's holiday camp.

When the week of fun was over, dad drove us to the riverside suburb of Port Glasgow. It's sad to say, but up until this period, we'd been ignorant to the facts that took our dad from Scotland in search of a new life in England. After skirting the city, we headed towards the Clyde. Along the way he explained how the riverside was a place where children grew up quickly. According to dad, it was a tough environment, and most youths knew their destiny lay in the shipyards, local factories, fishing boats, or at sea.

While we sat in the back of his Vauxhall Victor, he described how the docks were once a hive of activity. Those lucky enough became crane drivers, welders, fitters, riggers, labourers, or electricians. It was a working class, nononsense neighbourhood, united by unions but divided by football and religion.

By the time he was seventeen years old, spiralling unemployment was forcing people away from the city. The Merchant Navy were hiring and within weeks, he was onboard his first ship, employed as a stocker to load coal into the boiler. For years he sailed the seven seas, and on his return, Glasgow continued to decline. Instead of returning to his roots alongside the Clyde, he chose Luton, an industrial town 30 miles north of London. New ships might have been in low demand in Scotland, but car production was on the rise, and like many of his childhood friends, dad decided to call Luton home.

During our drive through the gritty riverside suburbs of Port Glasgow and Greenock, he pointed out landmarks that meant nothing to us.

'Over there is where your Auntie Nellie used to go dancing. It's a tatty old building now, but it used to be packed to the rafters every Saturday night. And see that wee house, near the corner? That's where Tom lived when he was a boy.'

Matthew and I exchanged blank looks and asked in unison, 'Tom who?'

'Tommy! Our next door neighbour.'

I remember saying to dad at that moment, 'So your friend from Port Glasgow moved all the way to England and ended up living next door to us?'

He laughed out loud. 'Half of the street moved to Luton, son. That's why I know so many people in the town. Many of them were school friends. We came for the work, but few of us ever went back to Scotland to live!'

He fell quiet while finding his bearings, and then started mumbling about derelict houses, missing streets, and graffiti. Just as he was deliberating whether to continue the mystery tour, he let out a yelp of joy. 'This is my street. I wonder if Annie still lives here.'

He parked the car and we walked towards a block of flats, three storeys high. Dad explained they were called tenements and insisted on taking a photo of us outside the communal front door. An elderly man walked past and dad began talking to him. I heard a name mentioned over and over. Annie Robinson. The man pointed to the adjacent tenement block before shuffling away.

Minutes later, we were on the second floor of the building, knocking on a door. It opened, revealing a woman in her fifties, dressed in a floral apron. Annie let out a squeal of delight and ushered us inside. While dad enjoyed tea, Matthew and I took up the offer of fizzy drinks and freshly baked bread. While we ate, they reminisced about the old days, exchanging stories, names and memories. When it was time to leave, Annie ushered Matthew and I to a window and asked us to look down at the streets below.

She pulled the curtains wide. 'Boys, this is where your dad played every day when he was a wee boy. The streets were filled with screaming children, all running after a leather ball. There would sometimes be scuffles, tears, and the odd fight. But they were great days, weren't they Sonny?'

Sonny was Dad's nickname. He stood nearby, smiling proudly while Annie recited those long-forgotten days of their childhood. Then she lowered her voice. 'Now, take a good look, boys. What do you see in the streets?'

I was still eating, so Matthew answered instead. 'I can see lots of parked cars, but there's no children playing football.'

Annie smiled and rested a hand lightly on his head, 'It's not always this quiet, son. The kids do play sometimes. But nothing like they used to, and each summer it seems to get less and less. It's all that TV, I reckon.'

She then offered us a Kit-Kat for the long journey home and said, 'Boys, promise me that you'll not waste all your time watching TV. Get out and explore the world. Just like your dad.'

By the front door, she knelt down and insisted on a hug. Then she said quietly, 'If you do decide to travel, make sure you visit your friends more often than your dad does.'

Before our departure from Port Glasgow, dad drove the short distance to the banks of the Clyde. Far in the distance, across the wide river, a dark smudge depicted the low-lying hills that led to the Highlands. The waterway was not as we'd imagined. Dad had described his childhood days, playing along the riverbank, and searching for crustaceans that he called clabby-doos. These would then be taken home and cooked in boiling water until the shells opened, revealing giant sized mussels.

As he pointed out local landmarks, we skimmed stones across the placid water and watched a fishing trawler head out to sea. On our way back to the car, he explained that by watching the cargo boats, he'd become inspired to travel the world. While in India and Hong Kong, he'd visited numerous tattoo artists, and the faded etchings on his arms and legs were testament to those adventurous days.

Later, in a backstreet café, he fed us burgers and explained that on our return we would not be seeing him at home anymore. During the long journey home, it finally struck me that our evenings by the TV would never be the same again — Dad relaxing in his favourite chair while mum sat nearby, drinking tea and laughing at the screen.

All of this had occurred about forty years earlier. As far as I knew, he never returned to see Annie. Despite the fact that I was close to Port Glasgow, I didn't have the time or energy to divert anymore. Besides, these locations were on the south of the Clyde. My journey was to the north. With thoughts of dad, Annie Robinson, and a street filled with boisterous kids I crossed back over the Millennium Bridge and set my sights on Helensburgh.

For a short while, I braved a dual carriageway, but soon found a marker that led me to a designated cycle way. Although the river was close by, I rarely glimpsed it until Clydebank. The track threaded its way through the outer suburbs, along alleyways, disused roads, and converted railway tracks, and then emerged onto quiet back streets.

My re-acquaintance with the Clyde coincided with a sighting of the Titan crane, a final reminder that this was once a dominant ship building area. There were no bungee jumpers aloft, just a pair of gulls, little more than specks, perched on top of the steel tower. As I approached the river, it was hard to imagine that close to this spot, some of the finest ships that ever sailed the seas were constructed. The list includes the HMS Hood and the RMS Queen Mary.

At the time of its launch in 1934, the RMS Queen Mary was considered the grandest ocean liner in the world. It was known simply as Hull Number 534 until the ceremony, which drew a crowd of 250,000 people. After the Queen named the ship, it slipped into the Clyde, where eighteen drag chains held it back, while the crowd roared in admiration.

The stretch between Clydebank and Dumbarton was pleasurable, as are most trips alongside canals. The land either side of the strip of water was flat. On the far side, rows of well-kept houses followed the gentle curves of the sedate waterway. From their vantage point, they had a perfect view of a lone rider, heading west along the embankment, flanked by meadows of tall grass.

The sunshine and showers continued, leaving me little alternative but to keep my new jacket on for the remainder of the trip. Besides, the air was cooling with the approach of evening. Scottish summers cannot guarantee sunshine, but there is always enough light. Being relatively close to the arctic does have its advantages at times. I estimated that dusk was still hours away, and by then I hoped to have basked in a hot shower and feasted on the remains of a meal.

Dumbarton was closer than I'd thought, and it was here that I bade farewell to the cycle path and took a fork in the road towards Helensburgh. In those last few miles, I hugged the northern edge of the Clyde. As the town grew nearer, I replayed the events that had occurred since waking. It had been an unusual day, unlike anything I'd expected.

After cycling into Helensburgh, I stopped alongside a municipal car park and gazed across the Clyde to the far side. Port Glasgow and Greenock were there, just visible under a dappled haze. I searched for the giant crane that stands at Greenock, still in use, despite the odds. But it was nowhere to be seen.

I rubbed my eyes, turned away from the water, and stole a glance at the high street. Like many Scottish towns, the houses and shops were constructed from granite and in the early dusk they stood mostly idle. A few places were open — a pub, fish and chip shop, and a local store — but I saw few people.

I was eager to finish the ride and reached into my front pannier for the phone. Mark answered and gave me clear, concise instructions on how to locate the house. He also informed me that a cold beer and spicy meal was waiting my arrival. The house was warm but damp with every radiator on full blast, each one decorated with sodden clothes. I received a warm welcome from my friends, pats on the back, and lots of questions about the route I'd taken.

At that moment, I felt weary but proud. I had no idea how their day had gone but would ask tomorrow when my strength returned. JP walked over with two cold beers and handed one to me. He was keen to talk and for a while we shared snippets of our day. Despite the weariness, I appreciated the gesture, and for a while we laughed as Alan ignited the party.

Despite the antics, laughter and music, I was unable to stay awake for much longer though. It had been a very long day!

Day 10: I Can See Clearly Now

'Life isn't about waiting for the storm to pass. It's about learning to dance in the rain.'

Vivian Greene

I woke early, tiptoed downstairs and headed for the kitchen. Once inside, I closed the door, switched on the kettle, and connected with Fran on Face Time. While she spoke, I wandered to and fro, searching for my gloves. The dining table was strewn with remnants from last night's gathering, and after turning on the light, I discovered my gloves next to a bowl of half-eaten chili. The sudden brightness woke up Colin, who was sprawled on the sofa nearby. He stirred to life, declaring the settee a better option than sharing a bed with Mick.

My gloves felt damp — as were my shoes, which had been placed against a warm radiator along with dank clothes from every other rider. While I walked through the room, Fran asked me a series of questions.

'Why are you whispering? Can't you stop moving for one second? Who's that person wrapped in a blanket standing behind you? Why is it we rarely talk these days, and when we do, you're always distracted?'

It was pointless trying to explain that mornings seemed to race past in a blur. By getting up first, I hoped to be able to chat with her briefly before the ride commenced. Even as she spoke, I heard the rumble of a toilet being flushed, followed by heavy footsteps on the stairs. Alan appeared in the kitchen doorway, bright-eyed and dressed for the road. He waved to the phone while filling the kettle. 'Morning, Fran!' he called out. 'How's life in Australia? You missed a good night here in Scotland.'

During her animated reply, and still holding the phone, I raided the cupboards for provisions and began scoffing a bowl of cereal. Halfway through, the next rider appeared, followed quickly by the others. Each was in a semi-state of dress, and while tea and toast were distributed, they chatted and hunted for dry clothes. I wished Fran goodnight and went outside to assist Nick, who was pulling a bike from the van.

176

A bitter wind tore along the quiet street, quickly forcing me inside again to find another layer to wear. By the time I returned, Colin was checking his bike. He rode up and down the street, making a few adjustments, and when happy, darted inside for breakfast. Mick stood at the doorway, studying the broody clouds massing overhead. 'One thing's for certain — we're going to get wet again today!'

The previous evening, Mark had read out the weather report. There was to be very little sunshine, plenty of showers, and a high chance of heavy rain throughout the day. Today was the one day I *really* hadn't wanted rain. Nick had picked a route that would take us through a glacial valley towards the historic town of Glencoe. We'd ride alongside steep-sided hills and mountains, including The Three Sisters of Glen Coe — a series of steep ridges, leading to the summit of Bidean nam Bian, 3,772 feet high. Subsidiary peaks and rocky outcrops combine to create a spectacular and — at times — dangerous environment.

Scottish peaks have a naming convention and, depending on their height, are categorised into three types. Those 3,000 feet and over are known as Munros, in memory of the Scottish climber, Hugo Munro. He later became Sir Hugo Munro, primarily due to his work — measuring, listing, and naming them all. In September 1891, he published his findings in the Scottish Mountaineering Journal, and ever since, his table of 283 Munros has been the cause of debate. This is mainly due to the lack of distinction between the mountaintops and the subsidiary high points that form a part of the peak.

Over the years, the official numbers have altered slightly. One mountain, called Sgurr nan Ceannaichean, was found to be three feet short of the magical number. The official figure now stands at 282. However, despite minor technicalities, the project was deemed a major success — not only in topography terms, but also as a means of promoting the Highlands of Scotland.

In a similar feat, John Rooke Corbett, a later member of the Scottish Mountaineering Club, listed another set of peaks. They were those with a height of 2,500 feet or more and less than 3,000 feet. This was mostly accomplished in the gap between the two World Wars. Unlike Munros, Corbetts must have a drop of at least 500 feet on all sides.

Finally, there are the Grahams. Initially, the hills between 2,000 and 2,499 feet were known as the lesser Corbetts, but after Fiona Torbet (nee Graham) undertook extensive research and published an accurate list in 1992, the name was changed in appreciation.

Knowing that Scotland has hundreds of Munros, Corbetts and Grahams does sound daunting. But it's the Munros that gain most of the attention. With so many of them in remote and appealing locations, it's inevitable that outdoor enthusiasts follow in the footsteps of Sir Hugo. The pastime of trekking to the top of each one has been termed Munro-bagging and the ultimate aim is to scale them all.

I've bagged a few in the past, but as I now live in Australia, my tally hasn't moved in years. Earlier in the book, I introduced you to three men — Fast Dave, Slow Dave, and the Android – who are actively engaged in bagging every Munro. I have no idea how many they have completed so far, but at their current pace, it will be a few more years before they finish!

The idea of bagging a new Munro did cross my mind when we crossed into Scotland. But with each mile travelled, the reality hit home that — although minor deviations were possible — scaling a Munro during a ten-hour ride was pushing the boundaries of sanity. Instead, my aim at Glencoe was to take photos of the craggy peaks while standing alongside coachloads of tourists in the lookout bay.

The sound of Nick's voice snapped me back to reality. He'd adjusted the brakes and was asking if I'd like to try out the bike before the rain set in. I sensed that departure was imminent. JP was already loading water bottles onto his bike, smiling too widely for such a dreary morning.

'Looks like the early night sorted you out, Ali,' he said. 'But I reckon we're about to get wet. Nick thinks we should get moving soon as there's a chance of storms this afternoon.'

A few whirlwind minutes, and we were prepared for the long day ahead. Each rider was either going up or down the stairs, and in or out of the bathroom. There was no sign of the girls though, and even Nick gave up the chance to wave us off, mumbling something about a warm bed before closing the front door.

Maybe it was the overcast sky, or because some riders had celebrated into the late hours, but — whatever the reason — as Mark took the lead, we set off silently in single file. At the end of the street, we turned left, then freewheeled towards the town centre. Directly ahead lay the River Clyde — wide, dark, and uninviting. Through gaps in the mist, the wind stirred the oily waters and far in the distance, a dark smudge of land signalled the shipyards of Greenock.

The road led us down to the banks of the river, and after turning right, we headed out of town. Apart from a lone jogger and a few parked cars, the waterfront looked deserted. The fish and chip shop, pubs and cafes were closed, with little sign of life apart from the sound of our wheels on the wet bitumen. Far across the water, a narrow band of light momentarily illuminated Greenock, its giant crane faintly visible. When I next looked up, it was gone.

During the first hour, we narrowly avoided a downpour and watched the rain fall in turrets across the water. We were no longer riding beside the River Clyde, but a wide inlet known as Gare Loch. The sight of a newsagent in the village of Rhu prompted requests from many riders for an early stop to purchase food and hot drinks. After dismounting, I thought back to all the funky coffee shops we'd dashed past on warm summer days to get to our destination. Now, on the coldest morning so far, with rain imminent, we chose a windswept, desolate shop.

The girl inside didn't look inspired by the expansive river view from her counter window. She greeted us curtly as we ambled inside and stood shoulder to shoulder in the close confines. She was about eighteen, in need of a good meal, with pinched cheeks and thin lips. Her auburn hair fell on slender shoulders, and as we searched the aisles, she flicked through the pages of a fashion magazine.

Unable to find anything worthwhile to eat, Alan stepped towards the counter. 'Morning! I don't suppose you do tea, do you?'

She pointed to a portable coffee machine, positioned by a window sill. Her voice was barely a mutter. 'You can make yourself tea or instant coffee, and its £2 a cup.'

'Excellent,' Alan said. 'Any chance of a freshly baked pie or sausage roll as well?'

She pointed to a shelf, stacked with packets of biscuits and mass-produced cakes. 'We dunnee do pies. It's no' a bakery, it's a newsagent with a coffee maker and a water boiler.'

'Six teas will be fine then please,' he said, with a slight raise of the eyebrows.

The drinks were piping hot, which should have offered some comfort, but the thin plastic beakers soon began warping. A passing shower splattered against the window, prompting us to stay a while, but when JP attempted small talk with the cashier, he was met with gruff replies. Instead, we ventured outside and huddled by the doorway, staring at the water as it lapped against the shingle.

While we sipped tea, gulls swept overhead, seemingly unaffected by the blustery conditions. Colin finished his drink first, crushing the plastic before dropping it into a bin. 'Come on, lads, it's a long way to Fort William. Rain is on the way and I'm not hanging around here.'

From the doorway of the shop front, it was hard to imagine we were in close proximity to Her Majesty's Naval Base, known as HMNB Clyde. The site was chosen for numerous reasons. Isolation is one, and the other is because the deep channel is perfect for storing submarines. These aren't run-of-the-mill vessels, but the Vanguard-class, capable of carrying up to eight Trident ballistic missiles and forty warheads.

Where there are nuclear bombs, there are those wishing to ban them, and near the village of Faslane, you'll find the longest running peace camp in the world. Set up to take action against the weapons, the group of activists live in what can be described as a hippy commune and have been doing so for over thirty years. We passed the camp not long after finishing our tea. It is set in woodland, surrounded by a fence, each picket a different colour to the next.

Through gaps in the foliage, I noticed caravans, tents, and awnings. Some were decorated in peace and love slogans; others were painted pink or orange. A banner was strewn between two trees, marking the entrance. Written in bold were the words, *Say No to the Trident*. Apart from the anti-nuclear symbols painted on the buildings, the location resembled the morning after a folk concert. There was little sign of life, apart from children playing on the grass.

That's not to say the residents aren't active at other times. Over the years, they've campaigned hard to promote their cause. In March 2014, two volunteers broke inside the naval facility and succeeded in getting on board the HMS Ambush — an Astute-class, nuclear-powered submarine.

Considering the rise in armed militancy across the globe, I was confident the broken fence had since been repaired. The military buildings nearest to the road resembled prison cells, with few windows and grey, concrete walls. The high, steel fence was ringed by barbed wire, and CCTV cameras, pointing in multiple directions, were positioned along its length. Just in case there was any doubt that the facility was off limits, numerous signs declared that photos and people were strictly prohibited.

After passing the base, the road edged away from the water, forcing us higher into swirling mist and sideways rain. It stifled any conversation. There was little to do but maintain the pace with the front riders and dig deep as the wind howled across the escarpment. Luckily, there were few cars, and very soon we were following the eastern edge of Loch Long. From the roadside, the lake was hard to view, either hidden behind trees or obscured by showers. When I looked again, the lake had vanished, and for a short while, we headed silently inland.

The next sighting of water caused a stir of excitement. JP rode alongside, pointing into the distance. 'Ali, there's Loch Lomond!'

It didn't look as bonny as I remembered from my first visit, as a teenager. There is something about rain, grey skies, cold, and hunger that diminishes the experience when you gaze on a location that once took your breath away.

Loch Lomond is the largest inland stretch of water in Great Britain, measures approximately twenty-four miles in length, and is up to five miles wide. It's dotted with twenty-two named islands, one of which is home to 'wild' wallabies. The marsupials on Inchconnachan were introduced in the 1940s by the landowner, Lady Arran, and have managed to survive, oblivious to the fact that they could be sunning themselves Down Under.

Loch Lomond forms part of Trossachs National Park, which encompasses a total area of 720 square miles. The fault line, which divides the low lands from the high lands, cuts through the park and rewards visitors with a wide choice of environments to explore. From wooded nooks to rolling hills and distant mountains, the loch and surrounding countryside hold a special place for many Scots. Over the centuries, it has managed to weave its way into folklore. Close to its shores, battles have been fought and hearts won over. Poets have searched for words and travellers have stopped to gaze.

There is even a song about Loch Lomond. Its origins are unknown and there are numerous interpretations about the meaning of the words. There are those who believe it is a love song and others who feel that it is connected to folklore. One legend suggests that if a native of Scotland dies outside of the country, their spirit will be transported home along the low road. Another theory is that it is about two captured rebels from the Jacobite uprising of 1745. One escaped and managed to take the high road back to Scotland. The English army executed the other, but the fairy people transported his spirit back to Scotland via the low road.

Ye'll tak' the high road and I'll tak' the low road
And I'll be in Scotland a'fore ye
Where me and my true love will never meet again
On the bonny, bonny banks of Loch Lomond

We didn't have the option of a low or high road. There was only the one, hugging the western edge of the loch. Far to our right, despite the consistent drizzle, tourist boats braved the choppy water while we stayed close to the verge in an effort to keep clear of passing traffic. The front riders continually threatened to pull ahead, and after losing sight of them around a series of bends, I rallied JP to catch up.

We found them minutes later, except for Colin, who we learned had raced ahead, intent on reaching Fort William before the expected storm. Although we rode in tight formation, the culmination of rain, winding roads, constant traffic, and a feisty wind eroded all chances of talking. Suddenly, without understanding of when or how it happened, JP and I were alone. For many miles, we pushed hard, but no matter how fast we rode, the other riders were nowhere to be seen. Not that it was critical. JP had his bike computer, and there was little chance of getting lost with the lake at our side.

Instead, we took it in turns to take the lead, bid farewell to Loch Lomond, and headed north through undulating country, broken by woodland, rivers, and streams. A break in the weather coincided with the chance to take a detour to view the Falls of Falloch. Dismounting, we entered the edge of a forest and pushed our bikes along a muddy track. The roar of the falls grew louder as we followed the trail onto a bridge, its sides and top covered in mesh. The water fell in turrets, making conversation difficult as we watched it cascade down the sheer sides of the rock into an angry pool. From there, it calmed before tumbling through a series of rocky beds to become a tributary for Loch Lomond.

By the time we resumed the journey, the rain had lifted and we talked of food. We rode as partners, pulling the back rider along, then changing places when the pace began hurting. At times, we shared tales of each other's lives, learning snippets as the miles vanished. We were convinced that we'd meet the main pack again, as they'd have to eat soon, and up until now there'd been nowhere to stop.

At a major intersection, JP turned around to check for traffic, swung his right arm out, and prepared for a turning towards Crianlarich. I sensed it was an unplanned move, so I shouted into the wind, 'Where are you going?'

He replied immediately. 'There's a train station nearby. It might have a café. The lads will probably be there.'

The road dipped, allowing us to freewheel until we came to a stop by the tracks. As befitting a remote location, the station was nothing more than a series of low buildings. There seemed little sign of life and no parked bikes. JP looked at me, the smile suddenly wiped from his muddied face. 'Can you believe it? There's no café or other bikes. Now we're miles behind again.'

I patted him on the back. 'Welcome to my world, JP. I'll race you to the top.'

The diversion had been short in distance but costly in time. We laboured up the incline, then returned to the A82. Twenty minutes later, we followed a sign for the Artisan Café and Art Studio, located along a slip road, and were rewarded for our efforts. Parked outside were only three bikes, confirming Colin was still riding solo to Fort William. The outside resembled the features of a small chapel, complete with an arched entrance and stout wooden door. The interior was framed by a high-pitched roof, and each wall was home to a range of paintings, prints, and artefacts. They were all for sale, and most had small print outs adjacent to each item, describing the artist and their inspiration to create.

The homely aroma of pea and ham soup filled the room, but it wasn't only broth on the menu. There was a wide selection of meals, sandwiches and wraps, made with local ingredients when possible. They even had blueberry muffins, each one bursting from its bake-proof wrapper. The two women behind the counter greeted us warmly, then guided us through the choices. After ordering, we stripped off our sodden tops and sat alongside Alan, Mark and Mick.

They'd already enjoyed lunch and were washing it down with hot drinks. We chatted about the rain, our late arrival, and Colin's decision to cycle to Fort William in the shortest time possible. In a way it made sense, as the morning had been a washout with few opportunities to enjoy each other's company.

The food was too tasty to rush, and the others waited outside while we ordered coffee. Before leaving, I browsed the stands and chose a print of a Highland Cow, sketched by a Scottish artist called Sarah Speight. This breed of cow is renowned for its long horns, placid nature, and ruffled hair, but I was yet to see one since arriving in Scotland. Speight had captured the mischievous cow perfectly, its long red hair and wet nose framed against a white background.

While it was being wrapped, I enquired about the café and its history. I learnt that the church was once called Strathfillan and last used as a place of worship in 2000. After extensive renovations, it became known as the Artisan Café. The name was chosen by the owners (Diane and Donna) who had always wanted to run a business that sold wholesome food and local crafts. The café also runs numerous courses, including candle-making, needle-felting, and children's craft.

Diane handed my package over. 'Take it easy on the road to Glencoe. The coaches get close, and car drivers are too absorbed in the mountains to think about cyclists. Mind you, on a day like today, there'll not be much to see.'

By the time we left, the rain had eased, which gave us the chance to ride and talk at the same time. Mark enquired about my gift, which was now jammed inside the rear panniers, and each of us estimated how far Colin had travelled.

An hour later, just after we'd skirted the glacial waters of Loch Tulla, I hit the wall. Initially, it was just a slight incline, but as the angle increased, so did the gap between me and the second last rider. In an effort to catch them, I reached into my panniers and ripped open a Mars Bar, chomping through the chocolate with little manners, but the sugar fix had little impact. Within minutes, they were no more than luminescent specks, inching away with each revolution.

By the time I caught them up, they'd all dismounted and were standing on a strip of land, converted into a car park and lookout. I hoped no one would ask any questions as I sucked in lungfuls of air. The riders were swigging on water and I noticed Nick and the girls amongst the group. A rare burst of sunshine prompted calls for a photo-shoot, and as the mist dispersed, a pearl shaped loch was revealed, glistening far below and nestled behind a pocket of woodland.

We set off again, Nick and the girl's behind, waving as they drove past us towards Fort William. With each mile, my strength faded. By the time we reached the turnoff for the Glencoe ski lift, I knew it was time to let them go. Since leaving the café, they'd already lowered their speed to cater for my needs.

At least, from here, there was no way I could get lost and instead of struggling to keep up, I craved the chance to ride at a moderate pace. They wished me luck and sped ahead. I felt a sense of relief, knowing I was no longer holding anyone back.

The first thing I did was dismount by the Glencoe ski lodge sign. I lay against one of the flag poles and devoured two muesli bars. Then, I weighed up my options. Now I was alone, there seemed to be so many things I wanted to do. My main aim was to ride to Fort William before the next deluge. But weather forecasts in Scotland are not always accurate. There are many variables to consider. One side of a mountain could be bathed in sunshine while the other side is belted by horizontal rain.

One thing that had niggled me since leaving Land's End was the lack of GoPro footage I'd managed to capture. Most had been from the vantage of my bike helmet, which had two main disadvantages. The first was that I was often at the back, which meant the material was mainly of JP's rear wheel. The second problem was that I was rarely in any of the footage. This wasn't helpful, especially when trying to convince the Guinness World Records that *I* was the one on the long book tour.

I now had the perfect opportunity and location to make amends. I spotted a side road, which looked as though it led deep into the Highlands. There was no signpost and it was too narrow for coaches. It looked perfect. I followed it for a few hundred yards, suppressing the urge to keep going as it threaded scenically through gaps in the hills.

I placed the camera on the ground, hoping to capture the peaks in the background while I rode back and forth in front of the lens. Initially I was worried that a car would turn into the road from the A82 and run the camera over. But with each attempt, I grew braver and eventually placed the GoPro in the centre of the road. This time I rode past it at speed and headed into the wilderness, smiling at the folly and determined not to look behind.

During this period, the mist and clouds began to ebb, revealing the true wonder of my surroundings. But I was conscious of time and the thought of evening rain, so I packed away the camera and headed back towards the road.

Just before the junction, a car pulled into the verge and a man got out to take photos. As we were the only two people around, it seemed rude not to make conversation.

'It's a magical location, isn't it?' he said.

His voice was distinctively English and I replied, 'Oh, yes. I can't believe the clouds are finally lifting. I've been hoping for this all day.'

He nodded in appreciation and ventured onto a mound of grass for a better angle. He was nearly six feet tall with unkempt hair, which tousled in the wind as he peered through the viewfinder. He was dressed for the office, wearing leather shoes, tailored trousers, and a recently ironed shirt.

Eager to assist, I said, 'Do you want me to take a photo with you and the mountain?'

He looked over and smiled. 'No, that's fine, mate. I live just down the road, but as you can probably tell, I'm not from Scotland. I moved here a few years ago, and since then, I've taken hundreds of photos of The Three Sisters but still can't drive past without taking another. The scenery changes every day. Sometimes the mountains are broody, like today. When the sun shines or when they're bathed in snow, there's no better sight in the world.'

We spoke for a while longer, which led to my own story and the quest to get to Fort William. Then he said, 'I won't ever be considered a local, but I can give you some advice. The road from here to Glencoe is notoriously dangerous, because of the tourist traffic. Look out for the alternative route instead. It's far quieter, and if you look carefully you might see the site where they located Hagrid's Hut for the Harry Potter movie. It's just past the Clachaig Inn.'

I thanked the man and set off. To my left, The Three Sisters dominated the landscape, and just like the tourists driving past, I couldn't steal my eyes away from them. The steep-sided buttresses glistened as water cascaded down each chasm. Far above, swirling mist wafted across the craggy ridgeline, giving fleeting glances of the false summit.

With so many tourists arriving by car, campervan and coach, it was inevitable I should find a place to stop. I stood close to the other visitors, listening to the wail of bagpipes, and after donating a coin, I managed to take a picture of the piper, framed perfectly in front of a faraway waterfall. I then clambered onto a nearby boulder to enjoy an apple.

The musician was warming up the pipes again, prompting me to stay longer. I recognised the first note and instantly thought back to dad, as the song had been one of his favourites. As the haunting sounds of Danny Boy echoed across the glen, I thought back to the precious times we'd spent in Scotland together.

I smiled at the tourists, ushering their children in front of the kilted piper for photos, and closed my eyes. I was happy for the chance to rest, and to enjoy the weak sunshine on my face. I mimed the words in time with the music.

'Oh, Danny boy, the pipes, the pipes are calling
From glen to glen and down the mountain side.
The summer's gone, and all the roses falling
It's you, it's you must go, and I must bide.'
[Frederic Weatherly]

During the gradual descent towards Glencoe, a broken-down vehicle caused a temporary traffic jam, resulting in a coach driving slowly beside me. As its wheels whipped up water from the road, I chanced a glance at the passengers.

I recognised a few from my time with the bagpipe player. When the bus sped up, I caught sight of two children, their wide eyes peering through the rear window. I gave them a wave and received a fit of silent giggles before they ducked behind their seats.

I took the quieter road towards Glencoe and passed a building on my left called the Clachaig Inn. A series of wooden chalets are set at a right angle to the main structure, its stone exterior painted a brilliant white. It looked perfect for those searching for comfort in a wild environment.

Just beyond The Inn, I passed the location mentioned by the Englishman where Hagrid's Hut may once have stood. Although there was no sign of a pumpkin patch or any remnants of a wooden shack, I could see why the setting would have been chosen. Its encroaching hills and narrow road meandered towards a wooded valley. I arrived in the village of Glencoe at the same time as another downpour. Instead of searching for a café, I raided my provisions, found a squashed banana, and kept on cycling.

The rain had managed to seep through every gap in my clothes, and with decreased visibility, all enthusiasm waned. I departed Glencoe and the surrounding mountains with weary legs, a grumbling stomach, and a strong urge to return another day. This too would make it to the list.

I raised my hand in relief while passing the Fort William sign and instantly began searching for the name of our accommodation among the small, detached hotels overlooking the loch. They all looked welcoming, some displaying vacancy signs. I stopped beside a parade of guest houses, all offering complimentary tea and coffee. It was time to call Mark.

He answered on the second ring and asked where I was. In the remote hope that he was close by, I said, 'I've made it into town, and if you pop your head outside, I'll probably see you. I'm surrounded by accommodation.'

I heard him laugh. 'I've got bad news, mate. Do you remember the hostel you stayed in twenty years ago with Alan and Nick?'

'Yes, of course. How could I forget? Nick hated it.'

'Well, he thinks the one we're in now is even shabbier.'

'Are we booked into a hostel?'

'Yes, it's written on the agenda.'

I reached into the front pannier, rummaged around, and pulled out the damp leaflet. As I read the name of the hostel, Mark gave detailed directions and explained I still had a few more miles to cover. Then he said, 'On the plus side, it's close to the Caledonian canal, which we'll be riding alongside in the morning. Hurry up if you can. We're all hungry but want to wait for you. At least you won't be distracted by Ben Nevis.'

When the call ended, I looked across town to where the peak loomed. But instead of appreciating the highest mountain in Britain, with the prominent scar made by the boots of thousands of walkers, all I could see were dappled clouds, encroaching from the hills. I clambered onto the bike a final time, forcing stiff leg muscles into action, and blinked away the rain. It had taken eleven hours to arrive, but I rode past the gift shops, historic hotels, and welcoming pubs without a glance.

Nick was outside the hostel when I arrived and greeted me with a pat on the back before stowing my bike in the van. He handed over my overnight bag, pointed to the front door and said, 'I chose a hostel, as I know you enjoy them.'

The receptionist wore a baggy woollen jumper, hung low over wide hips, and greeted me with a scowl. 'We don't allow parties in the dormitories, or loud music. If you get back after midnight, there's a call out fee, as the main door will be locked. In the morning, put all your sheets and towels into the basket by the door. Failure to comply will mean we have the right to charge your credit card. You're in dormitory number two with the others. There's a shower down the hallway, but don't hog it. Others in the hostel also need hot water.'

I smiled weakly. 'You're so kind. I've been on the road all day and it's comforting to hear such words.'

Without waiting for a reply, I hauled myself upstairs, eager to shower, before changing into dry clothes. Alan stood by the door of our room, studying a bus timetable, and greeted me with a handshake. He was freshly shaved, dressed in smart jeans, a T-shirt, and a waterproof jacket.

'Top man, Ali. I knew you'd be here before midnight! Did you manage to bag any Munros in our absence? We'll be waiting in the foyer. There's a bus into town in fifteen minutes.'

They all marched past me, one by one, with handshakes, pats on the back, and calls to, 'Be quick!' ringing in my ears.

After managing a smile, I grabbed a towel and found the shower. The door handle refused to budge. I rattled it impatiently and heard a deep voice from behind the panelled door.

'You'll have to wait, the shower's taken.'

Day 11: Caledonia

'Believe in yourself, even when no one else does.'
Harvey Mackay

'Sebastian, how many people do you know that have searched for the Loch Ness Monster?'

My ten-year-old son rolled his eyes and put down his toast.

'Dad, you won't have time to look for the Loch Ness Monster during your bike ride. Anyway, you must know it's not real.'

Before I could muster a worthy reply, Noah, my eldest, spoke up. Being two years older than Sebastian and feeling somewhat wiser, he informed me between mouthfuls of porridge that Loch Ness was the deepest lake in Britain. He also mentioned that explorers have searched the loch for years with no confirmed proof of a monster. I nodded in agreement, ruffled his soft curls and reminded them both that there was always a glimmer of hope.

Silence descended around the breakfast table, broken by the sound of Fran. 'Good on you for considering a swim, but it sounds a bit eccentric and the water will probably be freezing! All we really want, is for you to return home safely.'

Her voice trailed away, and suddenly I sensed the emotion in the room. Within forty-eight hours, I'd be on a plane bound for Ireland and it was finally hitting home. I tried to lighten the atmosphere by explaining the plan.

'After a few days in Ireland with Uncle Michael, I'll be refreshed and raring to go. Then I'll head over to England to start the ride. Hopefully it will be a nice, bright day when we reach Loch Ness. Maybe we'll have lunch by the shore, then I'll change and take a swim before we carry on the ride.'

Sebastian finished the last of his scrambled eggs, eager to talk. 'But Dad, the chances of finding the monster in that short amount of time are so small. It isn't worth the effort. Plus, it probably won't be deep enough near the edge.'

My expression turned serious for a moment. 'Of course, it's a silly venture, but it's also an opportunity I may never get again. We live a long way away from Scotland, and for me, it's important. Not to find the monster, but to have a mini adventure during my epic one.' My smile broke out again. 'The main problem I face at the moment, though, is that I haven't got any goggles.'

Noah dashed to his room, returning moments later with a pair of his own goggles and twirling the blue straps around his fingers. I stretched them around my head, causing a few chuckles as the undersized rims pinched my eye sockets. For a few moments, I pretended to swim, pulling my arms back in mock simulation, but the laughs soon vanished. Even the dog looked unimpressed, lying on the floor, watching with hopeful eyes and waiting for his walk.

I knew the idea of searching for the monster was absurd. Expensive studies have failed to find a sniff of the mythical creature and it's statistically proven not to exist. Still, it was worth a shot.

George Mallory the English mountaineer was once asked why he wanted to climb Mount Everest. The first three words of his reply to the New York Times reporter are now immortal. *Because it's there.* Of course, my mission to swim in the loch was miniscule compared to Mallory's heroic quest. But it followed the same logic, because — for a short while — it would be there. Within my grasp. It was as simple as that.

A few weeks later, not long after arriving at the hostel in Fort William, we headed into town on a public bus. During the meandering route through the outer suburbs of Fort William, the rain-streaked windows gave few clues as to what lay outside. Most passengers wore jackets, and some stopped by the door to shake raindrops from their umbrellas before greeting the driver.

Our arrival in town coincided with a lull in the showers, and most passengers disembarked simultaneously. It meant lots of company along the pedestrianised walkway, even though most shops were closed. Although I did chance a look along the way, our thoughts were on food, not memorabilia. Compared to the niche offerings on sale in the Artisan Café, most souvenirs here looked mass-produced. As expected, there were woolen garments, cuddly sheep, and glossy landscape prints. One shop setting even displayed a female mannequin, dressed in tartan, complete with sporran and dancing shoes.

There was no shortage of pubs to choose from, but the menu at the Ben Nevis Bar held the most appeal. Most tables were taken, and our waitress had little time for small talk as she whisked through the room taking orders. Most of us chose steak and all ate well.

Before leaving town, we were keen to experience one more pub. Nearby, we found The Grog and Gruel — an old-fashioned alehouse offering cask ales and local whiskies. A large, black and white print of a highland cow adorned one wall, alongside another of a lonely road inhabited by a single sheep. Dark wood panels and soft lighting added to the ambience, which tempted us to try their local ales. On any normal night, we'd have stayed longer to chat with the locals and overseas visitors. But tonight we were end-to-enders with a big day ahead. Before midnight, we headed home, this time by taxi.

Hours later, I woke with a jolt to movement from the upper bunk. It was Alan. If he was stirring, it was time to rise. My head was pounding. Not from a hangover but nausea and lack of sleep. Sleeping in a cramped dormitory with seven grown men, windows and door firmly closed, sure was testing. Earplugs would have helped keep out the noise from their groans and flatulence, but I'd forgotten to wear them and had paid the price.

Alan dropped silently from the top bunk, grabbed a towel and headed straight for the shower. Knowing there was just one toilet in our corridor, I rolled from the bed and scrambled into the corridor. When I returned to our room, the light was on and someone had drawn back the heavy curtains.

I peered out of the nearest window, expecting to see grey but hoping for blue. At least it wasn't raining. As I opened the curtains wider, each rider stirred to life. Very soon, we were sharing jokes about carnal noises, earthy smells, and grown men in cramped spaces.

'Lads, you need to leave by seven thirty,' Nick called out. 'An early start will hopefully give us a few hours to relax in Inverness. Ali, are you with us today? Or are you planning any more diversions?'

I replied brightly. 'I'll definitely be with you until Loch Ness. After that, who can say? I'm planning on taking a dip.'

Mick stopped packing. 'Are you serious? It'll be freezing!'

'Yes, quite serious. But let's see how we go. If it's lashing down with rain, it might be a different story.'

Breakfast was a sparse affair, consisting of tea, instant coffee, toast, jam and yoghurt. Considering the low cost of the accommodation, no one expected anything different.

Throughout the trip, I'd been impressed with the crew's ability to prepare quickly for each journey, and this morning was no different. The next few minutes were a frantic scramble to rub nappy cream onto my inflamed nether regions, clean my teeth, pull on my Lycra outfit, fill up two water bottles, add isotonic tablets, and unplug the GoPro camera. I also grabbed my goggles from my luggage and transferred them to my panniers, along with a set of bathers.

I ran down stairs in a state of semi-dress. They were already lined up and ready to depart. I held up my phone to display the time.

'It's seven thirty-two. What are we waiting for?'

It was time to find the Caledonian Canal. In 1803, an Act of Parliament authorised the construction of the canal, which was overseen by the Scottish Civil Engineer, Thomas Telford. At the time of its construction, during the 19th century, it gained recognition for its state of the art design, using advanced engineering techniques. Its purpose was to provide a direct link between the east and west coasts of Scotland, shaving off valuable time for merchant seaman.

It also meant the dangers of the open sea, where French pirates waited to plunder, could be avoided. Described as one of the great waterways of the world, the canal runs from coast to coast between Corpach (near Fort William) and Inverness. It officially opened in 1822 at a cost of £910,000 and boasts twenty-nine locks, four aqueducts and ten bridges.

It didn't take long for us to appreciate Telford's work. Within minutes of leaving the hostel, we crossed a small bridge that took us to the longest staircase lock in Britain. From the bottom, Neptune's Staircase resembles a man-made waterfall, blocked by a series of black gates. Each one is wide enough to walk across, with white handrails attached across the tops. We cycled parallel with the eight locks for 500 yards, each one higher than the last by about 70 feet.

The staircase was empty when we rode up the gentle incline, but when in use, a vessel takes ninety minutes to pass through the system. We took just a few. With a direct link between Fort William and Inverness, the towpath alongside the canal created a logical route for the first part of our journey. Very soon we were riding past moored boats, their occupants still resting behind closed curtains. We'd set off silently, but as ever, at a steady pace. The cool weather cleared my head and it was with a sense of relief I was able to slot into the centre of the pack.

The canal and its occupants finally began to stir, but the day was too young to slow down or stop, despite the opportunities around us. I wanted to capture those intricate moments that you sometimes experience when travelling. A family of swans, silhouetted by a carpet of mist, paddling across the water, would have made a lovely photo. But to stop would have cost us time and distance. An elderly man, waving from a moored boat looked an intriguing character to share tea and stories with. But we carried on cycling past.

Sometime during mid-morning, we came across a holiday camp billboard, advertising luxury accommodation close to the water and the chance for a cup of tea. We diverted from the road into a woodland setting, dotted with pine cabins. It was high summer, but apart from two men carrying a canoe, the complex looked deserted. We located reception and rattled the door to the adjacent café, but it refused to budge. Mark put his face to the window, peered inside and saw nothing but darkness. It was time to raid our supply of energy bars.

As we set off again, Mark pulled a piece of paper from his pocket and began firing questions at us. We had to guess the band, singer or title from the excerpt of a song, and for the next hour, as we called out answers, our minds were focused on music, not on food.

A bystander would have enjoyed the scene, watching and listening as six cyclists emerged from the mist, riding alongside the canal. The one at the front, dressed in a bright red waterproof, would call out a lyric above the clatter of wheels on the track, and a rider would answer with a shout. After a few minutes, they would be no more than fluorescent specks far in the distance, and the canal would revert to a place of solitude.

The first clue that we were approaching civilisation was the re-emergence of litter, strewn across the path. They were not large objects, such as abandoned shopping trolleys, but small items, including chocolate wrappers and discarded leaflets advertising boat trips, trodden into the ground.

There were other clues too, such as a solitary dog walker, followed shortly by more dog walkers. Then came the sight of slated rooftops, jutting above the tree line. We passed a canal boat, moored to the bank, and further along found many more. The dog-leg path led us through a wood, and when we emerged, the scene had changed. Suddenly there were people everywhere.

Some held umbrellas and others carried small children, while an assortment of crowded boats chugged lazily along the water. Tourists took photos, watching clouds as well as boats, and families wandered the path, mindful of their little ones getting too close to the edge. Signs were pinned to posts and onto buildings. Some displayed advice or rules and regulations. *No mooring past this point*, or, *Discard your litter responsibly.* Others displayed a call to action. *Keep Scotland clean and say no to litter.* Then, I saw an advertisement, posted on the window of a canal boat. *Explore the canal on a two-hour cruise. Please take a leaflet and call today.*

We'd arrived in the settlement of Fort Augustus, located partway between Fort William and Inverness. It is strategically positioned at the southwestern edge of Loch Ness, and reachable by boat, past a series of locks. The village is an ideal resting place for those walking the Great Glen Way, which stretches from coast to coast, across the Highlands for over 70 miles. Although we hadn't yet met many trekkers, we'd ridden on sections of the route all morning.

We dismounted and made our way towards a lock. The boat in transition was a tall ship named TS Royalist, and before crossing the narrow swing bridge, I stopped to watch it pass. The crew was dressed smartly in red tunics, and each wore a white sailor's cap with a black rim. Apart from the adult crew, most on board were sea cadets. During my youth, I'd also been a cadet and had known friends lucky enough to sail on tall ships.

My time as a sea cadet was hampered by the fact that I lived many hours from the sea. After three years of participation at the Lakeside Headquarters (every Friday after school), I still hadn't learned to sail and eventually gave up on a life at sea. The cadets on board the TS Royalist looked far happier than I'd ever been in a sailor's uniform. With the gates sealed and water rising, the ship fitted snuggly into the lock.

We crossed over the narrow swing bridge and walked along the port side of the ship. A female cadet stood on the bank, watching her friends on board, and I ventured nearer to talk. She was about fifteen years old with a confident smile and sunburnt cheeks. She explained they were on a five-day voyage, including their time at sea. I mentioned my time as a cadet, but she hadn't heard of TS Keyes.

She lived in Edinburgh and was a novice tall ship sailor, as were most other cadets on board, all from various parts of Britain. After crossing Loch Ness, they were bound for Fort William. The crew were oblivious to our land adventure and we knew nothing about theirs. For a few moments we were in close proximity, six cyclists cycling from one end of the country to the other, and a deck full of eager cadets in search of their own adventure.

Fort Augustus has a miniature cappuccino strip, which is located alongside the canal. Each café offers fine views of the water and most were enjoying brisk trade. We picked one at random and joined a small line of tourists waiting to order. When the food arrived, I sat with Mark and together we watched the tourist's come and go.

Damp rucksacks lay against a corner wall while their owners sat nearby, studying a walking guidebook. A passing shower chased in two grey-haired old ladies, and Mark steered them towards some empty seats. I reached for my bike helmet, prompting the waitress to ask if we were cycling.

'Yes,' I replied proudly, 'there's a few more of us outside. We're on our way to John O'Groats.'

'That sounds like fun. Will you be staying in Inverness?'

'Yes, and I might even take a dip in the loch on the way. I know it sounds a bit silly, but I live in Australia and it's not every day I get the chance to swim with Nessie.'

'It sounds perfectly fine to me. Mind you, it'll be cold. But I guess you know that already. If you don't find the real monster, you can always head into Drumnadrochit and take a picture of the model one.'

I'd forgotten about the sculptured Nessie, but the memory flooded back in an instant. I was in my earlier thirties, standing alongside the clay monster with my sister, Alice. The previous day we'd trekked to the summit of Ben Nevis with friends and family. I remember Alice's surprise at seeing pockets of snow in early summer. But north-facing gullies, high on Ben Nevis, are often deprived of sunshine.

The climb had been Alice's first and last Munro. A few years later, she died in a house fire. I tell friends I think about her every day. But at that moment, near the doorway of the café, it suddenly struck me that she hadn't been in my thoughts since Land's End.

'Are you alright, dear?'

I blinked away the thoughts of Alice and smiled at the waitress. 'I'm fine, thanks. Just daydreaming. Thanks for the tip on the alternative monster. I think it's time to pay him a visit.'

While I clipped up my chinstrap, she called out. 'You cannee miss the village. It's on the main road between here and Inverness.'

Mark overheard the final part of the conversation and smiled knowingly. 'Are you taking another diversion, Ali?'

'It seems that way, but don't worry. I'll get to Inverness tonight — no matter what.'

'I guess you're taking the low road again. We're taking the remote track on the other side of the loch. It would be lovely if you stayed with us, but somehow, I feel you're on a different type of journey. Am I right?'

When I nodded, he patted me on the back. 'Remember, you have my number so keep me posted and don't talk to strangers! I'll see you in Inverness.'

I bid them all farewell and went off in search of the monster. After crossing over the main swing bridge, I kept the loch to my right and followed the signs for Inverness. The single road stayed close to the waterline, offering panoramic views of the loch. During the journey I could understand why — despite the scientific data, hypothesising no such creature exists — visitors must feel a glimmer of hope they'll spot something mysterious in the water. In between dodging pot holes and listening for the familiar drone of tourist coaches, I found myself searching for a sea creature, rising from the depths.

My attention was soon diverted by a backlog of cars, waiting to pull into a car park. I spotted an attendant, assisting a campervan driver to reverse out of a tight spot. As the driver tooted his horn in acknowledgement and drove away, the attendant directed the next waiting vehicle into the vacant space. There were people and cars everywhere. I saw mums pushing buggies, heard the familiar jingle of an ice cream van, and noticed tourists with cameras at the ready. I stopped alongside the attendant, who was in conversation by two-way radio with a colleague.

I waited for a pause and asked, 'Excuse me, but why are there so many people here?'

He smiled half-heartedly, revealing a perfect row of dentures. 'They're here to visit Urquhart Castle.'

My blank look told him everything, until he pointed towards the loch. 'Can you see it? It's been there for centuries and is one of the most famous in Scotland.'

Urquhart Castle is strategically positioned on a section of headland, close to the loch. Even from afar, I could see many sections had survived the elements — and the ravages of time. The outer walls were mostly intact and the main turret stood proud against the water's edge. A wide expanse of velvet lawn stretched from the road to the distant gates, broken by a narrow footpath, filled with summertime visitors.

As I continued to stare, the attendant spoke again. 'It's hundreds of years old and has seen many battles, mainly between the English and Scots.'

He pointed towards the low-lying hills across the lake. 'Many of the clans, like the MacDonalds, wanted possession. They fought to the death to claim it.'

His green eyes flared with pride, but the spell was broken by the call of his radio. He ignored it though and kept his attention on me. 'Laddee, she's a grand old castle that's for sure, but you'll have to pay a grand old fee to visit her.' Then, he turned wearily back to the long line of cars.

I freewheeled towards the entrance, my thoughts unclear on what to do next. There are very few ancient monuments in Australia, and according to the attendant, I was now tantalisingly close to one of the most legendary castles in Scotland. But would I be able to park my bike, race across the lawn, explore the castle, and still have time to swim in the loch before nightfall?

I thought back to my Uncle Matt, who I'd met two weeks earlier in Ireland. Before commencing the long bike ride, I spent time with my family in the small heritage town of Ardara, which was once voted the 'best village to live in' by the Irish Times. The place is special to me for numerous reasons. It's where my mum grew up, which meant we holidayed there most summers during my childhood. It's also home to my brother Michael and his wife Maureen.

I'd planned to borrow a friend's bike, tackle a few hills, and then relax with my family before the 1,000-mile ride began. But the Irish rarely get to bed before midnight, and the Guinness proved as tempting as the mountains. With three days to go until the end-to-end ride began, jet lag had been replaced by sleep deprivation. At that point, I should have handed the bike back and booked myself a massage.

Instead, I convinced myself that one long ride would prepare me for the Cornish hills. I chose the narrow road through Glengesh Pass, a glacial valley that cuts through the steep sides of Common Mountain. At the top of the pass, the road zigzagged, resembling a miniature version of Alpine routes used in the Tour de France. Then it levelled onto a windswept plateau and past stacks of freshly cut peat. I cycled only from memory, past tiny settlements and isolated farms, convinced that with every mile I was getting fitter.

Throughout the day, I experienced many seasons and circumnavigated a series of coastal paths, rocky trails, desolate hills, and windswept bogs. By the time I returned, I was wearing a bright poncho to ward off the chill and approached the town in a state of euphoria.

Just outside Ardara, I spotted a familiar figure walking by the road. I stopped to rest, smiling at the unplanned encounter with Uncle Matt. It was only when I tried talking that I felt the dizziness in my head.

'Well, Alistair, it looks like you've been up in the hills again.'

'Yes, Uncle Matt,' I replied and stood patiently, waiting for him to say, 'Well done,' or, 'Good on you!'

Instead, he studied me with curious eyes and chuckled quietly. I looked around at the nearby hills and said, 'I can't believe my time in Ireland is nearly over. It won't be long until I'm riding in Cornwall.'

'Fair play to you Alistair, but please look after yourself. You're not a young man anymore.'

The words that followed were steady and serious. 'In fact, I think it's time you started to slow down and enjoy the ride.'

It was my time to be silent. I contemplated a witty reply, but my throat went dry. This was a man I'd known all my life and had always respected. He wrapped an arm casually around my shoulders. 'You don't need to push yourself anymore. Enjoy the time you have left in Aradra with your family. You're looking a bit worn out, and the real work hasn't even started yet.'

Had I pushed myself too hard? If so, what was driving me? He offered me a handshake and I locked mine with his, enjoying the feeling of strength. After bidding me farewell, his words continually played in my head.

I knew that when he talked about enjoying the ride, he wasn't just referring to the upcoming trip. He was talking about life itself. Uncle Matt is a sprightly figure, twenty years my senior. With a full head of hair, warm eyes and a strong back, he is known for his musical talents, quirky humour, and words of wisdom.

Were my fifty years of age too old for such adventures? No, of course not. But I'd noticed concern in his eyes. It was clear that during my travels, I needed to find some balance. With his comments still close to my thoughts, instead of cycling through the town and onto the next set of hills, I dismounted and walked along the narrow pavement.

A toot of a car horn from a distant relative eased out a smile as I made my way past the Corner House, a popular pub, partly owned by another of my uncles. All summer long, a wooden sign is positioned on the pavement outside. It reads, *Traditional music tonight. Visiting musicians welcome.* On most evenings, there are guitars strumming, fiddlers playing, and plenty of singing. Maybe tonight there would be recitals, poems, or a travelling musician, playing for the chance of a pint of Guinness.

I strolled onwards and around the corner towards Nancy's pub, once voted pub of the year by Georgina Campbell, Ireland's leading food and hospitability writer. Located on the main street, close to the Owentocker River, the white-washed building has been run by the same family for seven generations. I've seen tourists step inside, then walk back out again, convinced they have stepped into someone's front parlour. Each room is a different shape and size. Some are cosy and snug with just enough room for a few lucky patrons to sit amongst the knick-knacks, including ornate table lamps, cups, mirrors, and historical photos of local scenes.

Once inside, I found a seat at the front bar and ordered a Guinness. While waiting patiently for it to settle, I studied the extensive range of Toby jugs, hanging from the ceiling, and ran my hands across the Nancy's nameplate. I overheard a local, sharing a secret fishing spot with a German couple, and nearby, sitting alone at the end of the bar, another man tackled a crossword, at the same time nursing a whisky. As I sipped my Guinness, it suddenly struck me that I was sitting on a bar stool in an award-winning pub, located in the best village in Ireland.

During the short ride home, the sun made a late appearance. I stopped by the bridge to talk with a fisherman who was leaning over the side. He was dressed in khaki green, complete with rod and net, and pointed to a rock pool where apparently — only moments before — a salmon had leapt from the water. 'I visit Ardara every year on holiday from Belfast,' he said. 'It's a magical place.'

I couldn't have agreed more. During the final part of the ride towards Michael's house, I spotted a family at work, stacking hay, in preparation for winter. Grandparents, parents, children, and two dogs — all were enjoying the late afternoon sun. Instead of blitzing past, I rode slowly and they waved back. Further on, an old man in a flat cap and checked jacket stood outside his house, as though waiting for a lift. I stopped to chat, as you do in rural Ireland. There was no lift coming, or task that required completing. He was just outside, standing, watching, and enjoying the sun on his weathered face. Of course, he knew my brother, plus Uncle Matt and most of my family. He even remembered my mum.

When I finally arrived back at Michael's house, now enjoying tea and scones, Maureen came out and topped up my mug.

'So what's your strategy, Ali? How will you manage to get across Britain, keeping up with all your mates, considering you'll want to chat to every man and his dog along the way?'

I eased out a smile before considering my reply. 'You know me too well, but I think Uncle Matt has just about summed it up. I'll slow down or stop when I can and take the time to satisfy my curiosity. No doubt there will be times when I need to speed things up though. It's a balance I've been trying to work out all my life.'

Michael was outside now, standing close, nursing a tea, and smiling. 'Haven't we all, Ali,' he said. 'A few more day's in Ardara would have been perfect for you. By the way, I heard that Uncle Matt is playing in the Corner House tonight. Do you fancy popping into town for a Guinness later?'

Of course, so much had happened since then. Right now, I was contemplating options in a Scottish castle's car park.

My friends had one mission. To raise money for charity by cycling from one end of Britain to another in thirteen days. This alone was enough of a challenge, especially considering the intricate network of routes that Nick had handpicked. However, I craved more, as I'd soon be back in Australia. But how much more could I cram in?

I parked the bike and reached for my lock, but despite a frantic search, couldn't find it. After unpacking the entire contents of my panniers onto the tarmac, it was evident I'd left it in Nick's van. I placed everything back in, ensuring the goggles and bathers were at the top. Then, I hesitated. Surely it would be okay to leave the bike unlocked and run down to the castle for a super quick tour.

I studied the clientele milling around the entrance and felt reassured. After all, they were holidaymakers, not thieves or vagabonds. Dressed in shiny waterproofs and clean walking boots, some carried selfie sticks while playing on their phones.

But by the time I reached the counter, my thoughts had returned to Uncle Matt. Instead of purchasing a ticket, I smiled at the cashier. 'I think I'll leave it for today. Hopefully the castle will survive a few more years and I'll return one day with my family.'

I rode up the incline, waving to the attendant as I slowly continued my journey. The road led me west, towards the nearby village of Drumnadrochit. I was surprised but happy to find it had a village green. A highland piper stood in the centre of the lawn, attempting a rendition of The Flower of Scotland. He was watched by a toddler, licking an ice cream.

There were others appreciating the live music too, but they remained seated in the patio of a nearby cafe, enjoying cake and various hot drinks. The sight of so many holidaymakers, leisurely waiting for a break in the clouds, left me irritated. I also wanted to relax and felt the urge to dismount and listen to the piper. But a rare burst of sunshine on the wooded hills prompted me to keep moving in search of Nessie.

I tossed a coin into the open bag by the piper's side, rode onto a small bridge and stared down at the river, wondering where and when it merged with the loch. For a town that supposedly had a sculptured sea monster, I couldn't find a single expanse of water. But the throngs of cars and pedestrians led me to believe there was something else of interest in the area besides the village green, the cafes and highland piper.

I found the answer up ahead. A sign after the bridge pointed me left towards Nessieland, which I guessed was a themed children's attraction. Stopping at the junction, I noticed another sign, pointing towards the Loch Ness Centre and Exhibition. As this was also the way to Inverness, it provided a logical choice. Moments later, I stopped outside the entrance to a large stone building, once known as the Drumnadrochit Hotel, now home to the exhibition.

I picked up a flyer from the entrance. The choices sounded appealing but also time consuming. Perfect for a day tripper but too much for someone that still needed to find a clay monster and swim with a mythical one. Reluctantly, I gave up the chance to visit the six themed areas, which tell the story of the loch from the Ice Age to the present day. The exhibition also includes the equipment used in the monster hunts, including miniature submarines and sonar surveying tools. The thought struck me that maybe Noah's goggles would make it to the museum one day.

I needed advice, but the queue at the entrance looked too long. Instead, I visited the nearby gift shop. The aisles were filled with every conceivable type of memorabilia, for all tastes and budgets, from postcards to panoramic photos and woollen garments, handmade in remote Scottish Isles. One section was filled with monsters. Toy monsters, cuddly monsters, Lego monsters, and monsters bigger than a toddler. Some were green, others blue, but most were made in China.

On impulse, I purchased two small monsters. Would boys of ten and twelve be interested in cuddly Nessies? I couldn't be sure, but for me, it felt important. At the counter I asked the cashier if she knew where I could find the sculpture of Nessie. She placed the toys into a bag and called out to her colleague.

'Mary, is the statue of Nessie still nearby?'

The other woman was stacking shelves with *I saw Nessie*, fridge magnets and turned her eyes towards the exit as if to recollect a distant memory. 'I think it's near the back fence. I'll go ask Doug.'

She disappeared for a few seconds and returned with a man who I presumed was Doug. He had an impressive crop of auburn hair, despite his years, and wore a Nessie tie with obvious pride.

'Are you after the statue of Nessie?' he asked.

'Yes,' I replied, hopefully.

'Well, it's still here. But you'll have to go around by the carpark to find it. We don't promote the monster at the moment, as it needs a facelift! All the best to you now.' Then, he returned to the depths of the store.

I thanked the cashier and made my way to the adjacent carpark. Apart from a pubescent teenager working the summer as a part-time attendant, there was no one else around. I dismounted and asked where Nessie was. Without hesitation, he pointed to a wooden fence. 'There's a new one outside Nessieland, but the one through that wee lane has been there for years.'

I thanked him but felt hesitant during the short walk and turned back to the teenager. He'd been watching and shouted out, 'That's it. Just a bit further.'

I took a few more steps and there it was — just to my left, over a fence. There was no plaque or other tourists and only a small pool of water surrounding it. This wasn't the Nessie I remembered standing next to with Alice. This one was crumbling at the edges and a small part of its face had peeled away. Although tall with a prominent tail, the elements had taken their toll, leaving it cracked, unloved and forgotten. It was nowhere near the loch.

Had the waters retreated or had they moved the sculpture? I was too disappointed to ask. I was hoping for an impressive structure, close to the loch with people posing for photos. But instead I found a Nessie on the scrap heap. Back at the carpark, the attendant didn't bother asking if I'd found Nessie. I think the look on my face said it all.

'Excuse me, but do you live nearby?' I asked him.

'Yes, in the village.'

'Do you know where I can take a swim in the loch?'

He couldn't hold back a wide grin, revealing a set of braces. 'You cannee swim in the lake. Not near here anyway, and the water is freezing! Even in summer.'

'I don't plan on swimming far. Just a quick dip. Is there a reason why I can't swim? Is there an algae bloom or something?'

He stared at me, his eyes wide. 'No, the lake is fine. There's fish in it and all sorts of wildlife. I just meant that it's impossible to reach the water from this side.'

I got out my map and asked him to consider the road towards Inverness. Surely there must be one location where swimming was possible. While staring at the lines and contours, I could see his concentration wavering. His phone buzzed, distracting him for a moment, but I was determined to stay put until he could help.

He dismissed his phone for a moment. 'Your best bet is to cycle into Inverness and then head down the other side of the loch.'

I looked at him earnestly, my voice pleading. 'Are you saying there's nowhere between here and Inverness where I can get into the water? To be honest, I haven't got a lot of time or energy. I left Fort William this morning and I've lost all of my mates.'

I blundered on for a few more seconds, pointing to the road, my panniers, and the scrapes on my elbows from a recent fall. The poor kid didn't deserve this. But he kept eye contact and nodded compassionately. When I finished speaking, he said softly, 'Well there's one place, I guess. It's not a beach as such. But the public are allowed, as it's a slipway for tourist boats.'

My face lit up and I asked for directions. He was animated now too, completely ignoring his phone as it vibrated once again. 'It's easy, Mister. Just carry on for a few more miles and look for the Clansman Hotel. You cannee miss it. They have a tunnel under the road that leads to the loch. A company called Jacobite operates trips onto the loch from there. I suppose you can swim there, but it's not really a beach as such, and it's private land unless you're going on a wee cruise. I've heard their boats have sonar to help find the monster.'

His phone buzzed again and I knew it was time to depart. I called out my thanks and cycled away, my eyes drawn to the darkening sky. My arrival coincided with the docking of a boat, which deposited a horde of tourists, dressed in bright coloured ponchos. Although most of them walked past me to the shop and nearby café, others stayed by the water, posing for photos and throwing stones into the water.

I rested my bike against a boulder and took in the surrounding area. There was a wooden information hut at the end of the walkway where a solitary figure enquired about the next cruise. It was now or never if I wanted to take a dip. But my bathers were in the panniers, and in such an open area it was impossible to change without being charged for indecent exposure. I didn't want to swim in Lycra as I still had many more hours in the saddle.

To save on space, I'd only packed a hand towel and regretted the decision immediately when I tried stretching it around my waist. In frustration, I darted towards the back of the ticket office and began hurriedly stripping off.

Then I heard voices. Half undressed, I peeked out between the wooden stall and a tree. The pathway was filling with tourists returning to the jetty. If I could see them, they could see me, so I whipped my Lycra back on and walked innocently towards my bike.

I kicked a pebble across the slipway, muttering under my breath, and watched as it sunk in the cold, dark waters, a few feet from some trees. I hadn't noticed how near I was to the tree line, but it was only a short walk across the pebbles. I'd found myself a changing room.

After changing behind a tree, I focused on the task at hand to get into the water as fast as possible. Suddenly, Uncle Matt's words came back in an instant. *Slow down and enjoy the ride.* But was this diversion a scramble or enjoyment? I really didn't know anymore.

As for my children, would they even care if I swam in the loch? In truth, I was probably doing it for myself. To prove something. To prove I was still young enough to do these crazy things. Or to prove to the other cyclists I could ride from one end of the country to the other, and still take the time to stop and explore the sights?

I picked up Noah's goggles, stretching the elastic band to force them on, and within a few steps, I was out of the trees. Immediately I spotted an Indian man. He sported a trim beard, peppered with grey, and was standing close to the water, holding a single, red rose. I could see other roses too, bobbing close to the water's edge. For a few moments, we studied each other until he smiled briefly before returning his attention to the rose.

I waved and took another step forward. 'Hi there,' I called. 'I'm just going for a quick swim to see if I can spot the Loch Ness monster.'

He smiled again and nodded once before throwing the rose into the water. He then walked back to the jetty, his head low and movements slow. It seemed each of us had a very different reason for being there.

My first step into the water proved difficult. The shoreline was littered with rocks and most were coated in slippery moss. My heel skidded across the first rock, and then I wedged my toes into an unseen gap. With goggles on, it was akin to walking blind across a watery minefield. So I removed them and went on slowly.

After twenty steps, I was only knee deep but in full view of the Indian man, who was now standing with his family, watching my every movement. While contemplating placement of my next foot, a rose bobbed past, its red petals sodden and lifeless.

A cool wind brushed against my naked back. The clouds were re-forming, turning dark across the low-lying hills. I inched forward, probing for greater depths, hoping to soon feel silt or sand beneath my toes. In desperation, I took a giant step forward and gasped as my knee vanished. In an instant, the water rose to my torso, the chill quickening my breathing. Unseen boulders hampered my legs, and my feet scraped against hard granite. I attempted a lunge but couldn't balance very well on the uneven surface. It was hard to imagine I was standing in the deepest lake in Great Britain.

With time pressing on, I decided this would have to do and put the goggles back on. I caught sight of the Indian family still watching from afar and waved before ducking beneath the surface. The water was deeper to my left, so I held my breath and floated face down on the surface, studying the murky surroundings. It was deep enough to attempt a breast stroke, and as I lifted my head for air, a dark shape glided past, followed by a surge of water.

I surfaced quickly, pulled the goggles from my face, and looked out across rippling water. Was it Nessie, I wondered briefly? But no. It was a boat, barely 30 yards away, filled with tourists peering over the sides. I held up my hand and some waved back, a little confused. Somehow, I don't think it was me they wanted to spot.

Leaving the shores of Loch Ness, I continued on my journey towards a location regarded as the capital city of the Highlands. Inverness is home to nearly 50,000 people and is strategically located on Scotland's north-east coast, alongside the Moray Firth. I crossed over the River Ness, which splits the city into two, and stopped halfway to gaze up at Inverness Castle.

Unlike the bruised and battered Urquhart Castle, this one looked pristine and is currently used as a Sheriff Court. Back in 1836, it was constructed on the site of an 11th century defensive structure. Perched high upon a grassy embankment, the castle walls, ramparts and towers dominate the landscape. A Scottish flag fluttered high above one of the ramparts and from afar, I could see people walking around the perimeter of the red sandstone walls.

Far to my left, I noticed two church spires, jutting proudly towards a touch of blue. A bridge led me onto a busy road, lined either side by shops, pubs and restaurants. I stopped at a set of traffic lights and watched as pedestrians hurried across. Most were dressed for rain, despite the clouds showing signs of retreat.

The sight of a clock tower reminded me that evening was approaching, so I stopped to call Mark and tell him where I was. He informed me I was close, but there was just one more hurdle to complete. With the day finally drawing to a close, I hung up the phone, picked up my bike, and climbed the Market Brae Steps. Within an hour, I was back on the same steps, this time with a scrubbed body and clean clothes. I'd left my wet garments where they fell.

As we all walked through the city streets, I felt a vibrancy within the group. It might have been mid-week, but it was also high summer, and throngs of other tourists were also looking for suitable places to spend their time and money. We'd been recommended the Waterfront Bar, and while strolling over the River Ness, I spoke with Mick about their journey from Fort Augustus. As I guessed, it had been invigorating and remote with extensive views across beautiful Loch Ness. Once again, it seemed, my diversion had come at a cost.

It was still light when Alan pushed open the door to the pub and led us towards the bar. The décor was warm with soft lighting, piped music, and wooden floors. The barman was in his mid-thirties and greeted Alan with a vibrant smile. 'Well now, what can I get you?'

While speaking, his eyes darted across the room, as if checking earlier instructions were being followed.

'We're after a table for seven, please.'

'When for?'

'Now, please.'

'Have you booked?'

'No. Should we have?'

'Oh aye, for sure.'

Nick squeezed to the front. 'Sorry, but we didn't realise the pub was so popular. We've been cycling all day and were recommended to come here.'

The barman scanned the room and scratched his chin. 'Give me a minute will you, lads. I'll see what I can do.'

With professional ease, he shuffled a few tables around, casually chatting to the seated customers nearby. Then he pushed another table into the newly-formed gap and waved us over. Buoyed by this display of compassion, we settled down in comfort and ordered dinner. Partway through the main course, Alan appeared at the table with a glass of whisky. It was for Nick to enjoy as a token gesture for all he had done. It was dealt with swiftly, prompting another round of drinks for everyone.

Partway through the next beer, I heard the sound of a guitar being tuned. A musician was setting up in the corner. I found a good vantage point and watched.

'Good evening, ladies and gentlemen, and welcome to Inverness! My name is Davy Holt and this song is called Kishmul's Galley. I hope you enjoy it.'

And so began an evening of song. I wasn't the only one absorbed by the music and the words. For a while, Alan joined me at the bar, and on a nearby table, a stout man tapped his fingers to the beat. I leaned closer to the man and caught his attention.

'This is pretty special. Are you enjoying the music?'

'Oh! For sure! My great grandfather was Scottish and we've come over from Canada to see where he used to live. The lyrics are so enchanting.'

His teenage children also looked like they were enjoying themselves — as was his wife. They were all stamping their feet in time with the chords.

With each new song, Davy explained the meaning or source before strumming his guitar and singing. We heard folk songs about unreturned love, ancient battles, and factory closures. Other tunes were more uplifting — even more so when he explained the background behind the misty glens, the border skirmishes, and romantic trysts.

During the interval, I spoke to Davy and learned he was born in south-west Scotland, but now lives in the Highlands. This type of gig was his bread and butter, but he'd also travelled far and wide through Europe and even parts of America.

I purchased a CD, offered him a pint, and sat back with my group, all of whom were eagerly awaiting Davey's return to the stage. While we chatted, I thought back to my time in Glencoe — to the massacre, the wilderness, the steep-sided crags, and the haunting beauty. Alan placed a beer by my side. 'What a top night. I wonder if he'll sing a song for us,' he said with a smile.

With the sounds of Loch Lomond still ringing in our ears, we stepped into the cool night air, along with the last of the stragglers. At this point, we should have headed to our beds, but we were easily swept up in the moment and, without a thought, waltzed into the next establishment offering live music.

The dark interior of this next pub looked and sounded very different to the bar we'd just left. There was no food on offer and very few tables, although the bar was at least three deep. The musician here sounded grittier than Davy and had no CDs for sale. The songs were a mixture of eighties rock classics and folk, sung loud and without finesse.

It didn't take long for Alan to request Loch Lomond. By this time, we were all dancing, along with some of the regulars. Through the flash of strobe lights, I could see us all, hands held high, gyrating and laughing. No one mentioned our eighty-mile bike ride in the morning.

The last time I'd sat on Alan's shoulders was during a summer holiday in Tenerife, twenty years earlier. Suddenly, I was perched on his broad shoulders again, my head brushing close to the stained ceiling. From my distinct vantage point, I had a bird's eye view of the packed pub. I could see JP in deep conversation with a middle-aged woman who quite clearly loved tattoos. Mick and Colin were at the bar, shouting an order for drinks. Mark and Nick were on the dancefloor, re-enacting disco moves with strangers. A bouncer watched from the door, his arms crossed and expression blank. He'd seen it all before. In fact, most clientele were unperturbed by our actions.

When the musician stopped for a break and the lights came on, the mood lifted. It was finally time to head home. Outside, in the cool air, we reflected on the experience.

'Did you see that bloke with the tattoos staring at us?'

'That wasn't a man!'

'Are you sure?'

'What about the girl in the blue top who didn't stop dancing? Did you see the back of her hands, I swear they were hairier then Alan's.'

'I saw two women go into the toilet together.'

And so the conservations went on, each tale a little different to the last, exaggerated by fatigue and drunkenness. Yet, regardless of race, gender, sexual preference, fashion sense, or love of body art, the people we'd just met had welcomed us with open arms.

Since leaving Land's End, I'd craved a night when we threw caution to the wind, and finally, in Inverness, my wish had been well and truly granted.

Day 12: Things Can Only Get Better

'The Promised Land always lies on the other side of a wilderness.'
Havelock Ellis

An unseen hand shook me awake, followed by the sound of voices. After opening my eyes, I lay perfectly still, trying to shut out the slamming of doors and the footsteps pounding on the stairs. Mick appeared by the open door, dressed for a day in the saddle. His damp hair was dishevelled but his eyes were bright. He studied me for a second, then raised his eyebrows.

'Best you jump in the shower, Ali. Most of us have already packed and breakfast is about to be served. If I were you, I'd get your fill. We're heading into the wilds today!'

I mumbled a croaky response, threw back the sheets and made my way to the bathroom. The thought of cycling anywhere, let alone the Scottish wilderness, held little appeal. As I stood under the power shower, I remembered the evening's antics in a series of comical flashbacks. No amount of coffee could ease the pounding in my head and the thought of eggs turned my stomach. If any others were suffering, they didn't show it as they tucked into breakfast with gusto.

Back upstairs, I picked up my garments that lay scattered on the floor, then crammed all unrequired items into the holdall and filled up my two water bottles. Time was rushing past with still so much to do, including an urgent bathroom stop. In the meantime, my smart phone blazed into life with an incoming Face Time call from Australia. I ignored the beeps and ran off in search of my cycling shoes.

Although I held up the group for a few minutes, they didn't show signs of frustration. My guess is most were feeling some effects of the late night and I hoped it would slow them down. With this in mind, I declined the offer of using Alan's bike computer. Instead of tackling the stone steps on our bikes this morning, we took a curved track into the town centre. Foot commuters dashed on past while as usual we followed the beeps from the bike computers. I stayed at the back, slugging water and the first of many painkillers.

Within a few turns, we'd escaped the city into an industrial estate. Although surrounded by high fences and steel-clad warehouses, we weren't lost. The familiar blue cycle signs reminded me once again how Sustrans has managed to link many parts of Britain together. The path led us through gaps between each subdivision and deposited us parallel with the A9. We stayed on the bike track as it increased in angle, ignoring the heavy traffic next to us.

Up ahead, I could see the wide waters of Beauly Firth, an inlet of the Moray Firth. This was the nearest we'd get to the North Sea before reaching John O'Groats. The wind tugged at our jackets as we rode onto Kessock Bridge, which offered fine views of the water, over 100 feet below. The bridge is 3,465 feet long and links Inverness with the small village of North Kessock, located on the Black Isle. The name can be deceiving as it's not an isle but a peninsula, surrounded on three of its sides by water. Bottlenose dolphins are known to inhabit the fertile waters, but in truth, I rarely looked up during the crossing.

This was my second ever visit to the Black Isle. The first was twenty years earlier, and on that occasion, following the advice of a fish and chip worker, we'd headed north-east to the village of Cromarty. From there, we'd enjoyed a ferry ride on the Cromarty Rose, across the firth to the village of Nigg, which led us to the eastern flanks of Scotland. Nick had promised us a different adventure this time, heading inland towards the remote hamlet of Altnaharra. This site, along with Braemar in the Grampians, holds the record for the coldest temperature ever recorded in the UK, reaching minus 27.2 degrees.

On the far side of the bridge, we detoured away from the traffic, towards North Kessock, a linear village with far-reaching views across the Beauly Firth. It looked an ideal spot to relax, complete with a hotel, a quaint tearoom, and a one-stop shop for all essentials. But we'd hardly gained any distance and pressed on without a backward glance. On the water, anchored boats pointed into a stiff wind, and we dropped down through the gears. Although winter was officially four months away, the late summer sun was struggling to make an entrance from behind the hills that lay ahead.

Reluctantly, we veered away from the water, along country roads that hugged the A9. There were no steep inclines to test the group and the front riders seemed unaffected by the late night. Their speed wasn't excessive, but the pounding in my head refused to budge. I dropped away from the pack, unable and unwilling to respond. Partway through my second bottle of water, I came across them, patiently waiting by an intersection.

'I'm struggling to find my mojo this morning,' I said as I pulled alongside. 'I don't want to hold you back. Is there a direct route I can take instead?'

We were close to the village of Tore, and from their computer screen readouts, it looked like I could turn right onto the A9. Their route would take them towards the town of Dingwall, then alongside the Cromarty Firth. The decision was made.

'I'm going to take the main road to cut a few miles out. I've got a phone. I'll be in touch, OK?'

I'd forgotten to ask Nick for a tear out of his map, but by deviating from the planned route, I'd gain little in borrowing one of their computers.

'Ali, you don't have to do this,' JP replied.

The others nodded in agreement, but I refused to catch their eyes. I took another slug of water. 'Maybe I'm becoming a bit of a loner, but my mind is made up.'

It was Mark who spoke next, his voice carrying far. 'Well, you've always been able to liven up a party. Don't lose that appeal. Stay safe and we'll see you in Altnaharra. I know you'll be there somehow.'

I knew they were struggling to understand my need to continually split from them. But I could predict the future. If I stayed, within a few miles, an incline would appear and they'd soon be specks in the distance. Not out of malice, of course, but disciplined proficiency. I couldn't even rely on JP to keep me company at the back anymore. He'd gotten fitter and stronger each passing day, while I seemed to be wavering as the finish line approached.

They deserved the chance to complete the day's ride in a reasonable time without distractions. So I waved goodbye, turned onto the A9, and went in search of a shortcut. If it all went well, I'd cut in front. If my plan failed, at the very least I'd have a story to tell.

Described as one of the most dangerous roads in Scotland, the A9 is synonymous with accidents, some of them deadly. BBC Scotland once created a documentary called *Life and Death on the A9* in which they describe it as the 'road we love to hate'. The problem for cyclists is that heavy freight vehicles constantly use the road, as there aren't many other options nearby. Add the often-single lane to the inclement Scottish weather and you get multiple reasons why cyclists should avoid it whenever possible.

Apart from staying safe, my main goal was to obtain a map either from Nick or a roadside garage. Thirty minutes later, I remained clueless as to where I was. I approached a T-junction, right on the edge of a large expanse of water. With no idea if it was a loch or a river, I studied the area and weighed up my options. The idea of turning right seemed logical, as it would lead me across the water via a low-lying bridge. But the signpost pointed to Wick. From past experience, I remembered that Wick is located in the far north-eastern tip of Scotland, about ninety miles away. By taking the bridge, would I be sucked towards the east coast with mountains blocking my path into the interior?

The other arrow pointed towards Inverness where I'd woken with a hangover a few hours earlier. My stomach growled as if in disappointment of the limited options available — and the choices made thus far. A steady stream of vehicles approached the junction from behind me, slowing to a crawl before making their decision. No-one seemed to have as much trouble as me who stood nearby, conscious of time, uncertain about my whereabouts and frustrated at my ridiculous predicament.

Although Wick weighed heavily upon my mind, I eventually chose the turning for Inverness. Apart from getting lost, my other fear was the embarrassment of passing the others, riding full pelt in the opposite direction. At least this road offered the chance of solace as it wound through open countryside with views of the water that had barred my passage.

At the next T-junction, I turned right onto a bike path. Thankfully, the sign pointed away from Inverness and I was now on a downhill incline. I was happy for the chance to stop pedalling but concerned about my dwindling water supply.

Further ahead, I saw a parked car in a layby and pulled alongside to ask directions. I quickly explained the reason I was alone, as it always seemed to come up in conversation. The two people inside were called Thomas and Kate, and both looked to be in their early forties. They were on a touring holiday from Edinburgh and had stopped for tea and cake. They got out of the car, offered me a cup, and laid a map of the area on the bonnet.

When Thomas heard I was heading to Altnaharra he gave a thumbs up, followed by a smile.

'You're certainly getting to John O'Groats the best way. Though I've heard it's a wee bit wild and desolate out there. Hey, have you heard of a band called Runrig?'

'Yes, of course,' I said with a grin, thinking back to the CDs in my collection back home.

'I'm impressed. Have you listened to the song, *Summer Walkers*? It's a great wee tune about the very place you're about to cycle through.'

Runrig are a popular Scottish folk band, adored by millions and famous for the way they weave rock and folk music together. Their charismatic rendition of *Loch Lomond* brings everyone to their feet, and during Alan and Sam's wedding day celebration, the DJ belted out the tune to the enthusiastic (and drunken) guests. I hadn't thought about the band or their music for some time, yet here I was, cycling through the country they adored.

I'd listened to *Summer Walkers* long ago, but the places in the song meant very little to me at the time. As I tried to remember the words, Thomas pointed out our location on the map. I also found the T-junction with the bridge leading towards Wick, which I'd earlier dismissed. Studying the map, I could now see I had made the wrong decision. I'd ridden in a loop that was now taking me to the far side of the very same bridge.

I put my head in my hands and managed a strangled laugh. The situation wasn't funny, but I didn't want to crumple in front of two strangers. They both sensed the change in my demeanour.

Thomas prodded the map. 'Look, it's easy, Alistair. You just chunk it down into small steps. So, the first stop is Dingwall, which isn't far, and if I were you I'd stop on the way to get something to eat and drink.'

He pointed to a town called Alness and drew a line upwards with his finger across a jut of land. 'This is the shortcut you need. It avoids the loop around the eastern route. You might even catch up with your mates. From there, it's an easy ride to Bonar Bridge, and once you're across the Dornach Firth, take a sharp left and keep on going. As Runrig sang, "*And it's up by the Shin and up the Naver and the long winding shores of Loch Maree.*"'

The long-forgotten words eased some of the stress form my shoulders.

'Use your phone to take a photo of our map,' Thomas went on, 'but please, why don't you enjoy a sip of tea with a biscuit before you go?'

After taking a photo, as suggested, I eased two custard creams from the packet and offered my thanks. I now had a purpose and a plan. For years I'd been known as a man with a keen sense of direction, guiding friends and family across misty mountaintops in the Lake District with assured confidence. But since leaving Land's End I'd made numerous navigational errors, often at the amusement of the other riders. Curiosity was one thing, but stupidity was quite another.

Despite the upbeat meeting with two strangers, as Dingwall approached, dark thoughts clouded my mind, refusing to subside while I searched for a place to eat. In a world filled with supersized stores and retail parks, it was refreshing to find a town centre with a yesteryear feel. All the family stores, once found in every British high street — but now fast disappearing — were there. I passed a butchers, a florists, a seamstress, a newsagents, two chemists and numerous pubs. I even found a MacDonald's, but it didn't sell fast food. These MacDonalds were locals, with a slightly different surname to the fast food giants. Instead of 'Happy Meals', they offered an old-fashioned, family hardware service.

I dismounted and walked along the main street, watching, listening and thinking. Casual shoppers went about their business, chatting to shopkeepers on first name terms and making plans to catch up later. I chose a café at the far end of town and didn't bother locking the bike. The gloomy interior matched my mood, as if the wood-panelled walls were sucking up the light.

With no other customers, I was served promptly and also asked for a refill of the water bottles. Despite an extensive menu, the only item I could decide on was a strong coffee, served in a mug. While waiting for it to be brewed, I chose a seat in the middle of the café, discarded my jacket, helmet and gloves, then searched around for something to occupy my time. There were no books, magazines or castoff newspapers within sight, and getting up to ask for the Wi-Fi password suddenly seemed like a burden. Instead, I just sat and waited.

The clatter of heels on the tiled floor denoted the arrival of a group of ladies. They busied themselves with coats, bags, hats, and brollies as they settled into a corner table by the window. They were all grey haired and most wore glasses, which were soon put to use reading laminated menus. The women chatted noisily, discussing their choices and the weather. After they ordered, I noticed it got quiet. Their voices fell to a whisper and I caught one of them watching me. I had no idea why, as I hadn't done anything of note except stare into space.

My thoughts were on Colin, Mick, Alan, JP and Mark. At this very moment, they'd be chewing up the miles, sharing jokes, watching for the next turn, while I sat in a nameless café, waiting for a drink that I didn't even want anymore. I scanned the counter for the waitress and received a wave in return. The women were tucking into cake and drinking steaming tea by the time my tepid coffee arrived, along with an apology about a broken machine.

I couldn't hide the grimace after taking the first sip. Without placing the mug back on the table, I drained the remainder in one go, ignoring the bitter aftertaste. The morning was in danger of sending me into a spiral of despair. Not just because I'd taken a thirty-minute break for five seconds of warm coffee. But because it finally dawned on me this was the last full day on the road and I'd decided to ride solo again.

On the way out of town, the smell of fresh bread prompted me to try a sausage roll from a nearby bakery. It was piping hot with a crispy coating, and within a few steps, I'd devoured the lot. I returned for another, wrapped it in a paper bag, and stowed the valuable parcel.

The map captured on my smartphone was easy to read, and before setting off, I gathered my bearings. I had to get this right. The next location was Alness, and from there I needed to head inland. This route would cut out the road along the firth. The map also revealed I'd be riding towards a peak called Cnoc Muigh-bhlaraidh, located to the north of Alness. After that, the contours narrowed, which meant I'd be riding downhill again. With luck, if the clouds kept away, I'd enjoy impressive views of the straits. But I wasn't feeling excited about the diversion, just weak and lonely.

Then I heard the shrill of my phone, coming from the front pannier. I clicked connect and heard Nick's voice. 'I hear you've gone walkabout again! Where are you?'

I didn't want to sound desolate and moody. Instead, I cleared my throat and said, 'I'm in Dingwall. I took a small diversion for coffee and a quick bite to eat.'

There was a pause as he digested the news. 'Don't stay there for too long as there's still many miles to go. Can you meet me in Alness? I've got a few maps for you.'

The call ended and I set off in earnest, eager to meet within the hour. Along the way, I passed the Cromarty Bridge, which I'd ignored a few hours earlier. It was an impressive crossing, built on a base of boulders. Those who travelled across were only yards above the deep waters. There was no way I could avoid the A9 and its traffic without running late for Nick. Giving up speed for safety was a decision I didn't take lightly, but the weather seemed to be holding up.

Nick was waiting for me with the maps already torn out. He was eager to get to Altnaharra, as his wife and daughter were meeting him there, but his sharp eyes and ears didn't miss a loose water bottle holder and some misaligned derailleurs. After a quick pit stop, he declared me fit for the next leg, and with a toot of the horn drove off.

Just out of town, I passed Alness Golf Course and spotted numerous people pushing golf buggies along its wide and hilly fairways. The road changed direction again and rose slowly as it entered wooded farmland. I crossed small tributaries, rode through undulating hills, and glimpsed the flat-topped summit of Cnoc Muigh-bhlaraidh. In places, the trees dwindled, replaced by a carpet of purple heather. Throughout the entire shortcut, I didn't encounter a single vehicle. The only noise was the rasp of my breathing, competing with the bleating of sheep.

The road led me back towards sea level, providing an expansive lookout from a layby called Struie Viewpoint. The scene was dominated by Dornoch Firth, its dark waters stretching out towards Bonar Bridge and beyond that distant hills and mountains. To my right, I could see the route alongside the water that the others would have taken. But there was no sign of any cyclists, and with no phone signal, there was little else to do but continue. The road ended in a series of tight turns, then stopped at another T-junction.

Instinctively, this time, I turned left towards Bonar Bridge and rode alongside the Dornoch Firth. I didn't plan to stop in the village of Ardgay, but the sight of bikes parked outside a wooden-clad building called the Highland Café lifted my spirits. On closer inspection, there weren't any that I recognised. They were racing bikes without panniers and their owners were inside. I sat on a bench and stared out across the firth towards a ridge of hills, momentarily bathed in sunshine. A light shower quickly followed and made the next decision for me. Instead of reaching for my waterproof, I opened the door and stepped inside.

Although I didn't feel hungry, I couldn't resist the Highland Special — square sausages, black pudding, mushrooms, and chips. It wasn't just a café but also a shop, selling everything from breakfast cereals to chicken wire. One section was for diners with a few tables already taken. The three cyclists were there, along with a thirty-something couple sitting nearby. There was one other person — an elderly man, sitting alone by the window.

I picked a table in the far corner and decided to study the map. I located Altnaharra and ran my fingers along the winding road that would take me there. In such a remote location, there was little else on the diagram, apart from blue lines depicting tributaries or rivers. But there was a tiny square, described as the Crask Inn, which caught my attention. The thought of a welcoming inn out on the moors sounded appealing. But I dismissed the idea, convinced it would be nothing but a relic.

The cyclists were young, with broad Scottish accents that boomed across the room as they shared their adventure with nearby diners. It sounded like they were on a half-day ride, heading to Dingwall along the same route I'd chosen. I listened while they spoke passionately about Struie Viewpoint and explained how the locals called it the Millionaires View. On most days, I'd have shared my own experience at the lookout. Instead, I kept quiet.

After finishing their drinks, they reached for their jackets and walked outside. The couple they'd been talking with also stirred to life and very soon it was just me and the elderly man.

'Here you go.'

A plateful of food appeared before me, but before I could thank the waitress, she'd walked over to talk with the man. He'd hardly moved since I'd entered the café, and even as she took away his empty plate, he didn't flinch. He wore a tweed jacket, frayed at the edges, and a flat cap that sat snugly across a pair of large ears. Protruding from each was a forest of hairs, sprouting at right angles to his weathered face. In between each mouthful of sausage, I studied his features. Most noticeable were the long hairs spiralling from each nostril. His wrinkled, ruddy face led me to believe he'd enjoyed a lifetime working outdoors.

The waitress returned and placed a bottle of beer by his side, whispering a few words I couldn't hear. I wanted to make contact with the man, to ask him his name and to talk about simple things. Instead, I watched his hands shake as he sipped from the bottle and stared outside.

Unable to make a dent in the food, I pushed the plate away. I made eye contact with the man and waved on my way out. In reply, he touched the brim of his cap, his voice low and gruff. 'All the best to you now.'

Back outside, I packed my waterproof away, hoping that the hint of blue between the clouds was a sign of good fortune to come. I collected my bike and walked towards the road, my thoughts going back to the elderly man in the café. His eyes had been a steely blue and I wondered what he'd seen and done in his life that I'd never know or experience. It suddenly struck me that, for him, adventurous escapades were all but over. Not only was I still fit and healthy enough to undertake new challenges, I was actually on one right now!

At that moment, a weight lifted from my shoulders. I took in my surroundings, taking note of the wildflowers scattered across an adjacent meadow. There was nothing to hear but a gentle breeze, fanning the leaves of nearby trees. Yes, I'd pushed away my friends and still had many miles to go, but I could still salvage the day. I clipped into the pedals and set off towards a hotel in the wilderness.

It's no secret that the Scottish and English were at war during the 18th century. Like many conflicts, it wasn't as clear-cut as one country fighting another. Religion, politics, greed and corruption each played a part. Those in favour of Clan Stuart chose to join the Jacobite army, a force made up of patriotic highlanders and disillusioned British, all of them volunteers. In 1745, led by Bonny Prince Charlie, they broke out of the Highlands, and after capturing Edinburgh, they made it as far south as Derby, England.

However, the Jacobites retreated back to the Highlands when the planned support from the French fell through. It was in Culloden that the dream of putting a Stuart on the throne ended. The battle took place just outside Inverness and claimed the lives of fifteen hundred Jacobites, along with three hundred government soldiers. In the aftermath, many surviving Jacobites were rounded up, some imprisoned and others executed.

Riding towards the bridge, it was hard to believe that the surrounding landscape had once been a place of many fierce battles and hardships. The battle of Culloden led to calls to tame the north, resulting in a push to build more roads and bridges in the wild interior. Luckily, the culture of the Highlands managed to survive, and apart from football matches, fishing quotas, and trade disputes, the Scots and English reside peacefully — most of the time!

There was a sense of tranquility on the afternoon I crossed over the bridge towards the village. There was just one craft within view — a family-sized fishing boat, heading east in the direction of the sea. Bonar Bridge is home to about a thousand people, but most were evidently elsewhere. There was hardly a soul to be seen when I reached the far side.

I stopped by a triangular monument, which had a plaque on each of its sides. Each plaque carried an inscription, and the first was straight to the point, declaring that the Right Honourable Gordon Campbell opened the bridge on the 14th December 1973. The second plaque revealed there had once been another bridge, which lasted from 1893 until 1973. The third plaque was far more interesting to read, its etched words holding my attention.

Traveller, stop and read with gratitude the names of the Parliamentary Commissioners appointed in the year 1803 to direct the making of above five hundred miles of roads through the Highlands of Scotland and of numerous bridges, particularly those at Beauly, Scuddel, Bonar, Fleet, and Helmsdale.

I'd often considered the Highlands as a term for a mountainous area of Scotland. But the term is not all about height. It encompasses boundaries, culture and religion too. Geographically, the Highland Boundary Fault is what separates the low from the high. It traverses Scotland in a near straight line from Helensburgh, on the west coast, to Stonehaven in the east. It is a natural fault line, formed hundreds of millions of years ago when ancient continents collided.

Instead of rugged peaks, I was now surrounded by wide-open spaces. Dotted with farmsteads and woodlands, each new mile unveiled a landscape very different to what I'd seen so far — vast fields with sheep, crumbling stone walls, and narrow roads that wound into the distance. Time and time again I crossed over streams and pockets of water, some no larger than village ponds, others big enough to launch a boat on.

I came to another junction. I could either turn left or continue on in the direction I was heading. Maybe it was my imagination, but the road straight on looked narrower. However, a placard advertising the Altnaharra Hotel in nineteen miles, straight ahead, told me all I needed to know. I pulled out my phone, eager to inform Mark that I was on the home stretch, but there was no signal. It did tell me the time though. If I travelled at nineteen miles per hour, non-stop, I'd be at the hotel by five thirty. With the wind at my back, favourable inclines ahead, and the energy to keep the pace, I could be sinking an ale before dinner.

For ten minutes, I rode like a man possessed, convinced I'd be at the hotel in time for a hot bath before pre-dinner drinks with the lads. But the elements were turning against me. I felt the wind increasing, tugging at my fleece. I glanced left and saw the shower before it hit, sweeping unhindered across the moorland, its clouds as dark as the narrow road. By the time I'd dismounted and scrambled for the waterproof, the heavens had opened, causing tiny rivers to form on the tarmac.

Just as quickly, the rain eased and was replaced by a beautiful rainbow. Far away on the hillside, a herd of dishevelled sheep huddled close to a mythical pot of gold. I slowed to a steady pace, taking each bend with due diligence. Instead of racing, I decided at that moment to take my time and appreciate the surroundings. In a crowded world, it is becoming increasingly rare to be alone. I hadn't seen a car in some time, and the last person I'd spoken to had been the old man in the café.

During this brief period, I felt like a real explorer — someone like Alastair Humphries, who travelled the world by bike and described it in his book, *Moods of Future Joys — Around the World by Bike*; or a mountaineer, like Sir Edmund Hillary perhaps, about to reach the peak of an icy summit; or a sailor, like Captain Cook, bravely crossing the Pacific Ocean.

In comparison to these adventurers and explorers, I was merely an amateur, riding along a country road, a few hours' drive from the city, with overnight accommodation already booked. But for some reason, at that very moment, I felt invincible. With each new flurry of rain, I gritted my teeth and pushed harder. When a gust of wind threatened to drive me off the road, I laughed out loud and shook my fist. There was no one to hear me. Just the sheep and passing clouds.

The song from Runrig, Summer Walkers, entered my head. *And it's up by the Shin and up the Naver and the long winding shores of Loch Maree.* Loch Shin was to my left, hidden behind a ridge of pine trees. Loch Naver would be next, nestled alongside the hamlet of Altnaharra.

A shiver ran along my spine, but it wasn't caused by raindrops oozing down my neck. This was a sensory reaction, based on my current location and feeling. I had a deep sense of belonging, as though the whole trip had been leading me to this place and time. Suddenly, I began singing at random. It didn't matter what, as long as it was loud. When I grew weary of a particular song, I thought of another. Then I remembered the runners at Land's End as they sang, '*I would walk 500 miles and I would walk 500 miles more.*'

Close to the roadside, I noticed stacks of freshly cut peat, left to be dried by the wind and sun. The Irish term for peat is turf, and they use a two-sided spade called a sleán to slice it from the bog. The rustic scene reminded me of parts of Western Ireland, where turf is still used for heating. The similarities to Donegal were all around me, including the sheep, the streams, the boggy fields and endless skies. All I needed now to complete the scene was my late grandmother's house. The large family house is located partway up a hillside and can be seen from miles around. Two storeys high and painted white, the house is large enough to have once catered for fifteen children!

It is marked on Ordnance maps as Meenavalley Ho, with Ho being the symbol for house. Many years ago, two German travellers, armed with a map, mistakenly thought Ho meant hostel. At the time, Gran was in her sixties and lived alone. On a wet and windy spring evening, the couple, a man and a lady, rode in tandem up to her lawn on their motorbike. They only spoke German, while she knew only English and a little Gaelic.

Despite the fact she had no idea what they were talking about, one look at their weary faces was enough. After they'd warmed themselves in front of the hearth, she made tea and prepared a hearty meal. Later, she checked they were married, and once happy, lit a fire in the spare room and aired the double bed. In the morning, they enjoyed tea, eggs and soda bread. It was only when they tried to pay that the penny clicked. Gran waved them away, happy to have helped for no reward, and only glad of the company.

After passing the peat stacks, my thoughts turned to the sausage roll I'd purchased earlier. I stopped alongside a simple bridge that spanned a narrow but lively stretch of water. I tore open the wrapper, and partway through the first bite, glimpsed a flash of silver, leaping from the water. Nick had already explained that the Altnaharra Hotel is popular with serious fishermen, drawn to the pristine waterways in search of salmon and trout. I hadn't thought to search for fish on the way to the hotel.

I waited and watched, my camera primed for a snapshot, but there was no more excitement to be had. Then suddenly I remembered my GoPro and thought about all the footage I should have taken but rarely did. Further ahead, a curve in the road provided the perfect backdrop for a video, prompting me to set up the camera on a fence post. Oblivious to time, I rode back and forth along the road, hoping to capture a good recording. The hot bath and pre-dinner drinks would have to wait, and as for food — I still had one more energy bar left. By tomorrow afternoon, there'd be no need to eat it. We'd be in John O'Groats and the trip would be well and truly over. In fact, within forty-eight hours, I'd be at 38,000 feet, flying to Australia and my family.

But I was greedy now, wanting it all. The rain, the cold, and the feeling of isolation. Since leaving Bonar Bridge, I'd rarely looked at the map but I was still keen to find the Crask Inn. Maybe I'd passed the building during an earlier squall, and for a moment, I contemplated going back to check. I turned to stare at the lonely road I'd just traversed. I wasn't going back. The sky was paler now, showing the faint outline of the sun. Far to my left, it made its evening descent.

Riding onwards, I spotted a slight curve up ahead. Positioned behind a cluster of trees were two buildings on either side of the road. The faint aroma of turf caught at the back of my throat, its earthy smell instantly taking me back to winter evenings in Donegal. As I cycled nearer, the building on the right grabbed my attention, due to its similarities with my Gran's house. Like hers, it stood proud against the grassland and nearby hills. Even the design, with its slate roof and white exterior, looked similar.

One thing was different though. It had a small car park, positioned behind an open gate. It was an inn! There were no cars or bikes to be seen, leaving me doubtful it was open for business. I pushed the bike along a bed of shingles, past a window, and listened for the sound of music, voices, or laughter. But nothing. The familiar aroma of burning turf grew stronger, teasing my senses and emotions. I rested the bike against the wall and tested the door handle.

To my surprise, it opened with a satisfying click, swinging open with the help of a cool breeze. I stepped inside, embracing the warmth, and quickly closed the door behind me. Framed photos depicting Scottish landscapes hung on the walls and alongside the bar. Three wooden stools were lined up, side by side. To the left of the bar was an open plan area surrounded by tables. A fireplace took pride of place, its warm glow throwing lively shadows across the room. Instinctively, I made my way towards it and noticed a border collie, spread-eagled on the floor. I knelt alongside it and stroked its matted coat. The dog lifted his head, watched me with tired eyes, and greeted me with a wag of its tail.

I stroked its neck and whispered in its ear. 'Good boy. Are you the only one here?'

The dog wagged its tail, which bounced off the flagstones. Then, it closed its eyes. The pub was perfect. The only thing missing were my friends and a chatty publican. I eased off my jacket, gloves and helmet and called out, expecting to hear an apology. But my call was met with silence.

I studied the bar, taking note of the drinks and snacks on offer. My eyes were drawn to the real ales. The wall alongside me displayed a promotional poster for an upcoming Ceilidh, with traditional music and dance. I took note of the date and time and managed a half smile. By the time the Ceilidh would be in full swing, I'd be in a queue at Heathrow Airport, waiting to check in.

The wall behind the bar was taken up with a display of optics, including numerous whiskies. The last time I'd enjoyed a wee dram had been twenty years earlier on the final day of our bike ride. I was tempted again, but first I had to find the publican.

I found a corridor leading to other rooms and stopped to call out again. This time, I heard something. It was the distinctive sound of a metal blade striking wood. The door to my right opened wide and a man stepped into the corridor. He held a knife in one hand, and his face was dimly lit. Before I could turn and run, he smiled.

'I thought I heard someone calling. Sorry about that, but I'm down here in the kitchen, chopping spuds. I've got a party of long distance riders on their way for dinner and my wife is out for the day. They're staying the night at the inn.'

He studied my outfit then and said, 'Are you an end-to-ender too?'

'This time tomorrow I will be,' I said with a newfound pride.

'And will you be wanting a drink?'

'The organic ale sounds appealing.'

'Aye, it's a great wee drop, brewed in the Isle of Skye and very popular. Give me a few seconds and I'll be around to serve you.'

I selected a stool and sat at the bar while he poured the ale. He was about sixty years old with a full head of hair and a strong, straight back. He was taller than me and bent down to offer his hand across the bar. I learned that Mike and his wife Kai have been running the inn for over twenty years, and although I was their first customer of the day, the evening was due to be busy.

Located eighty miles from John O'Groats, the inn is a natural stopover for end-to-enders who cycle inland rather than skirt Scotland's flanks. Built in 1815 by the Sutherland Estate, it caters for intrepid explorers, offering a warm fire, refreshments, a freshly cooked meal, and a comfortable bed. After a long day in the saddle, I could think of no better location for a group of weary cyclists.

As for the ale, it tasted perfect, sliding down with ease. While I sipped the beer, Mike enquired about the ride so far, asking my opinion on what I thought of the route. He also wanted to know my thoughts on politics and the economy. I was happy to discuss such topics but was also curious to see if the other riders had visited. I was convinced they would have done so, but after hearing that they hadn't, I thought for a second I might somehow be in front. Just as quickly, the thought vanished when I caught sight of a clock on the wall. It was already six in the evening. I was definitely last again.

Mike broke the silence. 'What do you think of Brexit then?'

I explained I now lived in Australia but had been following the progress online. Mike's reply stunned me. 'You know, we've lived here without a TV and computer for twenty years.'

The inn had no power, apart from a generator, with no phone or internet connection, and it wasn't just an inn but also a working croft. They raised highland cattle and sheep, as well as an extensive vegetable patch.

'How do you keep up with what's going on in the world?' I asked.

'Oh, we drive into Inverness from time to time and keep up with the news from people like you. We get a lot of characters sitting at this bar and many put the world to rights!'

As I drained my ale, the empty glass left me in a quandary. The hands of the clock seemed to moving quicker than logically possible. I yearned to stay longer but needed to finish the day's journey. Mike could read my thoughts. 'Before you leave for Altnaharra, are you after a wee dram to warm you up?'

I was tempted, but one wee dram might lead to another and I still had a few more miles to go. I settled for another beer, leaving the whisky for the celebration at John O'Groats. After pouring the second pint, he excused himself and returned to the kitchen. I moved to the fireside and sat on a chair, close to the dog, both of us enjoying the warmth. I stretched out my legs and supped the beer while looking down at the sleeping dog. Maybe it was the heat, or the culmination of the day's events, but I was beginning to feel lightheaded.

Reluctantly, I drained the glass, patted the dog and prepared to leave. But first I wanted to study a display of prints, depicting the local landscape in various sizes and styles. I picked one up, admiring the way the artist had captured the solitude of the pub, surrounded by rugged moorland. Mike was back behind the bar. 'You can have that one, Alistair. It's on the house.'

'It's a perfect fit for my panniers. Are you sure? I'm happy to pay.'

'No need to pay. It's been lovely to chat with you. Sometimes it can get lonely up here.'

'Do you read travel books?' I asked.

'Not often, but I've enjoyed a few.'

'Good. The very least I can do is return the favour. I have a gift for you.'

He seemed pleased with the end-to-end book and was happy to pose for a photo. As I donned my clothes, he noticed the orange wind-cheater.

'Make sure you wear that. There'll be a chill wind from the Ben at this time of the day.'

'What's the Ben?' I asked while zipping up the jacket.

'Ben Klibreck. You cannee see the top now, but she is close by and broods over us. It's a fine mountain to climb but not on a day like today. You'll be glad to know that the road from here is mostly downhill. Nothing too severe, but you'll feel the cold that's for sure. You'll need to be quick though. They sometimes stop cooking after eight.'

We shook hands and I stepped outside, forcing the door closed behind me. I took a deep breath and inhaled the turf one more time. The Crask Inn had just joined the list of all those locations I'd visit again when next in Britain. It might even have slipped in as number one. Armed with the knowledge that the chef in our hotel might soon be hanging up his apron, I rode swiftly, my eyes hunting for pot holes and wayward sheep, a wide grin on my face despite the cold seeping into my bones.

Altnaharra couldn't come quickly enough, and after each bend in the road, I searched for signs of civilization. But apart from rundown buildings, there was little else except fields and isolated pockets of woodland. Then, I passed a farmyard and heard the bark of a dog. The road straightened and levelled. Coppiced woods were to my left and a stone wall was to my right. In the distance, I noticed a series of detached houses and a large white building, partially hidden behind trees. A prominent sign informed me the speed limit was down to forty miles per hour, and within seconds, I passed another, confirming I'd finally made it.

The hotel was set back from the road, framed by a river and moorland. The laneway was constructed from shingle, which meant I had to dismount to get to the entrance. Now, as I approached, I could fully appreciate the size of it, remembering Nick's advice that it was originally a shooting and fishing lodge. The rooms upstairs would command impressive views to the distant hills, and by the look of the car park, there were numerous guests staying overnight.

Our van was parked alongside a black Range Rover. Its owner stood alongside the open hatch, revealing a stash of fishing equipment. He was wide set with a ruddy complexion and thinning hair. He wore a tweed jacket, long trousers and gum boots. I said hello as I walked past, but he ignored the greeting, muttering to himself while sitting on the tailgate and wrestling with a boot.

A man approached from the lawn, walking a playful dog. It was only when he stepped onto the shingle that I realised it was Mick. But what was he doing with a Labrador? He welcomed me with a handshake and introduced me to his dog. Before I could ask, he pointed to a nearby window through which I could see some familiar faces, including partners and family of some of the riders. I was still mystified about Mick's dog being in the Highlands when the hotel door opened and JP bounded out to distract me.

'Ali, thank goodness you made it. We were getting worried.'

He guided me to the rear of the hotel and, on the way, informed me I had the bunkhouse all to myself. The others had all paid for an upgrade. I didn't much care for additional comfort or a bird's eye view of the mist covered hills. All I needed was hot food and a bed, along with a few ales if I stayed awake long enough. I was more than happy with the bunkhouse, and after a quick tour, JP directed me to an outbuilding. 'Your bike goes in there. I think it's an old cow shed.'

As soon as JP left, Alan appeared, smiling widely and holding a menu while cracking a joke. 'Top man, Ali. If you'd been twenty minutes later, we'd have sent out the Scottish Mountain Rescue Team.'

A sudden squall sent us all cowering towards the shed. In the semi light, Alan handed me the menu. 'You have to order straight away. The chef has called last orders!'

Horizontal rain lashed against the shed door as I quickly read the menu, picked the lamb cutlets, and then watched Alan sprint towards the hotel. It didn't take long for me to shower and change.

The moment I walked through the entrance, it felt as though I'd been transported onto an Agatha Christie movie set. The man from the car park had replaced his waterproofs with evening wear and leather brogues, and as he strolled past with an air of audacity, he called to an unseen friend in the whisky lounge. Framed photos of salmon hung from the walls, along with numerous landscapes of rivers and a winter scene of the hotel. Lounge chairs were positioned on the plush carpet, adjacent to an unlit fireplace.

We gathered around the hearth, telling stories about our day while enjoying pre-dinner drinks. Our final supper on the road was the grandest affair of them all. With waitress service and fine dining, the meal was a success. A new addition to the group was Lisa, Mick's girlfriend, who'd travelled up to Scotland with their dog to share the final part of our ride. After John O'Groats, they'd spend time together in Scotland before venturing back to England. Even now, the other riders were discussing plans on where to cycle for their autumn getaway.

Mark was sitting alongside me. 'So, Ali, will you miss all this? Or are you looking forward to getting back to Australia?'

In truthfulness, I was torn. The talk of another bike trip didn't enthuse me at all at that moment. I was too exhausted to even contemplate it. But there was something about their kinship I admired. Maybe I could replicate it in Australia. Although I doubted it. The bonds that form over many years of friendship are hard to reproduce. Mark was right in one aspect. I was looking forward to seeing my family again, as was he.

I declined the offer of dessert and asked if anyone wanted to try out the public bar. Some had been in there earlier while waiting for my arrival, so I was met with a series of headshakes. I left them with their drinks and found the door to the rear bar. Unlike the plush lounge, the décor in the bar was sparse. There was a long wooden bar with a few lonely stools, and a scattering of tables and chairs. Apart from two men chatting quietly at one end of the bar, the place was empty. I sat at the opposite end and ordered a beer. Then I took out my phone to study the photos I'd taken.

'There's no point looking for a signal. You won't find one here.'

The man who'd spoken sported long side burns, and his red hair was tinged with flecks of grey. Both men were in their late fifties, dressed in jeans, boots, and flannel shirts. They were both watching me as I placed the phone down on the bar.

'That's OK. I don't need Wi-Fi. I'm just looking at my cycling photos.'

The man nearest was keen to find out more. He studied me for a moment, his green eyes mostly hidden behind a frizz of hair. 'Are you one of those cyclists who's travelled up from Land's End?'

'Yeah. Do you get many at the hotel?'

'In the summer we get a fair share. I don't talk to them much. I'm always too busy with the fishermen.'

My blank stare opened up a new conversation about his life as a ghilly. I was soon to learn that a ghilly is the best friend a fishermen could ever hope to have. The rivers and lochs in the far highlands are a mecca for those in search of salmon or trout, and with strict rules on where and when to fish, local knowledge is critical. A good ghilly will advise on the best spots and the best type of fly to help catch the elusive salmon.

After a flurry of information, he then went quiet. I took a sip of beer and said, 'You sound very knowledgeable about the area. Have you lived here long?'

It was his friend's turn to talk now, the words tumbling from his mouth. 'He's born and bred in Altnaharra and knows every rock, river, and loch like the back of his hand. He even went to school in the village!'

The ghilly shrugged at the accolade and ordered another round of drinks. I was eager to find out more, including their names, but the outside door opened and in from the darkness stepped a tall, thin man dressed in an oil-skin jacket. Here was another character, perfect for a murder mystery. His eyes were narrow and he glanced my way with no more than a fleeting look. Soon he was stood alongside the two other men, and then they were joined by the barman, all in hushed discussions. Without a word, I placed the empty glass on the table and went off in search of my friends. I hoped they were all still alive!

I found them relaxing in the lounge and chose a seat alongside JP. He poured me a generous helping of wine and asked about my day. For the next hour, I joined in with the banter, fully aware that our 1,000-mile adventure was nearly over. With one day left, it was vital I stayed with them. There was no way I was going to arrive at John O'Groats on my own. With these thoughts in mind, I bid them farewell and made my way towards the bunkhouse.

The clouds had dispersed, allowing the moon to shine clearly in the sky. There was enough light to bathe the adjacent field, where a herd of red deer grazed quietly. I walked towards the fence line, not wanting to scare the creatures but eager to get nearer. The closest to me was a young buck, his antlers bathed in the moonlight as he lifted his head to investigate. I would go no further. He needed solitude and I yearned for sleep.

Day 13: Heroes

'You can't go back and change the beginning, but you can start where you are and change the ending.'
C.S.Lewis

I took a stroll around the hotel grounds before breakfast. My aim was to take photos of the deer, but the nearby fields now stood empty. Instead, I looked up and searched for clues about the weather. Like most British people, I've learnt to be optimistic whenever there is a hint of blue between the clouds. From the look of today's skies, both sunshine and showers seemed likely, but with any luck, there would be less of the latter.

In the pale-yellow light, the low-lying hills and grasslands were captivating. We'd soon be heading north, weaving our way through a landscape I'd never seen before. After today, this wonder would end. Within a few days I'd be back home, taking the same old commute. Until the next adventure.

Unlike many, though, my daily ride to work is not about traffic jams, traffic lights, or road rage. A life in the Australian countryside brings different challenges, one of which is the large distances to travel to get anywhere. During my ninety-minute journey to site, I've learnt vigilance, and to keep my eyes wide for stray kangaroos that might bolt at random from the bush. I know each turning, every straight, and have discovered all the safest spots for overtaking logging trucks. I also know the times and location where freight trains will halt my progress.

Yet here, out in the wilds of Scotland, I knew nothing of what lay ahead. I hadn't studied the map since arriving the night before and I didn't want to either. I wanted it all to surprise me. The slam of a car door snatched away my daydream. It was time for breakfast. On the way to the hotel entrance, I passed the man with the Range Rover. He was hopping about by his car, trying to squeeze into a pair of green waders. His cheeky were ruddy. I wondered if it were from the early morning exertion or the effects of late night whisky.

It's rare that I find smoked kippers on the breakfast menu, and with little regard for the fishy aftertaste, I ordered two. The waitress was blonde but going grey and wore a white blouse, black trousers, and flat shoes. With quiet discipline she busied herself around the tables, as did the other staff members, all of whom were dressed in black and white. The food was delivered swiftly and devoured with vigour. The dining room setting with its tablecloths, piped music, and heavy cutlery was notably different from the gritty, budget-style surroundings of Fort William. But despite the decadence, there was something missing. I couldn't quite grasp what it was.

One of the riders summed it up. 'Have you actually seen any of the staff here smile this morning?'

A murmur of agreement followed from around the table. While a waitress silently delivered a bowl of porridge to Mark, I pondered the situation. Hospitality is a difficult business at times. More so, if the accommodation is located in a remote area and certain standards are expected. Yes, the staff working that day did seem aloof. But I could only speculate as to why this was so. Maybe they just needed a break or we'd turned up at a difficult time. For hotel owners it must be testing when visitors come and go in such short spells. We arrive with baggage (physical and emotional), expectations, and demands — some within reason, others totally off the scale. By morning, we are gone.

All in all, I'd stayed at the hotel for about thirteen hours and was in a deep sleep for eight of them. Surely not enough time to for anyone to form a thorough impression of me. Why should I form one of them? In any case, the girl who took my payment seemed happy enough. She handed my receipt over with a smile.

'You're off to John O'Groats, aren't you?' she asked, looking me up and down. 'There's not many shops on the way. I hope you ate enough breakfast.'

She pointed towards the dining room then. 'There's plenty of apples. Make sure you tell your friends in case they want to grab one for the road.'

On my way to the exit, I grabbed an apple as suggested, then stopped to take a final look at the plush interior. Without doubt, the hotel had made it to my wish list. Hopefully, the wait staff would be a little chirpier next time I came, but in every other aspect, it fitted my needs perfectly.

The location is ideal for those seeking solitude and the food is delicious. I enjoyed the décor, the surroundings, and the sight of fishermen dressed in tweed while sipping whisky. I didn't care about the lack of Wi-Fi. In fact, I saw this as an attribute. In an overloaded world, the thought of snuggling up here by the fire, a good book in hand while a blizzard raged outside, sounded like bliss.

On the way back to the bunkhouse, I thought back to some of the wonderful hosts we'd encountered on our ride. Like Peter and Tessa in Callington, some had made lasting impressions by going out of their way to help us out. The bed and breakfast owner in Penzance had allowed us to park bikes in his dining room, and in Moffat, we'd been fed a breakfast fit for kings. All in all, we'd been very fortunate.

Being the final morning of our trip, I expected a rousing send-off speech by Nick, but he was being far quieter than normal. Maybe there was nothing left to say. He'd gotten us this far and our goal was only 74 miles away. He planned to drive to John O'Groats with his family today and then cycle back towards us. With luck, we'd converge simultaneously in the coastal town of Thurso. He watched from the doorway as we collected our bikes from the cow shed, wheeled them past the hotel entrance, saddled up quickly, and left with a wave.

First up, we crossed a small bridge, spanning a narrow but lively river. Next, we passed some isolated buildings, and further up, just past a farmyard, we came across the local primary school. The playground swings looked as though they'd recently enjoyed a lick of paint, but as it was the holidays, there wasn't a child in sight. From the roadside, the small, single storey building looked inviting enough for children. There were murals painted on the sides, and there was a grassed area, complete with goal.

I've since found out that the current number of students is just five. I've also learnt that the pupils and teachers were once involved in the creation of Bug Bombers Midge Repellent. It's now sold at the hotel, the proceeds going towards a charity called Cash4Kidz.

The sight of the school reminded me of my own children back home in Australia. Their school is situated about a mile from the Indian Ocean. Other schools in our town are so close to the bay that sometimes the students enjoy their lessons on the beach. Even our municipal football pitch offers views of the sparkling ocean. I tell my children how lucky they are and talk about the muddy, windswept pitches I played on in England. But all they do is roll their eyes.

A sudden sly thought came to mind. What if, next year, we could send the boys to a school just like the one in Altnaharra. What an experience that would be! A totally different culture and a chance to live in the Highlands. It sounded extreme, but the thought did bring a smile to my face. Cold, dark lochs and hills, compared to sunny, sandy beaches. I could imagine their faces now.

There was one more house in the village before we reached the open moorland. It resembled a static caravan, painted racing green with a wooden outhouse. Near the edge of its front garden, close to the road, stood a red telephone box, which I assumed was still functioning. Calls made from this glass box commanded panoramic views, but right now, there was no one inside.

The only creatures in sight were sheep. There were hundreds of them, dotted across the moors; their white coats prominent against the windswept grass. Some had managed to find gaps in the fences and were walking along the narrow road. Alan and Mark rode towards them, scattering a few towards the verge. The remaining three fled up a slight incline, bleating in confusion, but an open gate offered escape. They ran into a nearby field just as we caught up with them.

The road was barely more than a bitumen track and, in some places, hardly wide enough for a car. It followed the gentle contours of the land, past tributaries and streams towards a wide river that split the escarpment. With no traffic to worry about, we rode two by two, chatting amiably as the miles tumbled past, oblivious to the persistent drizzle glistening the road.

Nick had picked a route that took us alongside Loch Naver, a large body of water that feeds a river with the same name. We intended to follow the river to its end, where it flushes into the North Atlantic Ocean, 15 miles further north. We rode at a steady pace alongside the loch, its dark waters devoid of boats. At times, the road was so narrow that single file was best. We passed abandoned cottages and farmhouses, located at the end of muddy tracks and partially screened by pine trees.

If there were fish in the rivers, they didn't leap out when we rode alongside. There were others more determined than we were to find the salmon. We spotted a fisherman, dressed in a khaki oilskin, standing knee deep in the water, casting his fly up into grey sky.

Eventually the drizzle cleared, replaced by a light covering of clouds. Fleeting bursts of sunshine shone down onto the land, as though God was holding a torch. We rode through communities so small that they didn't even merit a welcome signpost. One had a tiny church, its white walls and red rooftop a beacon from afar.

We ate on the go, munching our complimentary apples and finishing off the last of the energy bars. The back road came to an abrupt end, and we stopped to allow cars to rush past at the junction. Finally, turning right, we joined the North and West Highlands Tourist Route. According to a road sign, we had 55 miles to go until John O'Groats.

A few miles later, in the village of Invernaver, we crossed a narrow bridge made of steel, spanning the River Naver. The river had blossomed into a wide, meandering body, flowing sedately between two ridges towards the sea. The road crept upwards and offered sweeping views of the widening river mouth as we approached the village of Bettyhill. The far side was dominated by a series of dark hills, their steep sides falling down to sand banks that stretched along the shoreline. There was a final chance to view the river as it flowed into Torrisdale Bay before merging with the North Atlantic.

At the top of the incline, the road turned east. It couldn't go north without leading to a dead end, as we were reaching the edge of the country. By boat, the next landfall would be the Isles of Faroe, approximately 250 miles away, and after that, it was Iceland. Despite being so close, the ocean was difficult to spot, hidden behind a gentle ridge that followed the contours of the coastline.

If you didn't know its rich history, the village of Bettyhill could be easily passed over. It looked pleasant enough, sat on top of a wide escarpment. It even boasted a moderately sized, modern hotel, positioned strategically on its western tip to ensure the guests enjoy the view of the river mouth, far below. But the real secret to Bettyhill's existence, dates back many years.

Crofting communities would once have played an essential role in the area, each given a few hectares for small-scale food production. During the

19th century, The Highland Potato Famine severely affected these communities, and for some residents, it triggered an exodus to countries such as Canada or Australia in search of a new life.

Crofters were also under pressure from the landowners who decided at this time that sheep pastoralism was a more lucrative arrangement than having tenants to work the land. This change of strategy meant forced evictions, which later become known as the Highland Clearances. During this dark, turbulent period, thousands of families across Scotland were displaced. The village of Bettyhill was constructed between 1811 and 1821 to house some of those homeless crofters.

The houses that we passed today, however, didn't look old at all. In fact, most were detached, with double glazing, manicured lawns, and neat flower beds. If any were up for sale, a canny real estate agent would — no doubt — add the words, *Ocean Glimpses*, on the literature. Not that we'd seen any real estates since leaving Altnaharra, or in fact a single shop!

From Bettyhill, the road continually dipped and ebbed, as though we were on a gentle rollercoaster. We passed tiny hamlets and farms but rarely any people. For a while, we had commanding views of the ocean, and long downhill stretches that allowed us one final chance to ride at speed. The road took us close to sea level, then turned away, forcing us into single file as we puffed our way to the next ridgeline.

The sight of golfers was unexpected, but those playing on the wide-open fairways of Reay Golf Course that afternoon would have appreciated the fleeting moments of sunshine as much as we did. The course stretched far towards the sand dunes, offering fine views of the ocean, just beyond.

Further on, just past the hamlet of Isauld, a familiar blue and white sign pointed us away from the main road onto narrow lanes, past small farms and isolated communities. The sight of a lone rider called Nick, heading our way, confirmed that John O'Groats was looming closer. His arrival boosted us, and as we headed back the way he'd come, we soon found ourselves riding through the outskirts of Thurso, the northernmost town in mainland Britain.

It felt strange to once again see housing estates, parks, schools, shops and people. The town of Thurso has a population of about 8,000 people, some of whom are still employed at the Dounreay nuclear power plant, even though it ceased operating at the end of the 20th century.

Decommissioning of aging power plants occurs right across mainland Europe, and ironically brings with it many job prospects. The Scottish government has invested large amounts of money into skills and training for the decommissioning of complex power plants and could potentially use this to their advantage in the future. Apart from dismantling power stations, traditional jobs still exist in the area including fishing, fish processing, and farming.

A few boarded-up windows in the high street shops, together with a chill wind, grey skies and dark, granite buildings didn't seem to affect the mood of those we cycled past. Most locals looked happy enough, going about their daily business without a second look at the entourage, riding slowly, in search of food.

Reid's bakery is located at the end of a pedestrianised area and after dismounting, the aroma of freshly baked pies wafted out to greet us. We joined the orderly queue inside to order food. Most tables had already been taken, and from what I could see, the clientele were tucking into their food with relish. Each of us peeled off our excess layers while waiting in turn to order. I heard Colin muttering to himself about what type of pie he'd order with his chips, and Alan was already at the front, collecting a mug of tea.

I heard a small boy talking to his mum at an adjacent table and decided to listen in. He was about five with soft freckles and a chubby round face.

'Mummy, why are those men wearing noisy shoes?'

'They're cyclists, Ben. The shoes help them ride faster, I think.'

'Why are their legs all muddy?'

'I suppose they've been out in the drizzle. Why don't you sit nicely and turn— '

'Where are they going?'

'To John O'Groats I suppose, or maybe just a day trip somewhere.'

'Why are they—?'

'That's enough now, Ben. Stop staring and finish off your chips before they get cold.'

I chose the homemade beef and mushroom pie, chips, gravy, beans and a mug of tea, then wrapped my arm protectively around the plate, eager to enjoy every morsel. After scraping the plate clean, I leaned back in the chair, rubbing my stomach in appreciation. I had no idea how many calories we'd burned and consumed since Land's End, but I was certainly trimmer than on day one. I also felt fitter than I had done in years.

A quick check in the bathroom mirror, however, showed that the culmination of sun, wind, rain, late nights, long days and diversions had taken their toll. The whites of my eyes had turned pink, and dark smudges sat beneath. I splashed my face in cold water and smiled at the wrinkled reflection. No matter. It was time to feel proud of my achievements.

Back in the café, the group were gathering up their gloves, helmets, and jackets. As soon as we stepped outside, each rider replaced the layers we'd taken off in the café. I wore a T-shirt, a fleece, a waterproof coat on top, as well as cycling gloves and a helmet.

Oblivious to the bitter wind, two teenage girls had opted to eat their lunch outside. They chatted amicably, long hair blowing, dressed in T-shirts, shorts and training shoes. Thurso is located 59 degrees north and faces the North Atlantic. It shares a similar latitude with Oslow, Moscow, and a town called Juneau in Alaska. Local teenagers, it appears, are bred tough.

The town also has a claim to fame. One bay in particular boasts the best right-hand reef break in Europe. With average water temperatures of just six degrees, surfing here is not for the faint-hearted. For many years, the O'Neil Cold Water Classic was held in Thurso, drawing surfing professionals from around the world, as well as thousands of visitors. The sport has helped transform the town, giving it an identity well beyond that of its geographical location and disused nuclear power plant.

We saddled up for the final stint and rode off towards a bridge. Pedestrians darted for cover as a sudden shower swept in from the ocean. By the time it passed, we were far from town, our sights firmly set on John O'Groats. Twenty years earlier we'd ridden to our final destination via the town of Wick on the east coast. This time, we rode along the north coast and enjoyed numerous glimpses of the North Atlantic. Somewhere during that final approach, the water became the North Sea.

Signposts counted down the final miles. I was desperate to spot a landmark from my first trip but had forgotten just how sparse the land was in this part of the world. It was devoid of a single hill and as flat as a popped bike tyre. Even the trees had vanished.

Far to our left, I caught sight of a multitude of stylish apartments, sitting side by side and each a different colour. The first was red, the next was yellow, then brown, green, and lastly blue. Their vibrant hues stood out proudly against the sky and I recognised them at once. I'd seen them once before but only on a computer screen. From afar, they resembled large beach huts, each with panoramic views of the bay.

They belong to National Retreats, an organisation specialising in luxury holiday accommodation in breathtaking locations. The colorful buildings are known as tofts and are located alongside the spired rooftop of the main building, lovingly restored after the original hotel at John O'Groats fell into disrepair.

Far ahead, sat a wide, two storey, whitewashed building. It is located on the main road to John O'Groats and as we came to a T-junction, I could see guests watching from some of its numerous windows. Instinctively, we all turned left, and immediately noticed a signpost, declaring that we only had a quarter of a mile to go.

After thirteen days and over a thousand miles, the end was approaching fast. Alan called out for everyone to slow down and took hold of the GoPro camera, lifting it high to get a panoramic video. Someone shouted a suggestion for us to form a line across the road, but by now we were fragmented, each rider grinning in anticipation.

It quickly came flooding back. The oval carpark, the row of shops, the tourist centre. Outside, a group of visitors stood together, hardly noticing the seven cyclists, threading their way through the middle. A middle-aged couple smiled knowingly, just as I caught sight of the sea.

Suddenly, I saw Samantha and Karen, standing by the famous signpost, holding aloft a smartphone, smiling and waving with excitement. They were playing music and at the sound of bagpipes, the hairs on the back of my neck came alive. They'd met us here twenty years ago and suddenly I was transported back in time. Back then, they'd been armed with frozen peas, champagne, a CD player and a speaker. This time, they were with Lisa, Tilly and an excited Labrador. We'd made it!

The first thing I did after leaping off my bike was hug Nick, and I followed up with firm handshakes all round. While congratulating JP, I caught sight of Alan and Sam in a warm embrace, the hotel creating a perfect backdrop. I knew our group was not the type to break into song. But, inside, I was singing like crazy. The dog seemed excited too, jumping up high to greet Mick before checking out everyone else.

Champagne was poured and a break between showers heralded plenty of time for photo shoots. After numerous solo shots, group shots, and shots with friends and family, Alan lined up alongside Nick and me for a photo by the sign. Twenty years had passed since we'd stood together at the exact spot. Just like before, we were grinning once again.

The years had by passed so quickly, but in that time, the hotel behind us had fallen into disrepair and been refurbished. And us? How had we fared? Alan and Nick had hardly changed. Both had a few more wrinkles and one had a dodgy knee. I studied them for a second, as they stood side-by-side, assured and confident, standing tall, sharing jokes, making plans for a celebratory beer.

My friendship with them had deepened, but was I a part of their close-knit group? Probably not. Perhaps if I hadn't made the decision to move to Australia, things might have turned out different. It's impossible to know.

I wondered if I were a wiser man now. Wiser than the one who stood here twenty years earlier? I'd certainly learnt a lot these past thirteen days. In fact, I don't think there's ever a point in life you stop learning. A few wrinkles, a head of grey, a dodgy back? None of these things will stop you growing.

Time had left its mark on us all in some way, but there was one thing it couldn't change — the distance to Land's End from John O'Groats, depicted on the wooden marker as 874 miles. While our photo was being taken, Colin announced that since starting our journey we'd actually covered 1,046 miles. We'd also worked off 40,166 calories.

I had no idea if I'd ridden more or less than his displayed amount. Sometimes I'd taken shortcuts to free up time; others times I'd gotten lost. But I was happy to claim the same amount. As for the calories burnt, we'd all earned an extravagant dinner.

While walking away from the signpost, I felt a sense of calm. I could finally put the memory of the first ride to rest, this latest ride now first and foremost in my mind. It had been a huge adventure, one that had tested me both physically and emotionally, far more than I'd ever envisaged. But I wasn't yet ready to leave. I needed more time to reflect on the journey and appreciate the extraordinary surroundings.

The others weren't so keen and made their way towards our overnight accommodation. I only meant to stay a short while but lost track of time in the gift shops. I took a stroll to the harbour wall, gazed out to sea, and searched for the smudge of land that signalled Stroma Island. The sun was struggling. It was getting late. But there was one more place to visit — the building now known as Natural Retreats John O'Groats.

I parked my bike at the rear entrance and walked inside. The old inn had been lovingly refurbished, reborn with a new name, a new look, and new feel. The plush décor immediately told me it was serious about comfort and luxury, and I stood by the reception area in awe.

Through sparking windows I could see the famous signpost, the small harbour and the seascape behind. Framed images of local attractions were hung neatly on a nearby wall, and as I stood admiring them, I heard someone walking confidently towards me.

Christine was bubbly, keen to talk, and passionate about her recent posting as the hotel's General Manager. I explained about our ride, the quest to raise money for charity, and my end-to-end book tour. I had one left to give away and asked if she minded being in a photo by the signpost.

Just as we headed for the exit, a man approached. Christine greeted him warmly and introduced me. His name was Tony. He had a mass of curls, a cheeky grin, and walked with a slight limp. He was about to start an adventure of his own and would be walking solo to Land's End. He walked alongside us as we made our way to the signpost, a walking pole by his side. By the time we'd reached the sign, I'd learnt that he has multiple sclerosis and was undertaking the walk in memory of his wife, Tina, who'd died of cancer 27 days after their wedding. During the trek he planned to raise thousands of pounds for the MS therapy centre in Rotherham.

'How long will it take you?' I asked.

'I have no idea,' he responded truthfully, his school boy grin masking any doubts.

'Do you have a support vehicle?'

'No, it's just me and my walking pole. I expect I've packed too much and will have to ditch a few items along the way. I've got a hashtag if you want to follow me.'

'I'm a bit of a beginner at hashtags but I'll give it a try. What is it?'

'It's hashtag Tony's wobbly walk. All one word.'

'You're a brave man,' I said and shook his hand one more time.

'Half mad, more like.'

He smiled widely and then pointed towards the hotel. 'I'd better head back and finish my packing.'

As he walked away, Christine said, 'We only met him yesterday. He's a lovely man and I hope he'll be okay. We get so many characters here. It's hard to remember them all, but he's a real hero, don't you think?'

I agreed wholeheartedly. A few minutes later, partway through a cup of tea in a nearby café, I was surprised to see Christine again. She was holding a LEJOG T-shirt and a completion certificate, which she handed over brightly. As I studied the gifts with glee, she said, 'Thanks for the book, Alistair. I'll store it in the library at the inn. Safe travels back home to Australia. You're very lucky to live in such a lovely country.'

I thanked her for the gifts and then stood up to shake her hand. 'Yes, you're right. But I'd forgotten how amazing Britain is. Next time, I think I'll stay much longer.'

'Well, if you do, don't forget to spend a night with us.'

'Absolutely. It's certainly on my list.'

Just then, I noticed the skies getting darker. 'Goodness me. I think it's time I got a move on. I've gained a bit of a reputation for being late these past few weeks. I'm going to celebrate with a wee dram tonight because tomorrow I'll be on my way south. I reckon, when I get home, I'll wonder if it was all a dream.'

Just Say Yes!

In 1996, during our inaugural ride, Alan and Samantha met in Gretna Green and fell in love. Twenty years later, unbeknown to us, another romance was blossoming. Later that evening in the Seaview Hotel, just as our celebratory dinner ended, Mick called for silence, fell to one knee and proposed to his lovely Lisa. He had carried the engagement ring all the way from Land's End to John O'Groats. There were tears of joy, followed by hugs, laughter and the ordering of champagne.

After toasting their future happiness, I sat at the bar with some of the riders. We were exchanging small talk with the barman. He was tall, fair haired and in his mid-twenties, with a relaxed, easy-going demeanour. While Mark scrolled through the jukebox looking for tunes, the barman cheerfully explained we were in the most northerly bar on mainland Britain. Despite the remote location, the choice of drinks was extensive. The beer we were enjoying had been brewed right here in John O'Groats, but there were over one hundred and thirty malts to choose from.

I was keen to make a toast, and with the barman's help, I picked a malt from a local distillery known as Old Pulteney, located in Wick.

'It's twelve years old,' he explained, 'and has won awards across the world.'

While he carefully poured whisky into numerous crystal glass tumblers, I called for a few moments silence. Some of the riders sniffed the malt in anticipation before returning their gaze to mine.

It wasn't a long speech. First, I congratulated Mick and Lisa and wished them every success for the future. Then I raised my glass, and to a chorus of approvals, thanked Nick for an amazing route and organising the trip of a lifetime. Someone called out that Karen had done most of the work, which caused some giggles. I was eager to chat about the highs and lows of the trip but sensed I might be heckled if I continued. Sentiment was not their style. So I paused to think how to end it.

Really, I'd wanted to thank JP for all the times he'd offered words of encouragement and kept me company along the shores of Loch Lomond. I'd wanted to thank Mick for the numerous occasions that he'd sought me out in the pub with a fresh beer. I'd wanted to thank Colin for the riding tips, the day he guided me along the Strawberry Line, and for the chats we'd shared about his life in Bedfordshire.

I'd wanted to thank Alan for his appetite for life, the constant jokes and banter, and the obscure way he enticed me up and out of bed when I was in agony. I'd wanted to thank Mark for all the times he'd called me on the phone, directing me to different places, and keeping his exasperation in check. I'd wanted to thank him for his trivia games, which had helped us through those long periods on the road.

Finally and most importantly, I'd wanted to thank the group for the times they'd helped me keep going or waited patiently for me to catch up. But I kept these words to myself. Instead, I raised my glass high.

'It's been eventful...to say the least. I'll see you all again in another twenty years, and next time, I promise, I'll even buy a bike computer.'

The End

End to End:

John O'Groats, Broken Spokes and a Dog called Gretna

When three friends set off on a 900-mile trip to explore Britain, using an out of date map to guide them, the scene is set for a wayward adventure. One cyclist didn't own a bike, but luckily, his brother was working out of town and had one in his garage. Painted racing green, with wide wheels and a robust frame, it was far from perfect for such a trip. But it was free!

Along the way they visited numerous country pubs, went in search of the remaining Beatles, discovered an ancient hideaway used by Scottish clans, and survived a storm in the Highlands. Each time they got lost they were helped by a variety of kind and quirky characters. If you like adventure travel books, then you'll enjoy this tale about three ordinary men, proving that extraordinary things can happen, just when you least expect it. For one of the cyclists, the journey would change his life forever.

Postcards from South America:
A Pig in a Taxi, Cotopaxi and Two Sticks of Dynamite

While deep underground in a Bolivian mine, running for cover from an imminent explosion, Alistair thought back to the parting words from his mother in law. "Don't do anything silly and please look after Fran."

Join Alistair and Fran in this fun-filled adventure story, as they travel by makeshift raft down the Amazon, climb volcanoes, teach English in the jungle and endure a hair-raising taxi ride with a pig. Along the way to Machu Picchu they hired a donkey called Angus, before venturing across a remote mountain pass, with just a mud map to guide them. From time to time they sent postcards from South America, sharing tales about their escapades and adventures.

If you've ever wondered what it's like to give up everything to follow your childhood dreams, this is the story for you.

Wild About Africa:

Sleepwalking on Kilimanjaro and Running from Lions

"Such a great read, oh my goodness." Jane Brown, A LoveReading Ambassador

"Was it my imagination or could I hear every footfall? Was it a gentle breeze that shook the side of our tent, or the brush of a lion's tail?"

48 hours after leaving London, Alistair was camped in the wilds of the Serengeti with his friend, Owen. He'd already had a close encounter with a marauding hyena and now lay perfectly still as lions stalked their camp. Africa was proving to be an exciting holiday destination, and within days, they witnessed the greatest wildlife spectacle on Earth: The Wildebeest Migration. But not everything went to plan. Partway through the trip, Alistair was robbed of all his possessions, hours before embarking on the hardest trek of his life, to the summit of Kilimanjaro, the highest freestanding mountain in the world.

Despite the robbery, he was determined to raise money for the charity that had supported his mum through her terminal illness, and set off for the snowy summit wearing discarded pink tracksuit pants and a borrowed Aran jumper. Days later he was turned back at the snowline by his guide, after suffering acute altitude sickness.

Many years later he returned to Africa, this time with his wife. During their overland trip they learned to track rhino, signed up for a white-knuckle rafting trip on the Zambezi and camped in the wilds of the Okavango Delta. There was also a mountain called Kilimanjaro, waiting to be climbed!

A Taste of Australia:
Bite-sized Travels across a Sunburned Country

'Get out of the bloody water, mate. There's a tiger snake behind you!'

Within seconds I was on the ledge, breathing hard as I caught sight of the creature. It looked to be a metre long, its banded stripes impossible to miss, as it moved silently across the pond with barely a ripple.

As a newly arrived migrant, Alistair was keen to experience the people and places that make Australia one of the most sought-after holiday destinations on the planet and home to the world's cutest animal – the quokka – but also to some of the deadliest. In *A Taste of Australia*, the author explores the 'Lucky Country,' from the top of Sydney Harbour Bridge to the hippy vibe of the East Coast and the boom and bust of Kalgoorlie, where everyone in town knows the price of gold.

Sometimes alone, or with family and friends, these escapades have taken him into the outback, foraging for bushtucker with Aboriginal guides. At other times he's travelled by campervan to Byron Bay and swam alongside turtles over untouched coral. Along the way he's stayed in remote mining camps and discovered a new way of working, where heat and dust are a way of life.

If you enjoy getting off the beaten track, these bite-sized stories will inspire you to travel far and wide – and perhaps to experience a different kind of life. Don't forget to slip on a shirt, slop on the sunscreen, slap on a hat and slide on your sunglasses, before seeking a shady spot to enjoy each tale.

Acknowledgements

Thanks to my wife, Francine, for giving me the space and freedom to lock myself away in the study to write. She lovingly supplied tea and biscuits at all hours and added inspirational advice during those moments of doubt. A debt is also owed to my two boys, Noah and Sebastian. Writing books takes time and effort, which means they've been neglected by me for too long. Maybe it's finally time for the family holiday I once promised! Thanks also, to Packard Images, for the creative cover design.

This book is dedicated to my Uncle Matt and big brother, Dave. I was once advised by Uncle Matt to slow down and enjoy the ride, and Dave showed me how to do it. Two years after this trip, he completed the end-to-end journey in three weeks, along with Fast Dave and the Android.

I hope you enjoyed *Slow Down and Enjoy the Ride* and wish you good luck if you are contemplating a similar adventure. If you have a few moments to spare I'd really appreciate an online review.

I enjoy keeping in touch with readers and you can find me at the following locations:

On my website @ alistairmcguinness.com

On Facebook @ alistairmcguinnesswriter

On Twitter @ amcguinness1

On Instagram @ alistair_mcguinness

Happy travels,

Alistair

Printed in Great Britain
by Amazon